Fault Lines

Tori Phelps

Fault Lines

Views across Haiti's Divide

❋

Beverly Bell

Cornell University Press
Ithaca and London

First published 2013 by Cornell University Press
First printing, Cornell Paperbacks, 2013
Printed in the United States of America

Library of Congress Cataloging-in-Publication Data

Bell, Beverly, 1962–
    Fault lines : views across Haiti's divide / Beverly Bell.
        p. cm.
    Includes bibliographical references and index.
    ISBN 978-0-8014-5212-3 (cloth : alk. paper) —
ISBN 978-0-8014-7769-0 (pbk. : alk. paper)
1. Earthquake relief—Haiti. 2. Haiti Earthquake, Haiti, 2010.
3. Haiti—Social conditions—21st century. 4. Haiti—Economic
conditions—21st century. I. Title.
    HV600 2010. H2 B45 2013
    972.9407'3—dc23   2012039141

Cornell University Press strives to use environmentally responsible suppliers
and materials to the fullest extent possible in the publishing of its books.
Such materials include vegetable-based, low-VOC inks and acid-free papers
that are recycled, totally chlorine-free, or partly composed of nonwood
fibers. For further information, visit our website at www.cornellpress.
cornell.edu.

Cloth printing   10 9 8 7 6 5 4 3 2 1
Paperback printing   10 9 8 7 6 5 4 3 2 1

To Bryan Bell,

Antoine Adrien,

and Magalie Marcelin

—their lives and their legacies—

Onè respè. Honor and respect.

Disaster shocks us out of slumber,
but only skillful effort keeps us awake.

Rebecca Solnit, *A Paradise Built in Hell:*
The Extraordinary Communities That Arise in Disaster

Contents

Foreword by Edwidge Danticat   xi

Acknowledgments   xv

Introduction: Thirty-Five Seconds   1

1. We Don't Have Enough Water to Make Tears: Surviving the Earthquake, or Not   12

2. What We Have, We Share: Solidarity Undergirds Rescue and Relief   19

3. Pearl of the Antilles: The Political Economy of Peril   27

4. Maroon Man: Social Movements throughout History   32

5. We Will Carry You On: The Women's Movement   41

6. You Can't Eat Okra with One Finger: Community-Run Humanitarian Aid   49

7. Fragile as a Crystal (Tales from Three Months Out)   57

8. Children of the Land: Small Farmers and Agriculture   63

9. Grains and Guns: Foreign Aid and Reconstruction   72

10. The Ones Who Must Decide: Social Movements in
    the Reconstruction   86

11. Our Bodies Are Shaking Now: Violence against Girls
    and Women   93

12. The Creole Connection: People-to-People Aid and
    Solidarity across Borders   102

13. We've Lost the Battle, but We Haven't Lost the War
    (Tales from Six Months Out)   112

14. Social Fault Lines: Class and Catastrophe   118

15. Monsanto Seeds, Miami Rice: The Politics of Food Aid
    and Trade   124

16. Home: From Tent Camp to Community   131

17. For Want of Twenty Cents: Children's Rights and
    Protection   140

18. The Super Bowl of Disasters: Profiting from Crisis   146

19. The Commonplace amid the Catastrophic (Tales from
    Nine Months Out)   154

20. Beyond Medical Care: The Health of the Nation   159

21. Hold Strong: The Pros and Pitfalls of Resilience   168

22. Mrs. Clinton Will Never See Me Working There:
    The Offshore Assembly Industry   176

23. The Central Pillar: Peasant Women   184

24. Elections (In the Time of Cholera)   190

25. We Will Never Fall Asleep Forgetting (Tales from
    Twelve Months Out)   197

Epilogue: Bringing It Back Home   201

Notes   207

Index   225

Foreword

When I was a girl in Haiti, I lived next door to three sisters who did piecework for an American evening gown company. In order to pay for their living expenses and another sister's education, the sisters strung together sequins and beads that would then be attached to gowns that, once completed, they carried to a factory near the airport.

Every now and then, Lina, Dieula, and Anisi Espérance would invite a few neighborhood girls to help them with their work. For this we would get a cent or two, a minuscule percentage of the very low wage they were being paid. Helping, however, would mean sitting at their feet, beneath the winnowing trays on which they had piled their materials and catching, along with sprinkles of their conversations, any beads or sequins that would accidentally fall or be blown away. Sometimes the sisters would let us hold the needles and thread that they used to attach the sequins and beads to the gowns, and I would see in the gorgeous penny-colored eyes that they all shared a great deal of pride in our efforts at replicating their carefully orchestrated movements.

Though this was for me child play, each time they'd allow me to dip my hands into the pile of tiny black, gold, silver, or copper circles, I would suspect an act of extreme generosity, an attempt at trying to teach me something about life. They had no reason to believe that my life would not at some point end up like theirs. And I was too young to realize that they were working toward a different type of life.

I would only much later realize that the sisters were poor and that I myself was poor and that my poverty was in part the reason I was not living with my parents who had emigrated to New York when I was a toddler and had temporarily left me in the care of my aunt and uncle while attempting to create a better life for themselves, and ultimately for me. But looking back now, I see that the Espérance sisters, like many of the Haitian men and women I knew, always seemed to be pushing a rock—be it a sequined one—up a hill, while constantly fighting a brave and valiant war against crushing and unrelenting poverty.

In the Greek myth, Sisyphus, a mortal, is condemned by the gods to endlessly roll a rock up a mountain, only to have it fall back down again. Each time the rock rolls down the mountain, he pushes it back up, and in the most optimistic telling of the story, he hopes that it will be the final time.

This is his punishment for defying the gods and for imagining his life, his fate, equal to their own.

Michèle Pierre-Louis, a former prime minister of Haiti, once compared the story of Sisyphus to Haiti. "Haitians are Sisyphean," she told a *Miami Herald* journalist in the film *Nou Bouke*. From the native Taínos who were wiped out by the Spaniards' greed, to the enslaved Africans who defeated the French and created the world's first black republic—only to invite the world's scorn—to the millions who survived the country's worst natural disaster, only to spend months in tent camps, then watch thousands of their loved ones die from United Nations–introduced cholera, Haitians are Sisyphean and much more.

Sisyphus in Haiti is the valiant Tibebe, who has been living on a cement slab since her house was destroyed in the earthquake. Even while suffering from a broken foot and heart trouble, she fights to protect herself from both rain and rape, all the while nurturing the dream of one day becoming literate. Sisyphus in Haiti is also Suze, a women's rights advocate who constantly answers 911-type calls on a limited phone card budget from women like Tibebe and their daughters and granddaughters. Sisyphus in Haiti is also Djab, a community organizer who lost nearly everything in the earthquake but continues to protest against human rights violations, especially those perpetrated by the United Nations forces. You will read about all these people and more in this insightful book. And you will travel with them, and the book's author, along the many fault lines that continue to shift above and below the ground in Haiti.

In May 2012 the Associated Press announced to the world something that many of us have always known, that Haiti has "gold hidden in its hills—and silver and copper, too." The same gold that led to the first genocide in the Americas, wiping out of the entire Taíno population who were forced to mine it to death.

Haiti's precious metals, we are told, could potentially be worth twenty billion dollars. Will this so-called windfall benefit people like Ti-bebe, Djab, Suze, and their families, or will it just be one more way that they and their children are robbed and—once all the riches have been pillaged—left to suffer the dire environmental circumstances?

In addition to mining, Haiti's future seems to be all about business. "Haiti is open for business" is at the heart of the rebranding of post-earthquake Haiti. But is this going to be, to evoke as Beverly Bell and others have, the Chinese symbol for crisis, more disaster than opportunity? Will it still be pennies-per-hour wages like those once earned by the Espérance sisters? Will workers' unions, like the ones Djab has fought for, be allowed?

The majority of Haitians are, the writer Langston Hughes famously said, perhaps symbolically, perhaps literally, the people without shoes. People "whose feet walked the dusty roads to market in the early morning, or trod softly on the bare floors of hotels, serving foreign guests. . . . All of the work that kept Haiti alive, paid interest on American loans, and enriched foreign traders, was done by people without shoes."

Yet these people are rarely sitting at decision-making tables that will either control the hotels and other businesses or the mines. There is rarely a representative of grassroots urban or rural sectors in the international commissions and panels that will decide the future of the country. In this book, thankfully they too are heard, not as victims or beggars, but as self-reliant and proud men and women who are the backbone of Haiti, and without whose full inclusion and participation the country will never fully succeed.

EDWIDGE DANTICAT

Acknowledgments

Fault Lines is the product of a robust gift economy. Big-hearted people have made it possible at every stage. I am profoundly grateful and inspired by their generosity and goodness.

Bishop Thomas Gumbleton and Jonathan Schwarz convinced me to write after the earthquake, when that seemed like a useless response. Michael Moore first offered a venue to publicize those writings that would later form the basis of this book.

In Haiti, old and new friends and colleagues gave interviews, revealed secrets, and solved mysteries. Others in both Haiti and the United States provided research, information, and an assemblage of essential resources. A limited list of those gracious providers includes Rose Anne Auguste, Rubie C. Bell, Nixon Boumba, Myriam Chancy, Carolle Charles, Christ in the Desert Monastery (especially Farid Ghilzai, Abbot Philip Lawrence, Brother James Rhoades, and Rosy Verdile), Eramithe Delva, Mark Donovan, Isabeau Doucet, Alex Dupuy, Patrice Florvilus, Allyn Gaestel, Conner Gorry, Steve Hellinger, Ansel Herz, Rosnel Jean-Baptiste, Maryse Jean-Jacques, Ricot Jean-Pierre, Margo Joseph, Annie Leonard, Michael Levy, Antonal Mortimé, Nicole Phillips, Jean Jores Pierre, Elizabeth McAlister, Jane Regan, Reyneld Sanon,

Mark Schuller, Nick Stratton, Ricardo Toussaint, Wayne Troyer, Matt VanGeest, Malya Villard-Appolon, Gina Vrigneau, Joris Willems, Dirk Wils, and the member organizations of the Haiti Response Coalition.

When I didn't have time to translate interviews, others' kindness did the job. Patricia Bingué, Larousse Charlot, Bill Davis, Monica Dyer, James Eliscar, Sylvia Gonzales, Agathe Jean-Baptiste, Joseph N. Pierre, David Schmidt, and Daniel Tillias volunteered or accepted solidarity wages for their fine translations. Rodney Jean-Louis checked all Creole spellings.

Patrick Bond, Ben Depp, Yolette Etienne, Susana Ferreira, Roberto (Bear) Guerra, Ruxandra Guidi, Guerda Lexima-Constant, Robert Naiman, Maya Panchang, Nicole Phillips, Elaine Poirier, Josh Steckley, Marylynn Steckley, and Claudette Werleigh read advance chapters. They improved them tremendously and kept many errors off them. The team at Cornell University Press was as remarkable for their expertise as for their patience with my everlasting delays. Many at the press touched this book, but the fingerprints of Susan Barnett, Karen Hwa, Katherine Liu, and Glenn Novak are everywhere on these pages.

Ben Depp, Roberto (Bear) Guerra, Jocelyne Joseph Mesilien, Wadner Pierre, Alice Speri, and Joris Willems donated their photographs to *Fault Lines*. Ben and Bear, moreover, have been the embodiment of solidarity photographers. Designer Cameron Benedict provided the long-sought, just-right cover image.

A sprawling assortment of friends, family, and colleagues gave the moral support that kept both this writing and me going forward in the two years after the earthquake. A few are Karen Ansara, Barbara Barrett, John Barrett, Jane Barry, Rubie C. Bell, Nixon Boumba, Kate Brown, Myriam Chancy, Valentine Doyle, Laurie Emrich, Bee Gosnell, Erika Guevara Rosas, John Harvey, Doug Hellinger, Steve Hellinger, Andy Lin, Laura Livoti, Laura Loescher, David Solnit, Toba Spitzer, Maria Suárez, Leslie Thatcher, and the krewes in New Orleans, New Mexico, and the Bay Area of California. Part of my sustenance came from my nieces and nephews, of the blood and cosmic kinds, who continually reminded me that laughter and joy are almost as vital as food and justice. This rumpus of children includes Brian, Constantino, Erika, Gisell, Hamilton, Karla, Kristopher, and Rikzi Avila Lopez; Henry, John, Matthew, and William Barrett; Cole and Lily Sky Bell; Amanda, David, Katherine, and Lydia Gosnell; David, Elizabeth, Jonas, and Lucy Rubie

Kletzing; Miles Larson; Jovani Milfort; Paul Montoya; and Emily and Stephen Taylor.

Among those who gave unusual gifts of immeasurable worth, a few stand out. Robert Naiman was a bedrock of guidance and nurturance during those first heartbreaking weeks. While Haiti's airport was still closed, Juana Ferrer welcomed me to the Dominican Republic and drove a whole night's journey to deliver me to Port-au-Prince. Tory Field was an extraordinary partner in traveling Haiti's devastated pathways in the earliest days. Jacques Bartoli and Josette and Fritz Pérard supported my stays in Haiti in a thousand ways that only old, dear friends would do. Mark Snyder hustled and sweated to track down people whose words appear here for permissions, and would not accept one centime for his troubles. Edwidge Danticat provided beautiful forewords for this as well as an earlier book and has been a model of grace and clarity for many years besides. Mark Schuller was the portrait of solidarity throughout *Fault Line*'s creation, offering a steady stream of analysis, feedback, and encouragement.

Following the earthquake, individuals and progressive foundations quickly jumped in with contributions for Other Worlds' work in Haiti (as well as for many of our ally organizations there), almost always without being asked. They are therefore also the funders of this book, which grew out of our work. They include many citizen donors as well as Aepoch Fund, American Jewish World Service, Karen and Jim Ansara, the CarEth Foundation, the Naomi and Nehemiah Cohen Foundation, Grassroots International, the Jewish Communal Fund, the Lawson Valentine Foundation, the New World Foundation, the Peace Development Fund, the PRBB Foundation, the Seattle Foundation, the Tides Foundation, and the Unitarian Universalist Service Committee. Grantmakers without Borders, the Institute for Policy Studies, and International Development Exchange offered invaluable institutional support.

Over the decades, I have been surrounded by an extraordinary collection of visionaries and front-line organizers who have molded my understanding of the world and the theories of change that underlie this book. They have also inspirited me and many others with their creativity and integrity in striving for new models of social relations and political and economic systems. A large subset are Haitians who have patiently taught me about their country, the meaning of global citizenship, and the prerequisites for justice. A very short list includes: Rev. Antoine

Adrien, Marie Simone Alexandre, Greg Asbed, Rosianne and Jesil Attis, Stephen Bartlett, German Bedoya, Patrick Bond, Dennis Brutus, Dorie Bunting, Bertha Caceres Flores, Alina "Tibebe" Cajuste, Ana Maria Carneiro, Gustavo Castro Soto, John Cavanagh, Camille Chalmers, Larry Cohen, Yannick Etienne, Yolette Etienne, Juana Ferrer, Debbie Fredo, Margarita García, Laura Germino, Bishop Thomas Gumbleton, Dorothy Healey, Juan Carlos Houghton, Shilpa Jain, Rev. Gérard Jean-Juste, Maria Diarra Keita, Pierre Labossiere, Helia Lajeunesse, Annie Leonard, Claudia López, Ilda Martines de Souza, Celia Martínez, Maria Elena Martínez, John Nichols, Emem Okon, Marcela Olivera, Oscar Olivera, Kathy Ozer, Marie Racine, Saúl Roque Morales, Peter Rosset, Grahame Russell, Lurdes Sánchez Sánchez, Ray Santiago, Miguel Santisteban, Virginia Setshedi, Marilene de Souza Santos, Jean Stokan, Neil Tangri, Coumba Toure, Rev. Hugo Trieste, Genevieve Vaughan, Rev. Jean-Marie Vincent, Mark Weisbrot, Scott Wright, and Daphne Wysham. So many more are part of this group, and I hope they know who they are. For those in this roll who are dead—especially Jean-Marie, who was assassinated in a hail of U.S.-funded machine-gun bullets—*lwanj*, honor, to their memories.

The ideas and hope that frame this book also come from social movements and popular organizations the world over, who have shown us all that other worlds not only are possible, but that they exist. It has been a privilege to collaborate with, and learn directly from, a number of them, especially the Coalition of Immokalee Workers, the Convergence of Movements of Peoples of the Americas (COMPA), the Council of Popular and Indigenous Organizations of Honduras (COPINH), Jubilee South, the Landless Workers Movement (MST) of Brazil, the Martin Luther King, Jr. Memorial Center in Cuba, Otros Mundos in Mexico, Red VIDA, Via Campesina, the Zapatista Army of National Liberation in Mexico, and most of the Haitian organizations appearing in this book.

Having saved my most zealous thanks for last, I now come to my beloved sisters at Other Worlds: Lauren Elliott, Alexis Erkert, Tory Field, and Deepa Panchang. They are standards in how to be the best one can be. They are, moreover, *makòmè*, co-mothers, in the gestation and delivery of this book. They helped shape ideas; sharpened analysis; pored over policy papers and social movement declarations; produced photos, images, the perfect phrase, and the essential fact; edited and reedited; pounded Haitian streets to check information; and assembled footnotes.

Alexis and Deepa contributed writing to many chapters. Almost as important to the realization of this book, they willingly put in many extra hours to pick up my organizational responsibilities that I neglected in order to write. Without these women, *Fault Lines*—and a lot of other things—would not be. This book is theirs also.

Throughout the research and creation of this text, Lauren Elliott held together most everything in my life as well as in my work. No job was too big or small, and each was performed with equal parts skill, love, and patience. She is an incomparable gift.

And finally, the big-spirited and super-talented Frances Benson of Cornell University Press again proved herself to be an exceptional human being and editor.

To you all, and many more besides, I bow low in appreciation, respect, and love. *Mèsi anpil.* Thank you very much.

Introduction

Thirty-Five Seconds

January 12, 2010

7.0 EARTHQUAKE ROCKS HAITI. That line burst onto the computer screen in my garret office in New Orleans as the Mississippi River Bridge eclipsed the late-afternoon sun. I stared stupidly. My brain couldn't shape the words into sense.

It was January 12, 2010. Haiti had just been shaken by the neck in what one survivor would later describe as "thirty-five seconds of hell."

Some would call the earthquake *goudougoudou*, for the terrifying sound that roared up out of the ground. Most would just refer to it as the *evènman*, the event. The day was so defining it simply came to be known as *douz*, twelve.

Haitian history had just cleaved into a new binary: before the *event* and after the *event*. What was thrown by the shaking land in that brief moment in January, and what would emerge from the divide, have irrevocably transformed the nation and its people. The full effects of the ensuing misery, destruction, and opportunism have yet to reveal themselves. The same is true of the citizen mobilizing that began as cement dust still wafted in the air, with grassroots movements hoping to rebuild a very different Haiti out of the rubble.

But before we get to that: The earthquake left one of the highest death tolls of any natural disaster. People threw around figures from 200,000 to 300,000, and the prime minister eventually put the toll at 316,000, but these sums were meaningless. No serious tally was ever taken of the corpses dropped from bulldozer scoops into shallow mass graves, or buried in relatives' yards, or left in the buildings between floors that were stacked like dinner plates throughout Port-au-Prince, Léogâne, Grand Goâve, Petit Goâve, and Jacmel. City blocks were cemeteries.

Down came so many structures that a Haitian official in charge of clearing the wreckage gave a high-ball estimate that removing all the rubble with a fleet of one thousand trucks could take twelve hours a day for an entire year.[1] Down came what Haitians called "the three Es": *état, églises, et écoles*, state, churches, and schools. Every single high-level gov-ernment building was left damaged or destroyed in a mess of detritus and dust: the National Palace, the prime minister's office, the parliament, every ministry, the Palace of Justice, and the police headquarters. The National Cathedral of the Catholic Church, the Holy Trinity Cathedral of the Episcopal Church, and many far more humble places of worship: decimated. The new, sophisticated campus of Quisqueya University and centers of learning from tall, bustling high schools to one-room kinder-gartens: flat. Because of Haiti's extreme shortage of schools, the standard was to have two shifts, one in the morning and one in the afternoon, so on that fateful Tuesday at 4:53 p.m. many were packed with students and teachers.

Haitians also suffered profound collective grief, psychological trau-ma, and disabling injuries. About six thousand to eight thousand lost limbs and/or digits.[2] An estimated 1.9 million were made homeless and dispossessed,[3] left to create their own replacement houses out of found materials and to survive in subhuman and life-threatening conditions in tent cities.

✖

Ground zero of the earthquake was near Gressier, close to my former home in Mòn Pitimi, Millet Mountain, which was not a mountain at all but hamlets strung across hills and flat land. I lived there for two stretches in the mid-1970s and early '80s, running a grammar school, literacy program, and shade-tree clinic. Most of my friends and adoptive sisters had long since passed away, life in Millet Mountain being a short proposition, but I was sick with worry over the fate of those who remained. Communications networks were down, but that community hadn't had access to telephone or e-mail even before the earthquake, back in what we never thought we would consider the good old days.

The days that followed were a frenzy, with far-flung family and friends trying to identify the dead and reconnect with the living. When cell phone reception returned to Port-au-Prince, I began getting text messages from women announcing that they were sleeping on the dirt in parks and drinking water from gutters, asking if there was any way to get funding for food and phone minutes for their grassroots groups, and urging *me* to be strong.

Family and associates began asking, "Are you going down?" This was a logical question, as I had worked closely with women's, farmers', democracy, and economic justice movements ever since those days on Millet Mountain. "I'm not a doctor," I replied. "I'd be useless." Instead, I tried to be as helpful as I could from the United States. In passing days, however, a few friends in Haiti and closer to home encouraged me to make the trip to explore how international support could be most useful. Already yearning to check on those whose fates I didn't know, I was persuaded. Thus it was that in the first week of February, I found myself on the island—though on the eastern part, in the Dominican Republic, since Haiti's Toussaint Louverture International Airport was closed to passenger planes. A friend from the Dominican small-farmers' movement drove me through the night in a truck to an unrecognizable Port-au-Prince, where survivors were still heaving with shock and the earth with aftershocks.

What I had suspected from the news and messages filtering up to New Orleans became obvious within my first hours in the capital. Even while corpses were a common sight, social movements—also known as popular movements, or mass-based, political-action groups—were already fixing their gaze on the horizon. It was the same one their enslaved forebears viewed more than two hundred years ago. They knew that their country's devastation—before the earthquake as now—was not inevitable. They knew that traditional "recovery" would fail to recover much of anything except the previous inequities. They knew that reconstruction could be, had to be, grounded in democracy, where all had a say. And they were organizing.

I found another silver lining. My friends on Millet Mountain had been safer than most. Their one-room houses of sticks and mud hadn't always kept the rain off them and never lasted long, but the banana-leaf roofs were so minimal, they didn't crush people when they collapsed. A rare instance when being poorer was better.

⌗

Fault Lines focuses on the first year after the quake, peering deep into the cracks opened in the society, economy, and polity. It casts a backward look at history to examine how such deep social fault lines developed in the first place. The book looks at what movements are doing to pry apart those cracks and wrest structural change from deep within. It studies ground level, where individuals are trying to straddle the divide every day, keeping their families alive and safe on shifting terrain. And it throws a forward glance at Haitians' visions for the future, in which they hope to find themselves on even, solid ground.

The book tells of the alternative principles and practices that the grassroots have tried to establish over time. You will read about the commitment to community and sharing, what Haitians call solidarity, which is not alternative at all but an ancient norm. *Fault Lines* describes how the old practices went into overdrive after the *event*, literally from the moment of the earth's heaving. They began with the search-and-rescue operations, which, contrary to international media images, were not led by foreign soldiers with German shepherds but by common citizens. First responders tell the stories of those they saved and those they couldn't as they toiled around the clock for days, sometimes with nothing more than their fingers, to free people from inside buildings and under rubble.

The book describes the citizen relief efforts that filled the gaping chasm between foreign donations and the urgent needs of survivors. You will read how these second responders who addressed recovery needs after the earliest moments of crisis—people who were more than likely homeless or hungry themselves—drew on the culture of solidarity to spontaneously offer lodging, medical care, food, and other sustenance. You will also learn about the organized aid programs that community groups launched, based in dignity, respect, and self-sufficiency. Some explicitly tried to model the world they wanted to see.

Fault Lines delves deeply into the agenda and endeavors of social movements. Leaders offer their analyses of Haiti's redevelopment, which is not principally about infrastructure, buildings, projects, or money. Instead, it is about power, about who gets to control what the future nation looks like. Women living under roofs of flowered bedsheets, farmers bringing food into the city for survivors, and rhetoric-filled university students explain how redistributing power, and creating a new society based on different theories and practices of it, are key to their work. They expound on how the moment is a critical one in which to create a cooperative relationship between state and nation, direct democracy, a domestic economy based foremost on satisfying the needs of all, and international relations premised on respect for each country's sovereignty.

The book also recounts what excellent business catastrophe is, like poverty and war. The Haitian story shows anew how one man's crisis can be another man's profit. Opportunists emerged from all over, from petty thieves roaming the internally displaced people's camps to so-called humanitarian aid organizations to well-connected UN officials to inside-the-Beltway contractors. You will read about how disaster capitalism, as Naomi Klein termed it in her book *The Shock Doctrine*, has run rampant.

The crisis in New Orleans, when the levees broke in the wake of Hurricane Katrina in 2005, weaves through the text as a point of comparison. Haiti's crisis reflects it in multiple ways. Yet the places were profoundly connected long before; nowhere else in the United States has a longer, deeper relationship with Haiti. Their histories crisscross, beginning with both having suffered colonization and enslavement by the Spanish and French. Louisiana even came to be part of the United States because of Haiti: France sold the Louisiana Territory to the United States in 1803 to recoup some of the financial losses it had incurred while trying to defeat the Haitian revolution (as well as to create a "maritime rival," as Napoleon called it, to England).[4] Blacks, mulattoes, and whites, free and enslaved, moved back and forth between the two places so much that, by 1809, one in two of New Orleans's inhabitants was from Haiti.[5] Today, the populations share gene pools and names via the same French, Spanish, and African ancestors. They have similar cultures, with connections between the music, the French language and the Creole ones, Carnival and parading (*rara*, traditional musical troupes in Haitian streets, and second lines and Mardi Gras Indians in New Orleans's streets), Creole food and Creole architecture, Catholicism, and the religion spelled Vodou in Haiti and Voodoo in New Orleans. Both places are rich in laid-back and highly interactive communities, and keeping them strong is what underlies a lot of the traditions like courtyard and stoop sitting, "speaking to" your neighbor, and communal street reveling.

The dual disasters stripped naked the trappings of difference between the richest and poorest countries in the hemisphere. New Orleans and Haiti are two predominantly black, low-income locales where the ongoing devastation has been only partly about nature. It has also been about inequitable distribution of power and wealth, and the race- and class-biased policies that have left certain groups highly vulnerable. It has been about government neglect, beginning years in advance when the authorities failed to heed experts' warnings about the disintegrating levees in New Orleans and the active fault systems under Haiti. The destruction has also been about corporate malfeasance and government disregard of it. Mirror images of disaster capitalism have been at play, even from some of the same companies. Construction has been driven more by developers, contractors, and profit-mongers than by those most directly impacted. Similar models have been patterned on privatization and market-driven solutions, and have led to highly unequal redevelopment. Only some—generally the lighter-skinned and wealthier—have been able to return to their homes. The places also have closely parallel patterns of racist media and public portrayal, community mobilization, and cultural resistance.

New Orleans appears here, too, because my vantage point has shifted back and forth between it and Haiti, both during the year in focus here and throughout life. I was born, raised, and now live in New Orleans, fourth generation. And though I wasn't residing in the city at the time of the flood, I became involved even while the category-five hurricane was still headed straight for it, as I frantically tried to regain contact with my octogenarian parents, much as so many of us would experience later with relatives and others we love in Haiti. I quickly became engaged with grassroots relief efforts in the Lower Ninth Ward, in an experience that was as illuminating as it was disturbing. As for Haiti, I have lived and worked with communities and social movements there off and on—mainly on—for more than two-thirds of my life. The two venues have been my central points of observation and engagement on the planet.

⁂

Three principles run through the words and events on the pages to come. First is "Nothing about us without us," an expression used by movements around the world to mean that those who are the focus of discussion must be allowed to speak for themselves and participate meaningfully in decisions. Nursing mothers, professionals, small business owners, and unemployed farmers all need to be included in planning and policymaking. Not only is it right, but their lived experiences and wisdom are essential to creating a society that functions through equal opportunity, peace, and rights. Second is that everyone must benefit from those decisions.

Typed out, those first couple of tenets look ridiculously simple. Yet neither is in operation in Haiti today, nor has either ever been. The vast majority of citizens have been excluded from public discourse, a share in the power, and fruits of the economy. Haiti is not exceptional in this regard. Yet the extreme nature of the long-entrenched disaster, coupled with the recent disaster, make it an especially revealing case study. As *Fault Lines* recounts, the silencing and erasure of grassroots civil society today is why all the policy prognoses, recovery blueprints, and humanitarian programs delivered from on high will fail to make any significant difference in the lives of the majority. It is why, in fact, they have already failed.

The third principle is that when people—even those with no capital or access—unite and organize, they can and do create dramatic, unpredictable changes. They can make the cost of maintaining the status quo so high that conceding land or wealth or power becomes in the interest of the landed or wealthy or powerful. As the book *Globalization from Below* puts it, "The power of the people is a secret that is repeatedly forgotten, to be rediscovered every time a new social movement arises."[6]

This is why no prototype defined by a current or former U.S. president or even a new Haitian president, or the Haitian business sector, or foreign agencies, is going to reconstruct Haiti. No clean, plunk-down development model will ever "build back better," to use Bill Clinton's slogan. Oil-drum artists and textile workers and sidewalk beauticians will end up impacting the future one way or the other, if not through inclusion in the discussion, then through their noncompliance or their rebellion.

That's why the stories told in *Fault Lines* are ultimately about hope. Never mind that forcing sustained change against the will of the local elite and political class, and the world's strongest forces, has been the most obdurate challenge of Haiti's life. Never mind the new challenges that the earthquake has provoked. Haitians still claim hope, along with fortitude and defiance, as badges of honor. Their premise, that things don't have to be the way they are, is still heartily alive. Citizens will proudly inform you that non-submission is an intractable element of their culture. Since *twelve*, I've heard from fiery activists and comfortable observers, and people somewhere in between, variants of "We are a rebellious people," and "We're not going to just be passive forever, you know."

Elitane Athelus, founder of the women street-merchant group Amen to Brave Women Martyrs (roughly translated from Fanm Martir Ayibobo Brav), put it this way: "We won't stop struggling until the conditions of our lives change. Remember that we already led a revolution with our own two hands. We haven't lost completely. The water is still running in the canal."

For Elitane and her compatriots, this source of hope is, as social theorist Roberto Unger put it, a "consequence of action, not its cause."[7] They already know their potential as agents of change, since popular pressure from them has been the locus of all positive systemic advances. People who have never had a history class or even learned to read can tell you about their ancestors having put an end to both slavery and French colonial rule in 1804. Each generation passes down the memories of martyrs and resisters, like Anacaona, the Arawak queen murdered by Spanish colonists; François Mackandal, the maroon leader who encouraged raids on plantations and the poisoning of slave owners during the 1750s; Boukman and Cécile Fatiman, the Vodou priest and priestess who led the 1791 ceremony where the slave revolution started; Toussaint Louverture and Jean-Jacques Dessalines, former slaves who served as generals in the revolution; Charlemagne Péralte, who led a guerrilla resistance against the 1915–34 U.S. military occupation; and Jean-Marie Vincent, Antoine Izméry, Jean Dominique, and so many others who have been killed in the quest for a new society in the past few decades. Others speak of how they and their comrades brought down the thirty-year Duvalier dictatorship in 1986, and still more can tell you what they have done since then to win social, economic, and political advances.

Another source of hope shines through the grim reality. As the chapters to come will demonstrate, Haiti's experience shows that large-scale, exaggerated poverty is unnatural and avoidable. It is the result of choices in policy, programs, and practices by the national elite and international community. This means that neither Haiti nor the world is condemned to its current state. Other choices can yield different, better outcomes.

Haitians are like so many alchemists trying to transmute hope into social transformation. But the challenge is not theirs alone, because neither the sources of the problem nor the solutions lie exclusively in their country. As *Fault Lines* discusses, the challenge is global, so that success will depend in large part on how much the rest of us choose to work toward a different world economy and body politic.

※

The interviews and information in *Fault Lines* were gleaned mainly during that first, shattered year, half of which I spent in Haiti and the other half of which I spent in constant contact with Haiti from New Orleans. Chapters dated sequentially, two per month, explore the vital issues as they unfolded real-time. Some chapters offer historical or political analysis, others interviews. Some feature investigative journalism, others stories from the streets.

Fault Lines was an unplanned birth. The surprise offspring came to be this way: Because much of my work involves collaborating with people's movements, in Haiti I wound up in dozens of discussions and strategy sessions. Also, so as to transmit to the outside world unheard perspectives and analyses, I interviewed hundreds of Haitians. Among them were the director of a UN agency and anti-UN demonstrators, former government ministers and former factory workers, environmentalists and those chopping down trees to make a living, architects and those living under cardboard, doctors and those dying for want of health care, antiviolence advocates and girls who had just been raped, historians and those making history. People shared their viewpoints from earthquake-sheared cement blocks, the new standard in seating, under tarps in displacement camps; at the neighborhood speakeasy on pitch-black nights during *blakawout*, blackouts, over warm bottles of Prestige beer; on mats of ant-ridden bagasse outside mud huts; on the veranda of a certain famed gingerbread hotel, which was the only place I could count on for food and Internet during the early, desperate days. One result of all this information-gathering, in that first year following the *event*, was publication of just shy of one hundred articles. Down the road, Fran Benson of Cornell University Press and I began discussing the conversion of this material into a book. Fran had already put her significant energy and talents into publishing an earlier book on Haiti with me, so I knew to expect a great collaboration. I consulted movement leaders in Haiti and colleagues at Other Worlds, the economic and social justice organization that I coordinate, and all were excited, so off we went.

Where not otherwise attributed, all quotations come from interviews done by me or, in a few cases, one of my coworkers. Each person whose words or stories are included here gave explicit permission. To request it, an Other Worlds staff person and a generous volunteer spent weeks climbing onto the backs of motorcycles and *taptaps*, the pickup trucks tricked out to look more like Carnival floats than shared taxis. They tracked down the farmer in his rice field, the cook next to the trash-strewn ravine in the dusty shantytown, and the famed journalist in his television studio—which was open-air and makeshift, like almost everything else post-earthquake. The team read back in Creole what I had written, explained the context in which I hoped to place the material, and asked whether the person wished to be included. Everyone did, fifty-one in all, and signed a form giving me permission to print their words but maintaining full ownership over them. On the occasions where we were unable to reach a speaker for authorization, or where I was sure someone had not intended his or her thoughts or actions to appear on a library shelf, I changed the name and disguised details. I also renamed all children, plus five people who asked to use a pseudonym; even in seemingly safe times in Haiti, the chance of a return to repression always looms. In the case of the woman referred to as Suze Abraham, she was happy to use her real name, but when I asked if we could change it because of the intimate nature of her story, she allowed as how that would be fine, too. I kept off of these pages all personal, cultural, and political secrets that people have asked me to guard over the years, and a few more just out of precaution.

My role, that of linguistic and cultural translator, comes with all the tensions that reflect the global politics of power. As a middle-class, white, U.S. American woman, I have had the literacy, passport, funding, time, and many other resources to write this book, so that the truths of people who have none of those things could find the world. I strive to apply my privilege toward shifting power and breaking down the inequities that caused the contradictions in the first place.

Though my name is on the cover, and though I alone am responsible for any shortcomings or errors, *Fault Lines* is an Other Worlds production. It owes its existence to the input of my extraordinary coworkers: Lauren Elliott, Alexis Erkert, Tory Field, and Deepa Panchang (more about their contributions in the acknowledgments). *Fault Lines* also owes its life to the organization's financial backing, which in turn comes from our heartful funder-allies.

Most of all, the book is possible because of the trust, teachings, and words of my Haitian friends and colleagues.

All proceeds from this book will either go back into Other Worlds' own program of supporting the organizations and coalitions you will read about here, or will be passed directly on to those groups.

A couple of clarifications on language: First, the word "peasant" is considered pejorative to some Westerners. I use it anyway, since it is how small farmers in Haiti self-identify, and since it accurately describes a socioeconomic position in an intact feudal society in a way that the descriptor "farmer," which describes only a profession, does not. Second, I use the term "U.S. American" to differentiate from all the other peoples of the Americas, who are also Americans.

Other Worlds and I offer *Fault Lines* with the hope that the next volume will tell a very different tale of Haiti and the planet, one in which the most powerful neither make the decisions nor take the winnings, but in which the people you will read about here—and their sisters and brothers everywhere—are closer to creating the world for which they are risking all. I offer it, moreover, with the desire that Alina "Tibebe" Cajuste, the poet gaining on her lifetime goal of becoming literate as I was writing this book, will be that volume's author.

1

We Don't Have Enough Water to Make Tears

Surviving the Earthquake, or Not

January 2010

"Oh, hey, you haven't wished me happy new year yet." That's what saved the Catholic leader's life, twelve days into a year that had had about as much happiness as it was going to get.

Monsignor André Pierre, rector of the University of Notre Dame of Haiti, was racing to a meeting at the archbishop's office next to the pink and yellow National Cathedral. "I waved to the archbishop up on the gallery from below and then I started running up the stairs," he said. Then someone stopped him for that new-year greeting:

> At that second everything went black. I thought I was having a heart attack. I shifted to the left, I shifted to the right, and then I went up in the air. Then the building fell on top of me. I said, "André, move." I rolled and crawled. I couldn't see anything; it was black. It was like being underwater, except it was earth. I ate so much dirt I can't tell you. It took me about forty-five minutes to get out. You couldn't see my clothes, my face, anything; I was just one solid mass of earth. Someone came by and wiped my face off and said, "Oh, it's you."

The archbishop and the other monsignor who had been awaiting him to start the meeting were both killed.

There were wounded people everywhere. I shouted "Bring the wounded!" I couldn't open the driver's door of my car; cement blocks and debris and a beam had fallen on it. But I got in through the passenger door. We loaded up five or six people to take to the hospital, but there was no more hospital. So I took them to [the neighborhood of] Delmas, and we set up a clinic there. I called my brother who's a doctor, and he told us how to clean the wounds.

Everyone can tell you an epic story of survival, their own or someone else's. Monsignor Pierre worked with a young computer technician, Kertus Viaud, who lived to tell this one:

I felt the ground shake and I knew an earthquake was coming. I'd heard you were supposed to get under a solid structure, but the best I could do was jump into my baby's cradle. When the shock hit, it turned the cradle sideways and shot me out into the air.

I landed and was about to run, and then I suddenly had the idea that if I ran, I could die. I stopped and let the dust settle until I could see, and that's when I saw that I wasn't on the ground, I was on a roof. If I had run, I would have fallen off and maybe died. I was standing there in just my boxers, still holding my cell phone I'd had in my hand when the *event* happened. I pulled two big shards of glass out of my feet that I hadn't even felt.

That night I slept on the sidewalk without a sheet or anything. The next night, I was sleeping on [the boulevard of] Champ de Mars when they said there was a tsunami coming. Everyone was yelling, "The water is coming!" We jumped up, but the man next to me didn't move, so I shook his shoulder and told him, "Hey, come on." That's when I realized he was dead.

Deriva Antoine, a young woman who had been a street vendor before she lost everything she had to sell, recounted: "When the earthquake struck, I bent over my baby like this." She crouched and braced, arms crooked. "I said, 'Even if I die, this little baby is going to live.'"

Josette Pérard, Haiti director of the grassroots development foundation Lambi Fund, shared this story:

Right in front of us a wall started to fall. Our driver veered really fast to the right, and the building fell where we had just been. That driver saved my life.

It was rush hour and the street was packed. A lot of cars all around us got crushed. They took a child out of the car in front of us and I thought for sure it was killed. But the child was so small, it came out alive.

Houses were falling left and right. I heard people screaming. A woman who'd just been pulled out of a house was lying on the ground bleeding, shouting, "Help! Help!" I said to two policeman, "Call an ambulance for her." Those police were going crazy; they had family somewhere, too. They said there was nothing they could do, which was true. There was no way an ambulance could get through; the earthquake had thrown cars into the middle of the street.

A little schoolgirl was in shock, panicking. She came to me sobbing, asking for my phone so she could call home. She called and called, but no telephones were working. I saw two people I knew putting a wounded man on a door to take him to the hospital.

People were walking in the streets like zombies. A man we knew said to us: "My wife? My children? Where are they?"

Three-year-old Ali turned to look at me as he was being dragged by his grandmother's hand into a rural community center turned refugee shelter. Apropos of nothing, he announced: "I was singing. I flew in the air. There was dirt everywhere. I slept in the street."

Wilson Dumas is a *taptap* driver who walks with a permanent limp from a crushed tibia. He is lucky to be alive, and knows it. "I was walking down the street. The next thing I knew, I woke up and I was on the ground with my legs buried in cement. I didn't know what had happened or how I got there. I looked to my left and my right; I was lying right between two dead people."

I had several conversations with the soft-spoken, ever-smiling auto mechanic Gary before he ever mentioned having risked his life to save his near-dead infant. He told the story as calmly as he might have described a car repair job he'd just completed:

For every home destroyed, a story of life or death. Photograph by Ben Depp.

My house collapsed with my baby in it. She was a year and some months. Two houses collapsed in front of mine, so I had to climb across the roofs of all three houses to get there, but every time I tried to climb up the houses kept dancing, so I had to wait a couple of hours. When I got inside, my baby was lying on the bed. My godmother had fallen on top of her, and lots of blocks were on top of them, and they were both passed out. It took me a long time to move the blocks away so I could get to them. I thought my baby was dead, but when I picked her up, I could feel a little breath. She was unconscious for three or four hours, all her limbs just splayed out. Now she's fine, and she wants to be with me every second.

Fanfan is eleven, as thin as a blade of grass. He was standing outside his new home, this one made of a blue tarp and sticks. One wall was completely open to thousands of new neighbors who had relocated to the same park. He had lost his sandals, his only shoes, inside his house when it fell. He told his story in a voice just above a whisper:

I was trapped in the house all day long until nighttime. My house was in a three-story building, and I was on the first floor. We all started running toward the garage. Some people got out, but I didn't. I couldn't move because when the building collapsed, cement blocks fell on my legs. My godmother was in the room with me, and I called to her, but she was dead. I kept calling out for help, but no one heard me. Finally that night, after ten, my father pulled some blocks up and found me there. He's a coffin-maker, and he got back from work. My mother helped him. They pulled me out.

Were you scared? "Yes." What were you thinking about as you lay there? "I was lying there calling for someone, and I thought I might die. But I didn't want to die, and I thought maybe God would save me."

⌘

The old downtown around Grand Rue looked post-nuclear. The streets were ghostly and silent, and even in daytime it seemed dark. Small fires burned in the middle of roads. Nothing was intact: no infrastructure, no commerce, no community, no electricity. Here the tall buildings didn't even pancake; they just crumbled. No vehicles moved.

Those who were out stepped slowly from high point to high point through the gray muck of the streets. Their clothes were rags, their bodies emaciated. No one smiled when I greeted them. A man sat alone on a broken chair. When I offered condolences, he shook his head and said, "It's bitter."

Where a bustling open-air market had recently been, several naked men pulled buckets of dark water up from a manhole. It was bathtime, post-earthquake.

Fourteen-year-old Donal appeared by my side from nowhere, wearing impossibly clean slacks and a neat polo shirt. He took it upon himself to narrate the scene. "You see these piles?" He pointed to what used to be sidewalks, where not long ago *timachann*, street vendors, had squatted over their wares of polka-dotted guinea hens, long-expired antibiotic pills, and dog-eared *Read English without Tears* paperbacks. The sidewalks had been replaced by ground concrete that looked as if it had been through a blender, and rebar bent like bread-wrapper twist ties. "All under these piles: *timachann*. They're everywhere in there. The day after the earthquake you could hear people screaming all over. But no help came; people just had to dig with their fingernails.

"Then there were piles of bodies in the streets. They were stacked high, here, here, everywhere. And the smell, oh, it was terrible."

Donal paused, then asked, "Do you think if you lost your three children you could go crazy?" Yes, you could. Do you know someone who lost three children? "Yeah. All her kids. I have another friend who came home and found every member of his family dead."

All day, every day, I asked acquaintances and strangers their experiences of January 12. Most told about family members and others they loved who hadn't made it. The stories of death were so profuse that a doctor told me, "They've become almost banal." A Haitian friend who lives in the United States said that, by day seven, she had learned of seventy-five people close to her who had perished. After that, she stopped reading e-mail.

A taxi driver who gave me a ride until his old car gave out told me,

I lost my child. He was my only son, four years old. He and his mother were outside, and he ran into the house. She went in to get him and just then the earthquake happened. She ran back out, and he didn't. That's the way it is. God said there is no life without problems. When my wife cries about losing our son, I tell her: "*Cheri*, sweetheart, God gives and God takes away. That's just part of what you have to expect from life." Tears have never come from my eyes once since January 12. Life, problems. Problems, life. You have to accept it.

One afternoon a few weeks after *twelve* on Delmas Road, a well-groomed man pulled a red car up to the curb. The car was in ruins. Its roof, sides, doors, windshield, and windows had been sheared off as though with a jagged-edged saw. Every seat but the driver's was mashed. And yet the vehicle was running. I walked over to look at this post-disaster innovation. "We have to take courage," the man informed me. Did you lose your house? I asked. "My house, yes, I lost it. And my two children." He exited the car by stepping straight out from the seat. Reaching into his wallet, he pulled out a laminated school ID of his daughter, ten-year-old Christianne Louis. In the picture, her shy smile pushed up her chubby cheeks, and her braided hair was festooned with red ribbons. "Her and my sixteen-year-old." He said earnestly, "We'll tell God thanks," and sidestepped back into the car. As he maneuvered it back onto the street, he called out, "Have a nice day." I stood stock-still and watched as he drove away.

Judith Simeon, a popular educator with women and peasant groups, told of the elderly Madame Saintilus, founder and director of a now-destroyed school. About two hundred of her students died within it. Day after day she, her sister, and her husband just sat in front of the school's remains, under the sun and the moon, broken with grief. Judith went over and strung a sheet of plastic over their heads to protect them.

In a meeting for the survivors of a women's micro-enterprise group, a young woman in a baseball cap said, "We've lost everyone. We don't have enough water to make tears anymore."

2

What We Have, We Share

Solidarity Undergirds Rescue and Relief

January 2010

"From the first hour, Haitians engaged in every type of solidarity imaginable—one supporting the other, one helping the other, one saving the other. If any of us is alive today, we can say that it's thanks to this solidarity," said Yolette Etienne. Yolette is an alternative development expert and a longtime activist who cut her political teeth in the youth rebellion against Jean-Claude Duvalier. At the time of the earthquake she was heading the national program of Oxfam Great Britain; today she does the same for Oxfam America.

Sitting in my courtyard because for many months she wouldn't set foot in a cement building, Yolette told how she had experienced solidarity right after the earth heaved. "It was a long night. Long, long, long. But you never felt alone. It was a huge collective grief without end. You saw people crying, then they'd sing. But it was sweet, too. Everyone was working together. No one shouted at anyone. We all spent the night trying to get people out of their houses with our hands. When we were finished, we'd go to another house and start over."

Amber Munger, a U.S. American human rights activist working with a community nonprofit, e-mailed out this account on day six:

> Never have I seen such motivation, determination, compassion, and solidarity among people. When we entered Port-au-Prince, the city had fallen and was continuing to fall as a result of continuous aftershocks. The streets were full of people sitting together. Everyone was sitting in the middle of the roads for fear that the houses would continue to fall on them. They were singing. The whole city was singing. They were singing songs of solidarity. They were singing songs of thanks and praise that they were still able to sing and to be together. These people have lost everything. The city is now a city of refugees. But they are putting their voices together to be thankful.

No help came from any officials. The Haitian government was invisible and impotent. My friend Djab Beaubrun said, "From the first second, the government disappeared. Not the first minute, the first second." Local police and firemen were left dead, overwhelmed, or without supplies because their stations had been obliterated. Most hospitals were damaged and unable to provide care. Several days passed before the UN, foreign governments, and international agencies began sending in search-and-rescue teams. When they did arrive, many were posted to the collapsed UN headquarters, upscale hotels, and supermarkets where foreigners were trapped. The professional international teams were required to be accompanied by armed foreign troops, severely limiting the pace of their response. Furthermore, they faced impediments like fuel shortages and the damaged airport and seaport. Though they worked very hard and under great risk, in the first two weeks they pulled out only about 130 survivors.[1]

Instead, ordinary citizens made up the largest force of rescuers and first responders. They strained to hear sounds from live beings buried under fallen buildings, and dug with bare hands, boards, and pot lids through broken glass, cement, and rebar to unearth people, live or dead. They reentered still-shaking structures to find more. Mesita Petit of the market women's support group Amen to Brave Women Martyrs said, "We shared our pain and our suffering. If you heard your baby in the ruins crying 'Mama, Mama, Mama,' fourteen people would run and help you. If you didn't have a piece of bread, someone would give you theirs."

People carried the wounded to hospitals on doors ripped from jambs, flattened cardboard boxes, or whatever could serve as a stretcher. Strangers offered use of their cars, trucks, or motorcycles to carry injured survivors to hospitals and corpses to mass graves. Medical personnel, despite their own losses and inadequate space and supplies, worked through the first night and following weeks to perform emergency amputations and treat hundreds of thousands.

The same solidarity and gift economy is what has kept this resource-poor people alive for centuries. Gifting is a time-honored means of keeping away hunger, prolonged illness, and early death. The circulation of objects and services has a second purpose, acting as a shuttle passing repeatedly through a loom to weave loyalty, gratitude, and historical memory. The warp and weft sustain values as well as relationships—not just between individuals, but between everyone as part of an inseparable whole. In theory, if not always in practice, the Haitian cultural understanding of community is that it is only as strong as its parts, only as healthy as its members.

When, as part of a research project, I asked journalist and TV host Konpè Filo whether Haiti was poor, he answered, "That depends on how you define poverty and wealth. Is Haiti poor? No, I would say Haiti is a rich country. One of Haiti's riches is the solidarity and community we have. We're raised in compounds with common courtyards, and we know that what you have, you have to share with your neighbors. You stand in front of your neighbor's house and you ask, 'Did you already have coffee today?' You know that your success and your family's success depend on the community's well-being. That's the model we have."

Yolette Etienne's story pivoted on that model. She recounted acts of heroism that were the everyday norm on January 12 and long after. "One man who was by himself, all by himself, he went into a collapsed building fifteen times to try to get people out. It was so dangerous. He pulled, he moved blocks, he found a saw and cut a steel door. He never did save anyone, but he wouldn't give up." How many people escaped from the wreckage and returned inside to save others, only to die in a violent aftershock themselves?

Yolette's eighty-seven-year-old mother was killed by a tumbling wall. Yolette said, "The man she'd been visiting with, a friend of the family, wouldn't leave her body until I got there. He didn't even know yet what had happened to his own family, but he wouldn't leave her."

Getro Nelio was a twenty-five-year-old basketball coach whose stature approximated a stalk of sugarcane and whose face had lost all affect. He said,

> What hurt me most was that my father died in front of me and there was nothing I could do for him. His head was crushed, and I told myself there was no way he could live. Meanwhile, there were people under the cement screaming, "Getro, here I am!" I had to abandon my father to save those people. I couldn't forget him, but the only thing on my mind was to save people who might live, who were injured, especially women. My father's house was a three-story building, and all the stories fell and made a sandwich. We took twenty-eight out alive, but for those underneath, we didn't have any way to get them out. Thirty-seven total died. So many people were inside just then because that's when *Frijolito* was on.

Frijolito, or Little Bean, is what Haitians call the Mexico-based soap opera that is actually named *Amarte así*, To Love You Like This. "*Frijolito* saved him" or "*Frijolito* killed him" became common expressions for whether someone lived or died while watching the show during the earthquake.

Getro said, "Foreigners always think badly of Haiti; they think it's full of thieves and insecurity. But Haiti is a beautiful country. Don't underestimate Haitians."

Some villains were at work, too, disaster profiteers taking what they could get in the chaos, be it money from a deserted home or a girl to rape or foreign aid dollars to cadge. Overwhelmingly, their actions during those days were exceptions to the rule of helping and giving.

❊

Beyond acting as the first line of rescue, Haitian people were also the number one source of emergency humanitarian aid. Even before the end of the desperate effort to save those who could be saved—before all those still trapped were presumed to be dead—survivors' urgent needs had to be addressed. Though most people were on the razor's edge of survival themselves, they compiled what food they had or scrounged it from abandoned stores (what outsiders often referred to as "looting") to distribute to the hungry. They located charcoal and cooked meals to give out. They shared slim reserves of water, sheets, and money with loved ones and those they had never before seen. In the dearth of professional medical care, small groups organized their own triage and decided who should be treated first—with whatever was on hand, be it a newspaper for a splint or traditional leaf medicine for wounds. People who had a place to sleep took in those who didn't: orphaned and abandoned children, injured and ill, elders, or whole families. Some took it upon themselves to organize education or recreation for children, since no schools were functioning.

(Spectacular daily actions of solidarity were alive and well in New Orleans just after the storm, too, as anyone who was there can tell you, though accounts of them were largely absent from the public record. People with no official function or training or resources took great risk to rescue others from attics and rooftops, by foot or boat; tracked down lost children; undertook treacherous journeys to evacuate and care for senior citizens, wheelchair-bound and sick individuals, and those left in hospitals; took into their homes abandoned neighbors and pets; and performed many other unheralded acts of valor.)

The computer technician Kertus Viaud recounted that, the day after the earthquake, he watched a young man on a street pass four candies and one palm-size plastic sack of water around to strangers who happened to be next to him. Kertus heard the youth tell them, "Don't take too much water; it's for all of us." Kertus also said that his wife, who was nursing their three-month-old, took to her breast and kept alive another baby whose parents couldn't be found.

U.S. American human rights advocate Dr. Sasha Kramer sent out an e-mail on January 19 with this account:

> A large yellow truck was parked in front of the gate and rapidly unloading hundreds of bags of food over our fence. The hungry crowd had already begun to gather and in the dark it was hard to decide how to best distribute the food. . . . Our friend began to get everyone in the crowd into a line that stretched down the road. We braced ourselves for the fighting that we had heard would come, but in a miraculous display of restraint and compassion, people

lined up to get the food and one by one the bags were handed out without a single serious incident. . . .

By the time we got back into the house, the food had all been distributed and the patient [whose leg had just been amputated] was waking up. . . . At one point one of the Haitian men working at the hospital came in and leaned over him and said to him in Creole, "Listen man, even if your family couldn't be here tonight we want you to know that everyone here loves you, we are all your brothers and sisters."

So, don't believe Anderson Cooper when he says that Haiti is a hotbed for violence and riots, it is just not the case. In the darkest of times, Haiti has proven to be a country of brave, resilient and kind people.

The popular educator Judith Simeon said, "It was truly those who had nothing who did the most." She recounted her own activities only after I prodded her.

I put together a group of people; we each went and helped others. People didn't have any food, so we shared what we had. The youth could walk to get what they needed, so they weren't my priority. I was interested in people who couldn't get by. I used what I knew with dehydrated people, especially little children and elders who were so weak. I gave them oral rehydration serum with water, salt, and sugar. I also used my knowledge of herbal medicines, natural remedies with plants and leaves, to help people heal.

For two weeks, two friends and I took care of a group of fourteen kids whose parents had died, while we tried to find their family in the countryside or other cousins and neighbors who could take them in. The kids were as young as three. . . . No, I didn't have any relation to them. It was our citizen obligation to take care of those who needed it.

Immediately, the newly homeless and those worried by so many violent aftershocks—basically everyone—congregated in open fields, public plazas, school yards, and streets, as far as possible from buildings that might yet topple. Private landowners allowed or actively encouraged displaced people to set up shelter on their lands (though this would later change). People elected camp presidents and committees. They organized themselves to seek out shelter materials and other supplies, and to designate areas for toilets and bathing. They compiled lists of camp residents: names; numbers of families, children, pregnant women, and sick people; and special needs. They hammered signs asking for assistance on telephone poles, like "Camp Africa. Need: food, water, medicines, tents," "Bodies inside," and "Jesus save us"—in English, since the appeals were directed at foreigners. Later, some camp leaders would attempt to navigate complicated external aid structures on behalf of their camps.

To provide safety in the insecure environment of camps and streets, some women kept a vigilant eye out for women and children who were at high risk of violence, intervening where necessary. Some men, like Getro, left their own families to provide added protection to women-headed groups.

Throughout the countryside, rural farmers cared for the six hundred thousand who had fled earthquake-hit urban centers.[2] Some of the emigrants had headed home to their families to avoid sleeping in the streets, while others had simply jumped on the first bus out. A lot of those buses had been sent to Port-au-Prince by authorities from non-struck areas, to evacuate people for free. The rural second responders took in multitudes, usually without any organization or financial support.

In one example, Arianne Jean, a street vendor, and her husband, Destin Monfortin, a farmer, hosted eighteen guests from their extended family. This brought the number of mouths to feed in their household to twenty-seven. When I encountered them one night in the village of Papaye, a rural outpost in the Central Plateau, their home had been full for five weeks. "If it had been for money, we would never have done it," Arianne said. "We did it because we wanted them to have a life. If God saved the lives of some of us from a catastrophe of that size, it's so we could protect the lives of others. People have to live; you have to receive them.

"It's been a big knife stab for us to find food for them all. But since we're peasants, what we have, we share so they can live, too."

Over recent decades, in Haiti as around the world, insecurity in stranger-filled cities has deterred the free flow of solidarity. Perceptions of scarcity, which encourage people to believe they have to hold on to what they have because there isn't enough to go around, have frayed it, too. The capitalist message that to succeed, one must accumulate (otherwise called hoarding), contradicts the impulse to pass on; that, too, has worn down the tradition. The earthquake has been a reminder to most Haitians, and to others paying attention, of the value of nonmonetary transactions of services, care, and goods.

Some say that mutual aid and gifting, writ large, should be recognized as explicit parts of an alternative economy. Ricot Jean-Pierre, advocacy director of the Haitian Platform to Advocate Alternative Development (Plate-forme Haïtienne de Plaidoyer pour un Développement Alternatif, or PAPDA), said, "Our work is to show that we can enter into another development logic that's not just via the market but that's through the community, with a solidarity economy."

This culture of generosity has been a redeeming element post-*twelve*, both a lifeline and a source of pride. Yolette Etienne said, "The tremendous chain of solidarity we saw from the day of the earthquake on: that is our capacity. That is our victory. That is our heart."

Yolette buried her mother in the garden behind the flattened family home and bordered the spot with rocks and flowers. At the funeral ceremony, she told those of us assembled next to the mound, "From now on, let nothing we do be for the individual. Let it all be for the collective."

3

Pearl of the Antilles

The Political Economy of Peril

February 2010

The geographic catastrophe was natural. The magnitude of death and injury was not. Many earthquakes have registered higher than 7.0 on the Richter scale but resulted in only a fraction of the casualties. Chile, for example, was flailed by an 8.8-er six weeks after *twelve*, but only 723 people died. The astronomical destruction in Haiti came down to politics and economics. It can be traced to structural violence—the policies and systems that reflect colonialism, imperialism, racism, and patriarchy and that play out in very stark and gritty ways in the lives of the poor.

You can track the devastation, in part, to two International Monetary Fund (IMF) standby agreements in the 1980s and 1990s, which compelled the Haitian government to lower tariffs on food imports as a condition for receiving loans. The consequence was a flood of U.S. commodities with whose low prices Haitian farmers could not compete. In the 1990s, hundreds of thousands of failing farmers fled their land for foreign soil or the capital. They came to Port-au-Prince to *chèche lavi*, make a life, as red-light windshield washers or vendors of Kellogg's Corn Flakes long past their use-by date. By 2010, a city meant for 200,000 to

250,000 was home to two or three million people. More than eight in ten lived in shantytowns,[1] in overcrowded housing of substandard materials perched on steep hillsides and ravines and on former marshlands infilled with garbage. An unknowable number of deaths on *twelve* were caused by the collapse of those inadequate houses in those precarious locales.

You can also link the casualty rate directly to government disregard of the rural poor, in an unbroken legacy from slavery times. Another reason many came to be in those houses on January 12 was that state services were all but nonexistent in the countryside. ID cards, colleges, specialized health care, and much else have always been available almost exclusively in a few cities. Countless people met their end because they were visiting the capital to test an egg-sized growth on their neck or study English or get a driver's license.

The roots of Haiti's structural violence stretch all the way back to 1492. Then, the island of Quisqueya—the Taíno name for the island that today hosts Haiti and the Dominican Republic, variously translated as "cradle of life," "mother of the earth," and "fruitful land"—became one of Christopher Columbus's points of entry into the so-called New World. The Spanish colonists who arrived with him enslaved the Arawak Indians, killing off almost all of them within twenty-seven years through grinding labor practices and European diseases.[2] To replenish their workforce, the Spanish began bringing in Africans, stolen mainly from the West and West-Central parts of the continent. Later, following a 1697 treaty to settle a land dispute with the French, the Spanish retreated to the eastern part of the island, now the Dominican Republic. The French who replaced them brought in labor-intensive sugarcane, along with vastly expanded numbers of Africans each year to work that cane.[3] Haiti became the most profitable colony in the world, known as the Pearl of the Antilles because of the wealth derived from the slaves' labor.

In 1804, an army of enslaved and free blacks and *gens de couleur*, people of racially mixed ancestry, won a complicated war that they had been waging since 1791. The victory created the only nation ever born from a successful slave uprising, the first black republic in the world, and the second independent republic in the Western Hemisphere.

But the revolution did not resolve the underlying issues over which it had been waged, and thus did not grant full liberation to the people. A few Haitians replaced the French in controlling land and power. The new elite were a combination of black military leaders from the war and light-skinned descendants of the colonists who, once the masters had fled, claimed the land based on parentage. When Jean-Jacques Dessalines, Haiti's first postcolonial ruler, attempted to redistribute some of the land, the new latifundia murdered him. Over the decades, self-proclaimed emperors and presidents-for-life exploited the poor for their own benefit, as well as the benefit of the landholding class in the countryside and the merchant class in the cities. Security forces—at different times military, paramilitary, police, rural sheriffs' good-ole-boy networks, and hired hit squads—aided and abetted the leaders by violently repressing dissent, while helping themselves to their own share of the booty. Economic and political benefits remained far from the reach of the new citizens.

The outside world opposed the free Haitians, too. All Western powers embargoed the sovereign black nation in an attempt to keep its message of freedom from other enslaved populations. (They failed, however, to stanch either trade or the call to liberation.) Moreover, France imposed an indemnity of 150 million gold francs in 1825 (later reduced to 60 million) for the value of income and property lost from the revolution, meaning slave labor and land. The combination of the embargoes and those debt payments crippled the country financially. France didn't recognize Haiti until 1838, with other Western powers doing so around the same time—except the United States, which held out until 1862.

Subsequent attempts to gain submission of the restive nation have included embargoes (from 1991 to 1994 and 2001 to 2004 by the United States, other nations, and financial institutions), coups d'état (with the United States playing leading roles in two as recently as 1991 and 2004),[4] and occupations (including one by the U.S. military from 1915 to 1934, and one by UN troops from 2004 until today).

During the first of those occupations, U.S. Marines ran Haiti with a leaden hand, drafting a new constitution, forcing Haitians into unpaid corvée, and creating a vicious new military. Haitian peasants calling themselves Cacos launched another guerrilla insurrection from strongholds in the mountains. They disrupted control until the marines brutally suppressed them in 1919. Broad-based political mobilization was key to finally ending the occupation, with a series of student strikes in 1929 leading to a nationwide general strike and international condemnation of the U.S. presence.[5]

You can see the roots of structural violence in more recent foreign treatment of Haiti, which ranges from exclusion and resource deprivation to direct, militaristic assaults. Many Haitians say they are still being punished for challenging slavery, white colonists, the French empire, and the hegemony of the United States and other powers. One Haitian told me, "The war against us, from back when we fought for our independence, has never ended."

The same roots push up all through the ground. You can see them in Haiti and across the planet in the social status of women and the sacrifices they have to make to keep their families alive. You can see them in the market-magic doctrine imposed by Washington and its allies, especially since the 1980s with structural adjustment (conditions on loans imposed by financial institutions) and economic globalization, which have given corporations free license to profit off the precious resources, people, and environments of sovereign nations. The policies have included lowering import tariffs on foreign food, as mentioned earlier; less government spending on health, education, and agriculture; privatization of essential services and industry; and new free-trade zones to house sweatshops.

The roots have damaged in extreme ways the lives of most of the individuals described within this book. They lie beneath the current concentration of resources and power. Haiti is the most unequal country in the Western Hemisphere.[6] It still hosts two disparate societies in an unofficial apartheid. The first group claims the lineage of colonizing Europeans as well as enslaved Africans, is biracial and black (and occasionally white), speaks French and Creole, is preponderantly Catholic, and is culturally cosmopolitan. Though only a small percentage of the population, this set controls money, land, industry, and—throughout almost all of Haitian history—government. The second group is almost exclusively black, Creole speaking, predominantly Vodouisant and Catholic (both at once, though Protestantism is growing), rural based or rural descended, culturally African, and destitute beyond reckoning.

Per capita income is $1,123 per year.[7] That means the average person makes $3 a day, but that average is skewed by the multimillionaire elite (or, to paraphrase the language of the Occupy movement, the .01 percent). On the other end, 80 percent lives below the poverty line, meaning less than $2.00 a day, and 54 percent lives in extreme poverty, meaning less than $1.25 a day.[8] That doesn't mean $2.00 or $1.25 *every* day, though; some days bring no income, and therefore no food, whatsoever.

In rural areas, 88 percent lives in poverty, and 67 percent in extreme poverty.[9] The country has one doctor for every 4,000 people, and one nurse for every 9,091 people.[10] Only 45 percent of school-age children are in school, and only 49 percent of adults are literate.[11] Haiti ranks 158th out of 187 countries in the 2011 UN Human Development Index,[12] though the conditions may actually be worse because of the impossibility of collecting reliable data post-quake.

Statistics aren't necessary to paint the picture, though. Anyone who knows anything about Haiti already knows the tagline, so common that the poet Jean-Claude Martineau calls it Haiti's last name: "the poorest country in the Western Hemisphere." The conditions of life are excruciating enough that Creole shares one word, *lamizè*, for both "poverty" and "misery." In all rural areas and many urban ones, the standard reply to "How are you?" is "*Pa pi mal.*" No worse.

The talk of structural violence, and why it has so harmed Haiti through the ages and the 2010 disaster, does not imply that a conspiracy is at work. None is needed. Haitians have not been harmed intentionally. They have simply been collateral damage in the global political economy.

4

Maroon Man

Social Movements throughout History

February 2010

Le Marron Inconnu, the Unknown Maroon, faces the presidential palace from the edge of Champ de Mars, the once-elegant plaza at the center of Port-au-Prince. He balances on his right knee and his left leg, which is extended tautly behind him. Around his left ankle remains a shackle from his days of captivity. He has thrown back his muscular chest and shoulders and raised his head to the sky to blow a conch shell, the ancient summons to revolution. He's a little worse for wear—the blade of the machete he wields in his fist has broken off, and the busted links of a chain that used to be attached to the shackle have long since disappeared—but that hasn't dampened his spirit.

Many Haitians call the bronze colossus by the familiar Nèg Mawon, Maroon Man. The maroons were slaves who, at the turn of the nineteenth century, fled the plantations and took to the mountains, where they lived in underground free communities that doubled as revolutionary bases. From them, they launched the attacks on plantations that would lead to their freedom and would incite similar uprisings across the Caribbean and the U.S. South. (One of the largest rebellions in U.S.

history was north of New Orleans in 1811; it took its inspiration from the Haitian revolution, and one of its leaders actually came from Haiti.)[1]

This monument to Haitian resistance and liberty was commissioned by President-for-Life François Duvalier, a man not known for either of those things. Duvalier claimed Maroon Man as a symbol of the *noiriste*, or black pride, movement he purported to represent. When the people toppled his son's regime in revolution redux, they took the statue and his conch as icons of their struggle.

When the earthquake struck, Maroon Man adapted yet again to the state of his nation. Like so many others, he became a resident of a displaced persons camp. His mighty frame was tightly hemmed in by newly slapped-up tin and cardboard shacks, sheets of plastic, and drying laundry.

✻

For the grassroots, the fight for change that Maroon Man represents has been as constant as the beatings they have taken. As a group, they have never acquiesced, never consented to live quietly with a status quo they oppose. Yannick Etienne, an organizer with the labor rights group Workers' Struggle (Batay Ouvriye), characterized this element of the political culture as "We are a people that resists what we don't like; that's one of our trademarks." An oft-cited expression is "*Nou pap bay menm yon zong*." We won't cede so much as a fingernail.

François "Papa Doc" Duvalier started one of the most repressive and corrupt regimes (1957–71) in a long history of such regimes; his son Jean-Claude or "Baby Doc" (1971–86) took over from him and finished it. From under the boots of these dictators, the population employed what social scientist James Scott called "weapons of the weak."[2] These are means of exerting power by those without much of it, tools of resistance for those who have neither the personal safety nor the social power to openly make grievances or change systems. The weapons were acts of noncompliance that could generally escape notice, like foot-dragging or gumming up the works or slow, subtle sabotage. From time to time, revolutionaries attempted insurrections from within or invasions from without, only to be rounded up and killed, sometimes along with every member of their families.

Under Jean-Claude, another liberation struggle simmered. Movements crafted ways to get around what from the outside appeared to

be complete control by the despot. Church groups, popular organizations, leftist intellectuals, and anonymous individuals worked from
underground, sometimes avoiding repression, sometimes not. People
devised covert ways to organize, from going to a river to wash clothes
so they could talk out of earshot of state agents; to playing music with
messages disguised in the lyrics; to passing gourde bills (Haiti's cur-
rency), on which cryptic information was scrawled, from hand to hand
in the marketplace. Some media disguised news and exhortations to
rebellion in its programming, especially Radio Haïti Inter, which the
hero Jean Dominique (immortalized in the movie *The Agronomist*)
ran for four decades until he was assassinated in 2000. Periodically,
the quiet dissent broke open into a free-speech or human-rights
campaign.

Then came the final-drop phenomenon. The millions of instances
of murder, torture, imprisonment, beating, savagery, and degradation
had raised citizens' anger and resolve. They, in turn, had increased quiet
acts of defiance. Like drops landing in a reservoir, most were virtually
weightless and invisible on their own, but they accumulated until one
finally broke the dam. That drop came after the Tonton Macoutes, the
tyrant's personal henchmen, gunned down three youths in the town of
Gonaïves in late 1985. Decades of latent fury and clandestine organizing overflowed into a crashing torrent of rebellion, with strikes and daily
protests and fierce refusal to submit. The dictatorship survived the uprising by a mere ten weeks.

The U.S. government had provided the Duvaliers with financial
and political support all the way along, except for a brief period under
Kennedy and then in the final weeks of the dictatorship, when the wide-
spread resistance made it clear that the autocracy was doomed.[3] Want-
ing to preempt the ascendance of a left-wing government, on February 7,
1986, the United States flew Duvalier to France aboard one of its own
airplanes, and installed a military junta the next day.

Too late. It was too late to put the cork back into the bottle, people
told each other. They had lost their fear. Women, peasant farmers, street
vendors, youth, students, clergy and laity, journalists, professionals, and
others were already engaged in a full-on struggle to turn their alternative
vision into reality. The movements knew the message articulated by Frei
Betto, Brazilian friar and activist: "Government is like beans—it only
works in a pressure cooker."[4] They knew what Indian writer and activist

Arundhati Roy would later say at a World Social Forum, the quintessential gathering of social movements, in Brazil: "Remember this: We be many and they be few. They need us more than we need them."[5]

The demands of organized groups and spontaneous crowds at the time of the uncorking remain the dominant ones today. They include the following:

- Participatory democracy, not where people merely vote once every few years for leaders to make decisions for them, but where all participate in major decisions. A prerequisite is government that is freely elected, transparent, and accountable.
- Full civil liberties.
- Sovereignty from the intervention of other nations.
- The fulfillment of social and economic needs as the centerpiece of government focus and budgetary expenditures, with priorities of housing; food; water; health care; adult literacy; free, quality education for all children; sustainable agriculture; and humane, fairly compensated employment.
- Transformation of the domestic economy, wherein wealth and other resources are more equally divided among all and managed so as to benefit all.
- Legal, social, and economic rights for women and their children, including the right to be free from violence.
- Decentralization from the metropolis, what is commonly known as the Republic of Port-au-Prince, so that services, jobs, and government exist in and respond to the needs of rural areas, too.
- Rejuvenation of environmental health. This necessitates enforcing existent environmental laws, nurturing programs of ecological restoration, and providing rural livelihood alternatives to cutting trees and overexploiting the earth.
- Land reform, with guaranteed tenure, for farmers.
- A new place in the global economy in which Haiti's economic enterprises truly benefit its people, rather than provide cheap labor for middle- and high-income countries and a market for goods produced in those countries.

✳

One of the very first public political acts of the post-Duvalier moment was to unseat a leviathan stone statue of Christopher Columbus—who began Haiti's long history of colonization—from its post on the seawall in downtown Port-au-Prince and to heave it into the ocean. Over the next few years, the beaten-down population created one of Haiti's most fertile periods of transformation. The people were inspired by their own history as well as that of recent revolutionary movements elsewhere in the Caribbean and in Central America, Southern Africa, and the Philippines. They engaged in a campaign of *dechoukaj*, pull up the roots, to rid the country of Duvalierism. They forced the dictator's cronies out of high posts. Some engaged in vigilante justice, killing a few especially cruel Tonton Macoutes as punishment for their atrocities. Workers tried to wrest power from the old Duvalier-affiliated unions and to build a worker-accountable labor movement. Women came forward forcefully to demand rights for all, especially for themselves. Radio journalists created a free-speech format in which regular citizens got to share their opinions. Peasants demanded redistribution of land. Students and youth organized school walkouts and street demonstrations and challenged every source of illegitimate authority they could. Priests, nuns, and laypeople streamed out of the old Catholic Church, with its fealty to the elite and to hierarchy, and into the *tilegliz*, the little church or church of the poor, part of the worldwide liberation theology movement, which taught that justice was God's will and which galvanized critical thinking and political engagement. Taking its cue from the successful Sandinista campaign in Nicaragua, progressive Catholic leaders commenced a national adult literacy program. Teachers fanned out across the country to teach the three R's: reading, writing, and root causes of poverty and oppression.

For the remainder of the 1980s, the United States propped up, with money and arms, successive military councils that killed and disappeared activists, church lay workers, journalists, and even those literacy teachers. Yet there was no stopping the momentum of the masses, and from then on they have continued to win advances in fits and starts. They popularly ratified a constitution in 1987, replacing one that had demanded obeisance to the dictators. They won a first-ever free election in 1990, bringing the populist priest Jean-Bertrand Aristide to the National Palace by a landslide and, with him, hopes for a government that would finally serve the people. Yet before that could come to pass, Aristide was ousted by a coup d'état in 1991. It was engineered by those who preferred the status quo: the military, some in the Haitian bourgeoisie, and the U.S. government.[6] Aristide was ousted again in 2004, during his second term. The coups, the role of foreign governments in them, and the subsequent vote tampering were central targets of popular protest and mobilizing. Yet along the way, movements split bitterly over positions on the president and whether he was fulfilling or betraying his mandate.

A steady part of the movements' work, then as now, has been *konsyantizasyon*, consciousness-raising, to transform individuals into political actors. Marc-Arthur Fils-Aimé, who directs the Karl Lévêque Cultural Institute (Institut Culturel Karl Lévêque, or ICKL), a popular education center named after a liberation theology priest, explained: "We help groups know we don't have to wait to get our reward in heaven. We teach that it's human beings that created the system that makes them poor, and it's human beings who can destroy that system. They're the ones who carry the burden, and they're the ones who can bring about the solution." Among other effects of the consciousness-raising have been a greater awareness by the people of their rights and a higher level of organization across sectors.

No Haitian leader has ever addressed poverty in any real way, because of lack of will or of ability. The overthrow of Aristide, a mere eight months into his first term, demonstrated what could happen when one tried. Unyielding, many of the movements' campaigns during this century's first decade continued the age-old project of trying to force the state to meet its people's needs. On occasions when the angry grassroots was able to shut down the capital with their protests long enough so that transportation became scarce, offices had to close, and construction projects came to a standstill, the frustrated elite had to make some concessions. Though the people never attained anything close to what they had hoped, they did gain lower gas prices in 2006, blockage of a free-trade agreement with the European Union that would have further undermined local production in 2007, government adoption of short-term subsidies on rice in 2008, and an increase of almost 300 percent in the daily minimum wage in 2009. The raise to 200 gourdes, or US$5.00, was still far from livable, and laborers in the export assembly industry did not even get that: pressure by Haitian company owners, backed by the U.S. government, kept their raise capped at only 125 gourdes a day, or US$3.13.[7] But the extra coins meant something for people's stomachs, as well as for their confidence in the latent strength that they possessed between them.

Movements succeeded in annulling much of the foreign debt, if not in getting their government to stand up to the financial institutions that control debt negotiations. Since the 1980s, citizens' groups had fought the government's policy of stripping social essentials from the national budget so it could pay interest on the debt instead. The injustice, they said, was all the greater since much of the payment was for "odious debt"—that is, loans that never went to the nation's people but rather into the pockets of kleptocratic leaders. Collaborating with the networks Jubilee South and the Committee for the Abolition of Third World Debt, Haitians took up the call, "*Nou pa dwe, nou pap peye.*" Don't owe, won't pay. They insisted that not only did they have no debt to the North, but the North owed *them* for all the resources and labor it had extracted, and should pay reparations. They brought their campaign to the streets, the halls of power in Washington, and global public opinion. Finally in 2009, the World Bank, the IMF, and the Inter-American Development Bank pledged cancellation of most of the debt, though interest continued amassing on loans issued after 2005.[8] It took the spectacular devastation of January 2010 for the international community to commit to full cancellation of remaining payments; more than $825 million was wiped off the books shortly after the earthquake. Six months later, though, the IMF issued a new $60 million loan with the potential for more economic conditions.[9]

Over the past quarter century, the grassroots has also been forcing the integration of Creole, the single language known by all, into a growing number of social domains. French—spoken fluently by fewer than 10 percent, according to authoritative linguist Yves Dejean[10]—was traditionally the only language employed in the courts, government, media, schools, churches, and formal commerce. Those who didn't speak or read the colonial tongue suffered under a linguistic apartheid, in which they could be condemned in a trial they did not understand, robbed blind by the merchant who bought their harvest, and completely barred from the affairs of the state. Creole's adoption as a second official language in the 1987 constitution, its recent evolution as a written language, and its spread to new terrains have been slowly but steadily swinging open doors to participation by all in affairs that concern them.

Another advance by activists has been prominence in the cross-border social movements that have burgeoned since the 1980s, in response to the economic globalization that has everywhere pushed inequality and exclusion to new levels. Haitians have assumed leadership, taking the microphone at mobilizations against the World Trade Organization in Cancún and the World Bank in Washington, imparting lessons from their history in conference rooms of World Social Forums, guiding Americas-wide strategy meetings in Mexican villages controlled by the revolutionary Zapatistas, and much more. In the process, they have been winning anew the respect and acclaim they first earned during the revolution, as powerful protagonists for justice.

※

When and how fast movements rise and make change are, always and everywhere, unpredictable. Also unpredictable is what Haitians call *konjonkti a*, the conjuncture, meaning the context of a given historic moment—like a coup or catastrophe—and how that widens or constrains possibilities. Still, in Haiti one can reasonably expect that certain variables will raise or lower the movements' potential for effectiveness. These include levels of popular participation, strength of leadership, and clarity of strategy. Financial resources help but are not a critical factor, as the grassroots has rarely had any. One essential ingredient, unity among and between organizations and sectors, has remained elusive throughout modern history. The problem has been aggravated by divide-and-conquer strategies employed by Haitian and foreign governments: turning neighbors into gun-toting paramilitaries, creating fake activist groups and controlling unions to subvert organizing, planting provocateurs into organizations and campaigns to break them apart, etc. After *twelve*, organizations that hadn't spoken in years came together to join their strength into coalitions, then fought and ruptured again, then united into new configurations, and so on.

Throughout history, the movements' gains have been one step forward, one step back. Konpè Filo was once at the forefront of a group of young journalists who widened the boundaries of free speech; he has also been active in the struggle against Duvalier and for cultural pride. Not long ago he said, "Look at all this white hair. What did I ever accomplish?" He has a point. Sometimes it's hard to tell with the naked eye what has been definitively won.

Despite continual setbacks, the grassroots has never given up on what their ancestors began. Dr. Lise-Marie Dejean, a former Minister for the Status and Rights of Women and a member of Haitian Women's Solidarity (Solidarite Fanm Ayisyen, or SOFA), expressed a variation of what I have heard said by literally thousands of Haitians over the decades: "We have an expression that says '*Nap kontinye lite jouk mayi mi.*' We'll continue struggling until the corn has ripened. But corn is never ripe, you see; you harvest it green and then you cut the kernels off, you grind it, you do what you want with it, but it's never really ripe. That means that until we cannot go another step, until the bitter end, we'll fight."[11]

5

We Will Carry You On

The Women's Movement

March 2010

Magalie Marcelin liked to sit very still and twist her braids between thin fingers—languidly, the same way she walked, the same way she responded to something you said. If you didn't know her, you might not have recognized her capacity. But Magalie was a force of nature.

She began her activism as a teenager under Jean-Claude Duvalier, when she was part of a political theater group. Some of her fellow actors were arrested, and Magalie went into hiding. She later went to Canada and studied law, returning after the dictatorship to resume her advocacy, especially for women. Under the 1991–94 coup regime, Magalie once again lived underground. Even then she never stopped organizing, and hosted meetings at her clandestine residence.

She was a midwife in the birth of the modern women's movement in Haiti. She also started the Women's House (Kay Fanm), which led the nation in feminist and antiviolence activities, alongside its counterpart Haitian Women's Solidarity. The Women's House headquarters doubled as Haiti's first shelter for battered women. On a Saturday morning, you might have found Magalie in the kitchen in relaxed conversation with several young women taking refuge from an abusive partner, a group of women from a shantytown in a side room having a political meeting, a lawyer in a back office preparing testimony on military-sponsored rape for National Truth and Justice Commission hearings, and middle-class women and their daughters on the patio learning folkloric dance steps.

Magalie was instrumental in getting laws passed for women's equal rights in marriage and for the criminalization of rape and domestic violence. As a lawyer, she helped prepare abuse cases but didn't argue them herself; instead, she found other lawyers to do so. She once managed to get a fair hearing for a woman who, after having been beaten for many years, killed her husband. In another trial, of a socially prominent man who abused his wife, Magalie organized women to pack the courtroom to offset the man's influence. The woman won.[1]

Magalie wasn't paid for any of this work but rather supported herself by consulting for a nonprofit agency, doing sociological investigations in rural zones. She lived at the Women's House, sleeping on the floor on a thin foam mattress. That way she was available twenty-four hours for the needs of the survivors taking shelter there.

Magalie was a free spirit. Her e-mail moniker was the playful *ti-landeng*, hard-headed. Part of her philosophy was that, to do this work decade in and decade out, she had to keep her soul nourished. She found that nourishment in part by visiting her hometown of Jacmel whenever she could. She was an actress, too, and when she was very young appeared in a full-length film, *Anita*, about a *restavèk*, literally "stay-with," or child servant. She always hoped to get back into theater but never found the time; there were too many women to defend and support.

Magalie was dead serious about things that really mattered. She didn't play political games and told it like it was. She particularly angered people with a statement she made repeatedly: "A penis is not a weapon." In a context where synonyms for penis are "machete" and "club"; where having sex is usually called "crush," "cut," or "clip"; and where violence against women has almost total impunity, Magalie chose not to worry about alienating others.

Many of her gestures were quiet and unseen. She helped women find jobs, money, or whatever they needed to survive and be safe, and advised those who wanted to start women's groups. She was doing just that when the earthquake struck: meeting with someone wishing to launch a women's organization.

Three others who were in the woman's home were rescued, but for some reason Magalie was not. Jacques Bartoli, her close friend, told the rest of the story:

> The morning after the earthquake, [Magalie's son-in-law] alerted me and [another friend] where Magalie was, in a house on Avenue Poupelard. I got together a sledgehammer, hammers, and heavy picks, and we headed down. The street was blocked, so we walked and walked. Magalie's daughter and her husband met us at the house. We got together a group of volunteers and extracted her four or five hours later, but she was already dead. Two other women that Magalie had just helped the day before, women who were having trouble with their mates, joined us to go to the morgue, but the morgue had collapsed. So we took Magalie's body back to the Women's House, where they laid it out with ice. We knew she wanted to be buried on her land in Jacmel, on the other side of the river, but we couldn't get there. Someone suggested burying her temporarily and exhuming her body in a year to take her to her land. So Magalie's daughter found a place in Port-au-Prince and buried her the next day.

Three additional founders and shapers of Haiti's contemporary feminist movement and discourse died in the earthquake. Anne-Marie Coriolan founded Haitian Women's Solidarity and the adult education and training Center for Research and Action for Development (Centre de Recherche et d'Action pour le Développement, or CRAD). She also served as a top adviser to the Minister for the Status and Rights of Women. Myriam Merlet was chief of staff at the same ministry and was instrumental in the group WomenInfo (EnfoFanm), which promoted women and their writings. Mireille Neptune Anglade's research and writing broke new intellectual pathways on gender and economics.

The catastrophe also took the lives of countless women who toiled without title, recognition, office, or resources to make life as a female more just and equitable. Each was part of a vibrant tradition of women's activism whose roots stretch far back in history.

※

Haitian women have largely been erased from history. We are left to imagine, extrapolate, and reconstruct what we can about their roles. Part of the task of re-creating their place in history involves changing our perception of what composes resistance and where to look for it. From the outside, many actions may appear private or personal. An observer may miss the significance of daily acts of resistance in unremarkable or household-based realms, and yet profound change often enters through them. An onlooker may also misunderstand what appears to be compliance but which may, in fact, be a strategy where conciliatory activity or relations with opponents are essential for survival or for quiet opposition.

What gendered records do exist show women appearing early on, sometimes as leaders, in national resistance struggles. In 1791, the Vodou priestess Cécile Fatiman helped lead the ceremony that launched the war of independence. Marie-Jeanne, Sanite Belair, and Marie Claire Heureuse were noted actors in that war. An uncounted number of unnamed slave women took part in the poisoning of slave holders, subterfuge on the plantations, marooning, and rebellions. Women played key roles in opposing the U.S. occupation of 1915–34, smuggling ammunition and information to rebels.[2]

Advocacy for women's rights is documented at least as far back as 1820, when a group of wealthy women changed the law that had deemed all women minors. (The law was subsequently reinstated, and remained until 1979.) The founding of the Feminine League for Social Action (Ligue Féminine d'Action Sociale) in 1934 was an outgrowth of women's opposition to the U.S. occupation; with it, a feminist movement dawned. Composed primarily of middle-class intellectuals and professionals, the league and other groups launched the move for women's full political rights, rights and autonomy within marriage, an equal minimum wage, a three-week paid maternity leave, and protection for children. The league founded offshoot organizations to protect women's rights in the workplace (1935), to support homemakers (1937), and to defend children (1939).[3] Its advocacy won legal and constitutional rights, including the right of women to hold elective offices, except the presidency, in 1944, and then full political rights, including the right to vote, in 1950. Yet repression and electoral fraud denied women, like their male counterparts, a truly free vote until 1990.

Though evidence exists of some cross-class political collaboration,[4] the elite nature of the Feminine League for Social Action and feminist organizations that followed did not include poor women either as members or as a focus of their political programs.[5] And because poor women were socially disenfranchised, the rights that feminists won effectively did not include them. For example, for indigent and illiterate women—the great majority—the right to hold political office was meaningless. This changed under the Duvalier dictatorship, when distinctions between women were partially leveled because the regime denied political freedoms to *all* women, equally. Losing their safety and the fruits of their victories pushed middle- and upper-class feminists into the national liberation struggle. By 1965, their movement effectively merged with the mobilization of the poor masses against the dictator.[6]

During the 1980s, some women again began organizing for gender-specific rights and power. Once again, state repression was partially responsible, for in their forced exile around the Americas and Europe, they became exposed to new strands of rising feminist thought and to greater women's rights and status in the home and society. When they returned home, they brought these new ideas and experiences with them.[7]

The birth of a contemporary women's movement can be pegged to the political opening that accompanied Duvalier's ouster in 1986. Within two months of his exit, two major women's marches demanded justice for all Haitians and for women in particular. Almost two thousand turned out in the remote village of Papaye, where a peasant group had been organizing underground, while in Port-au-Prince, more than thirty thousand women from all social sectors took to the streets.

Then as now, their claims have been directed toward the state for full legal, political, and economic rights. Women demand government investment in social services that serve them and their children: health care, reproductive rights, education, potable water, and rural infrastructure such as roads. They demand employment with dignity, a living wage, the right to form unions without reprisal, and protection from sexual harassment. They demand enforcement of their right to own and inherit land and other property. Advocates have also been lobbying for laws that would grant rights to domestic workers, civil and property protections for women in common-law marriage equaling those in legal marriage, and the enforcement of paternal responsibility laws. Women are, moreover, pushing the government to implement the UN Convention on the Elimination of All Forms of Discrimination against Women, which was ratified in Haiti three decades ago but has never been applied.

Another cardinal demand is that the state protect women from violence. Two coalitions of women working inside and outside of government have won legislative victories and are working on more. They are the National Coordination for Advocacy on Women's Rights (Coordination Nationale de Plaidoyer pour les Droits des Femmes, or CONAP), a grouping of eleven feminist organizations led mainly by the Women's House, Haitian Women's Solidarity, and InfoWomen; and the National Coalition against Violence against Women (Concertation Nationale contre la Violence Faite aux Femmes), a working group of Haitian government representatives, civil society groups, and international agencies. With Magalie playing a prominent role, they won a 2005 decree stiffening prosecution for rape. It is now legally classified as a "sexual aggression" instead of the prior "moral offense" and carries a mandatory minimum sentence of ten years of imprisonment where it involves a woman, fifteen years for a girl. The decree also did away with gender bias in laws regarding adultery and spousal murder. Before, as one example, it was legally permissable for a husband to murder his wife if he caught her in the act of adultery, but punishable for a woman to do the same. Advocates are still working to move these protections from paper to reality.

A second set of claims has been aimed at men in civil society for rights, security, and equitable power and access. Prominent demands have included an end to violence and abuse; the right of women to make decisions for themselves and to share in decision making regarding the family; the right to leave the home, to associate freely, and to speak and be heard; equal control over household earnings and property; and child support.

Women's assertions of agency and activism have met substantial opposition from repressive governments, as well as from some fathers and husbands who have prohibited them from becoming involved or even leaving the home. Women have also been shut out by other men in activist spheres who have refused them entrée into meetings or organizations, especially in rural areas. This has changed dramatically over time, though, and today it is more common that women's voices are silenced and their participation thwarted because they have to attend to chores and to children.

Despite the opposition, their strength, identity, and voice are crescendoing. Their engagement in the intertwined struggles for a more equitable

International Women's Day demonstration. Photograph by Ben Depp.

gender power balance and a more just nation has grown consistently.[8] The balance between organizing for the good of the whole and the good of women as a group remains delicate, though. This is especially true among peasant women, whose precarious survival necessitates tight cooperation with their male counterparts. Most are adamant that their work to change gender relations must be done in close collaboration with men. Even in those cases, though, women have been steadily forming their own committees within peasant and worker collectives, as well as their own autonomous organizations.

Tensions have remained bitter among some activist groups, with historical mistrust between social classes and organizations enduring in the sharply cleaved society. At the same time, many have recognized that the social crisis of the post-earthquake context has provided new opportunities for making common cause.

The road ahead was already long on *twelve*, and now presents more detours and switchbacks. Under excruciating conditions, women have borne the primary burden of caring for children and the vulnerable, and of keeping family and community intact. Poor women's economic status has further deteriorated, while the physical safety of women and girls living in the camps is at a crisis point.

※

On March 8, International Women's Day, in the year of the earthquake, women organized gatherings and street marches all over the country. One of the commemorations took place on the grounds of the Ministry for the Status and Rights of Women. That is, it had been the grounds of the ministry, but the ceremony occurred on a freshly bulldozed lot. The ministry had collapsed during the *event*, crushing employees inside.

When constituting the ministry in 1994, Aristide had decreed that it be housed in the former headquarters of the Armed Forces of Haiti that he had just disbanded. One of the first gestures of ministry staff was to bedeck their new building with lavender flowers and ribbons, making clear to everyone that the locale that had once governed death now nurtured life. For sixteen years, the ministry bustled with energy for women's agency, equality, and rights, and for new paradigms of power. On International Women's Day 2010, the ribbons rustling in the breeze were black. They were affixed to a big funeral wreath for the staff who had perished. On each ribbon, inked in white, were the words: "We remember, we advance."

Nearby was another event, this one organized by a coalition of feminist groups. One of the speakers was Yolette Jeanty, who had replaced Magalie as director of the Women's House. Yolette closed her presentation with this vow: "Magalie is not here and she is here. We are her feet. We are her words. We are her heart. We are her path. Magalie, we will carry you on."

6

You Can't Eat Okra
with One Finger

Community–Run Humanitarian Aid

March 2010

Christroi Petit-Homme, a member of Heads Together Haitian Peasants
(Tèt Kole Ti Peyizan Ayisyen, Tèt Kole for short), lives in the Artibonite
Valley—a long walk, a motorcycle ride, and three bus rides away from
Port-au-Prince. Like most everyone in his village of Piatre, Christroi lives
without access to a doctor or a nearby water source or electricity or a
road. Making it past childbirth is not at all assured, and families have few
other resources but each other, so mutual support is a survival strategy.
Community members are expected to help each other harvest the crops
when it's time and to pass on a little food when someone's need is urgent,
even if they haven't really got any to spare.

Besides farming, hardship and the need to stand with one's neighbors
are two of the things the people of Piatre know best. Christroi explained
the community interdependence through the old proverb: *"Yon sèl dwèt
pa manje kalalou."* You can't eat okra with one finger. Jean-Jacques Henrilus, one of the national coordinators of Heads Together, elaborated.
"Solidarity is a principle of our group. When there were massacres in
Jean-Rabel and Piatre, when there were arrests, when there is work to

be done, when there are political fights, there's always solidarity. When we know we need political pressure, we give it. Some people bring food. Some bring wood, some bring water. Those who only have a little change put it in a sack as a collection for other members."

So it was logical that when word of the scale of devastation reached Piatre, and when the village began receiving emigrants from the city, Heads Together members snapped into action. On day four, the peasant group, the local church, and the general population convened to decide their collective response. They adopted a three-pronged relief strategy: taking food to survivors in Port-au-Prince, housing internally displaced people and, if they themselves had no guests, contributing food to homes that did.

Jerome Toussaint explained this one afternoon a few weeks after *twelve* under the shade of a towering mango tree, where he and other Heads Together members sat on plantain leaves cut for the occasion, since chairs are a rare commodity. Jerome said that he had sent bananas, coconuts, and breadfruit he grew, along with water he bought, to thirteen people "in difficulty" in the city. He admitted it was hard because he was already supporting his wife and four children, but said, "It's my contribution." Like other farmers, he carried his produce down a steep path on his back. When he hit the flat dirt trail, he paid part of a day's income to sit behind the motorcycle-taxi driver, with his goods strapped behind him. Then, once on the main road, he wrangled a ride into inner, devastated Port-au-Prince, with its unnavigable roads and shifted geography.

In a survey of the forty-two farmers at the mango-tree meeting, twelve said they were hosting displaced people. Justin St. Fils, for example, took in seven orphans after his brother was killed. Fifteen said their burden had just multiplied, too, because they now had to feed their children who had returned home after their schools in Port-au-Prince had been closed.

Less than two weeks after the quake, nineteen Haitian organizations from human rights, women's rights, media, peasant, alternative development, and other sectors issued a joint statement, which read in part: "The emergency aid effort we are involved in is alternative in character. . . . We are advocating a humanitarian effort that is appropriate to our reality, respectful of our culture and our environment, and which does not undermine the forms of economic solidarity that have been put in place over the decades by the grassroots organizations with which we work. . . .

Solidarity and gifting thrive. Here, a volunteer work collective clears a neighbor's land.
Photograph by Roberto "Bear" Guerra.

Massive humanitarian aid is indispensable today, given the scale of the disaster, but it should be deployed in terms of a different vision."[1]

As in Piatre, peasant, church, student, neighborhood, and activist groups all over hastily established programs rooted in the same solidarity we saw in the individual rescue and relief responses. (In New Orleans, too, community groups filled the vacuum left by government neglect. They set up clinics in living rooms, sent out alerts via national radio to learn where neighbors had relocated, created free restaurants in yards and Internet centers in gutted buildings, collected tools that were free for the borrowing; converted churches to shelters, drew in volunteers from around the country to help with cleanup, etc.)

Most of the organized Haitian community responses had limited funding and capacity, and so were small scale and short term, usually lasting only a few months. But while operating, they offered a different vision and experience of what "humanitarian" can mean. At their best, they embodied society premised on respect, democratic participation, generosity, and dignity. Embedded in the small and local models were the seeds for a just and equitable nation.

※

While a lot of community-based aid and giving goes unnamed and publicly unnoticed in most of the world, in Haiti much of it has been formalized into systems. Three elements are common to all. First, no one ultimately has more than she or he started with, but the sharing allows each to do more with meager resources than would otherwise be possible. Second, unlike micro-credit, which demands interest (sometimes for program costs and sometimes for profit), in these systems no one takes any fees or makes money off anyone else. Third, the exchanges are based in human relationship and trust. Some of the solidarity customs follow:

- *Konbit* is a collective work group in which members of the community labor on behalf of one another without compensation. Like a barn-raising, *konbit* allows people to harvest their fields or undertake major work projects when they have neither the hands to accomplish the task nor the money to hire them.
- *Twòk* is an informal exchange with, for example, one family giving its cow's milk to another family that has a newborn, while the baby's father repairs shoes for the first family. *Twòk* was heavily used in earthquake evacuee-flooded communities—fish from one village for breadfruit and yams from another was one exchange set—as each area tried to stretch what resources it had.
- *Sòl*, a revolving loan fund, works when people put an agreed-upon amount into a common pot each week or month, and then give the total to a different member each round. This allows each to have enough capital to make a significant payment at some point, like for materials to fix a leaking thatch roof or a cooking pot for a street-corner spaghetti lunch operation. The individual receiving the kitty doesn't ever pay back the money.
- *Sabotaj* works like *sòl*, but daily. It is practiced among market women who have learned that it's worth giving up a little cash each morning so that they can make a big investment on the days when the bonanza comes around to them—like on a carton of soap bars, which, bought wholesale, increases profits. The name is thought to imply sabotaging poverty.
- *Men ansanm*, hands together, functions through community organizations. Each round, a different member of the organization receives money from the common fund, holding on to it for a period to bolster his or her business. She or he returns the principal but keeps the profit made in the interim.

⌘

Many of the emergency responses were launched in rural areas like Piatre, for several reasons. First, little of the countryside was seriously harmed by the earth's moving plates. Second, astronomical numbers of people were fleeing disaster-struck urban centers for the country. Third, that is where food is produced.

The response took on new dimensions in the Central Plateau region because of the volume of displaced people showing up there: in the first month, ninety-one thousand in the province that incorporates the Central Plateau.[2] The principal group that became involved there was the Peasant Movement of Papaye (Mouvman Peyizan Papay, or MPP), one of Haiti's largest and most influential peasants' organizations. Members took up a collection of $519.60, and the organization's directorate contributed another $128. With that, MPP took sixty refuge seekers into its guesthouse, people known to the group as well as strangers who showed up at their door. MPP provided lodging, three meals a day, clothes, shoes, medical and dental care, Internet access, entertainment like movies (*Titanic*, dubbed in French, was the feature film during my visit), and excursions. Evacuated youth organized a soccer team, which competed against the MPP team. MPP members took a pregnant woman to the hospital to give birth and enrolled three children back into school. They even slaughtered two of their cows so they could bring meat to patients at the nearby Partners in Health hospital.

In addition, MPP supported its members who took displaced people into their own homes, like Arianne Jean and Destin Monfortin, the couple we met earlier who was hosting eighteen guests. Arianne said, "At first we bought a little sack of rice and three cans of beans [twenty-seven cups]. I milled ten cans of corn [ninety cups] we'd grown. Each morning, Destin went to the fields and came back with plantains and vegetables. There came a day I realized I couldn't go on. All my funds were gone, and the payments on my micro-loan were at risk." She turned to MPP, which gave her money to keep buying food until the visitors returned to the city.

�֎

The cash-poor, community-rich Carrefour-Feuilles region of Port-au-Prince hosted one of numerous urban-based alternative aid programs. This one benefited three populations: families who had difficulty getting food aid, market women who had difficulty staying employed, and farmers who had difficulty selling their food. With support from international grants, the Association for the Promotion of Integrated Family Health (Association pour la Promotion de la Santé Intégrale de la Famille, or APROSIFA) contracted with sixty women who were *timachann*, street vendors, from the neighborhood. Each *timachann* got money to purchase food and cook one large meal a day for ten or fifteen specified families, the same set each day, usually with upward of seven members per family. Officially, the project provided food for approximately forty-eight hundred people daily. Actually, according to the association's founder Rose Anne Auguste, the numbers were much higher, because when the women finished serving those they were responsible for, they kept dishing out food to hungry folks who dropped by until their pots were empty.

The meals' ingredients were all bought from Haitian farmers. Rose Anne said, "I would like to tell the international community that we can grow food."

One of the *timachann* operations took place in a communal courtyard of three extended families, where houses had all been replaced by tents. On a Sunday afternoon, just as the Protestant services being held in the middle of several streets wrapped up, Madame Riveau finished preparing three blackened, industrial-size pots of rice, bean sauce, and vegetables. Her contracted food recipients, what she called her "family," filed into the courtyard and awaited their food under a mango tree. Two seventy-something identical twins, sporting house dresses and gray braids, held court for all within earshot. Teenagers flirted with each other, and the little kids did what they do everywhere: amused themselves with scraps of nothing. Once the food was ready, Madame Riveau ladled servings into the containers they handed her: many-times-recycled Styrofoam to-go boxes, plastic Thermos lunch buckets, and tin bowls.

The scene could hardly have diverged more from the distributions of sacks of imported rice taking place under the armed surveillance of U.S. and UN soldiers only a few blocks away. Except for the context, in fact, the scene was not much different from that of many Sunday afternoons pre-earthquake. Rose Anne said, "We have our own vision of reconstruction of our country. We have a philosophy that corresponds to our reality, not the reality of the international community. What we want is for the international community, the foundations and agencies, to hear our philosophy and our dream for our people, our country."

Another urban response took place in a damaged kindergarten building in the low-income neighborhood of BelAir, where the activist group
Solidarity among Youth / Watch Out (Solidarite Ant Jèn / Veye Yo,
known as SAJ / Veye Yo) had a long history. According to Lenz Jean-
François, an organizer with the group as well as director of the psychology department at the State University of Haiti, people who had already
been part of SAJ / Veye Yo's program made their way to the school
spontaneously after the earthquake. SAJ / Veye Yo activists claimed that
they were able to offer care to homeless and traumatized residents of the
neighborhood in a way that only organizations with sustained relationships could do. Tania Felix, co-organizer of the shelter, said, "We are the
principal actors in our own reconstruction. The aid we're giving is not
something that foreigners can give us. It's not soldiers who can help us;
it's people helping each other as people."

Each day, the team fed four hundred people and sheltered two hundred. SAJ / Veye Yo also offered medical care and sessions on topics such
as antistress techniques and women's health. Their resources were a
combination of free truckloads of water from a Canadian nonprofit
and a local company, funds given by a German company, and volunteer
Haitian doctors, nurses, psychology students, and organizers.

The walls of the main room were lined with stacks of the residents'
remaining belongings, bundles tied up in sheets. On the wall above
the bundles, someone had taped white paper banners reading "love,"
"solidarity," and "respect." On one morning, the main room held a family huddled in conversation, a naked baby trying out his singing voice
in a yellow plastic tub, and an elderly man resting on a slatted chair
with his cane between his knees. A boy and a girl played checkers on
a piece of cardboard, the boy assuring me that he was the best. A toddler dressed only in a T-shirt lurched toward a photographer friend's
camera, beaming and calling, "Photo! Photo!" When I asked a woman
if she wanted her picture taken, she replied in perfect English, "No. I
don't want my family to see me in a shelter." In a classroom, student
volunteers arranged first aid supplies on shelves. Out back, a couple of
women in a cooking hut handed around glasses of orange juice they had
just squeezed.

Lenz said, "A danger of aid is that it infantilizes people. We say that
what will traumatize the Haitian people even more than the thirty-five
seconds of the earthquake is finding themselves, from one day to the

next, standing with bowls in their hands and waiting for someone to give them a sheet so they can sleep. This dependence is terrible for people's identity.

"People need to know that we can count on ourselves. We have the capacity. That's what's behind this initiative. We accept support that comes, but in the framework of respecting people's dignity."

7

Fragile as a Crystal

(Tales from Three Months Out)

April 2010

One Saturday night, Djab Beaubrun and Marco Desir came by to get me for a goat roast. Djab had talked so much all week about the happening that he'd taken to just calling it *kabrit la*, the goat. Though it was clearly a celebration, no one would call it so out of respect for national mourning.

Djab had some six-part name, but everyone called him Djab, Devil. He and Marco were part-time research and education contractors with Haitian nonprofits—part time being when there are contracts to be found—and full-time political rabble-rousers. That night Marco looked dapper in a checked cotton shirt and a boating hat he'd found somewhere. I know Djab had cleaned up for the occasion, but he still looked pretty much the same as always: scruff on his chin, pants sliding down his butt, sneakers just barely tied. In a nation where most everyone invests scarce resources to look highly presentable—precious water to wash, cash to buy starch for clothes and ribbons for hair, and time to heat charcoal to fire up the iron, for example—Djab was insouciant.

Djab was so unswervingly good-humored you could have forgotten that his good friend, the professor and hero of the left, Jean Anil

Louis-Juste, had been shot down by a gunman on the morning of *twelve*, and that a falling wall had killed his son in the afternoon. You could have forgotten that Djab was homeless because his apartment was too badly damaged to inhabit and was moving between various lodgings. Or that his wife had wanted no part of a transitory life or the endless torment that Port-au-Prince had become, so had left him to go stay with family in Cap-Haïtien, taking their two-year-old Karl with her.

You would never have known how dire finances had become for Djab and his family, either, except for rare comments he let slip. Like about milk, which Djab claimed was Karl's primary passion. "The quality of milk I can give him corresponds to the quantity of money I have," Djab said. Karl now gets the lowest-grade milk available.

The goat was being hosted by the Toussaint Louverture Front (whom I have renamed because the members did not ask to be part of a book). The point was to bring together those who had been thrown hither and yon by a shaking earth, either moving to new parts of town or leaving Port-au-Prince altogether. Physical structures were not the only ones that had fissured; relationships and social institutions had, too. Like all else, the future status of the organization—who would return, in what state, and what the group's capacity might be—was shrouded by the unknown. Those days, the only certainty was uncertainty.

Djab, Marco, and I cut behind buildings, past dead-ends, and through alleys. Marco held my hand gallantly as though I were unused to the lunar-like terrain. All was black, the only electricity anywhere being in the generator- and inverter-enriched homes of the well-to-do and the offices of foreign nongovernmental organizations (NGOs), and there were none of either in this neighborhood. We arrived at the site of the goat, which was a narrow, cement corridor between two rows of houses, pungent with the smell of sewage. The darkness was so complete that when people introduced themselves to me, they held their glowing cell phones up to their faces.

Prestige, Haiti's only beer company, had stopped distributing because its building had been damaged. Djab, who would never admit to being a nationalist, was nevertheless boycotting imported beer and drinking only *tafya*, a type of raw rum that would knock you flat. He was in luck at the goat: the hosts had provided a whole stash of the stuff. With each recycled glass jar of it, someone poured libations for the brothers and sisters lost and then launched it around the circle. When one jar was drained, a host stepped gingerly over or around sleeping neighbors—shining the dim green light of a cell phone to avoid treading on anyone—to fetch a fresh one.

The conversation reflected what one heard on the streets each day: disgust at the Haitian government for its negligence and at the international community for its advantage-taking. But it was also full of jokes, like the one about President René Préval going to a reception at the donors' meeting in the Dominican Republic. There, he was offered the choice of Prestige or Presidente, the premier Dominican beer. He selected Presidente. A Haitian standing by said, "But Your Excellency, you're the head of state of Haiti. How can you take a Dominican beer?"

"Because," Préval replied, "I am a president without prestige."

"Heard that one," someone called out, and you could almost see the eyes rolling through the darkness.

As with Djab, you could have forgotten that everyone here had just lost children or parents or jobs or homes. They all reveled—some, like Djab, with way too much *tafya* in them—knowing this could be their last festive occasion for a while.

※

Mostly, the Port-au-Prince scene was one of unmitigated misery. "It's a nightmare from which you never wake up," said Loune Viaud of Partners in Health. SOS signs, hung across streets and on corrugated tin walls just after the quake, were now filthy and battered. On the road to Léogâne, a cement sign painted in soft pastel colors declared, "Please help us rebuild. We lost everything. Our girls orphanage, schools, medical clinic, pharmacy, village for the needy, church, guesthouse, vehicles." The desperation wasn't less now than when the signs were first hung, though the hope that foreign aid would eventually come to the rescue surely was.

One steamy-hot afternoon as I jumped down from a public bus, a young woman stepped up and grabbed my arm tightly. "Get me a visa," she demanded. I told her I couldn't; my government was not hospitable to Haitians, and visas were almost impossible to come by. She leaned in very close and said, "I have to leave. This country smells."

In a clinic, a very young girl I'd never seen before approached and said out of the blue, "My mother died. My little sister's name is Timarie. Did your house get crushed?" No. "My house got crushed."

I was participating in a meeting in a camp one day when a woman planted herself in front of me. In a deadened voice, she said, "I have one son, a strong young man of ten. He lost his foot in the earthquake. What are he and I supposed to do? A ten-year-old with a stump." Before I could compose myself enough to give my condolences, she had turned and walked away.

The mother of a teenage girl who was raped in a camp asked, "Can you help us find a psychologist? This whole nation needs a psychologist."

Anxiety was aggravated by the aftershocks. In the first six weeks, there were fifty-nine of a magnitude of 4.5 or greater. One was 6.0.[1] A nation of newly minted geologists argued about whether and when there would come another earthquake. Panicked people went running outside at the slightest unexplained noise. My friend Suze Abraham called at 1:30 a.m. after a 4.3 to tell me to go sleep in the courtyard.

As usual, Alina "Tibebe" Cajuste had just the right image for the moment. A former *restavèk* and now child rights advocate, Tibebe, Little Baby, kept this name which her keepers used, which she called her "slave name." It was the only one she ever had, since she was never given a birth certificate or baptized until well on in life when her half-sister Alina Cajuste died; then her biological family passed that name on to her. Tibebe spoke in spontaneous, imagery-filled poetry, though she neither read nor wrote a word, and recited long, evocative poems aloud from memory whenever she got a chance. Occasionally someone from her women's group transcribed one of her pieces for her. As she told everyone, becoming literate was one of her dreams. The other was the end of the child servitude system.

Clasping her long arms around her knees on a cement step in my courtyard, Tibebe said, "Haiti is as fragile as a crystal."

�֎

"*Kay kraze, nimewo efase.*" House collapsed, number erased. The old expression meant that someone's flimsy home of sticks and mud had finally given up altogether. It could have served as the new national motto.

Beside the loss of loved ones, loss of housing was the primary preoccupation. The standard "How are you?" was supplanted by "Where are you sleeping?" This was a multiple-choice question, with possible answers being house, yard, car, street, or camp.

Djab observed, "They've always said, 'The street is the living room of the people.' Now it's the bedroom of the people and the kitchen of the people, too."

Even many who had homes didn't enter them, let alone sleep in them, because they were too structurally damaged or because of the fear that the next rumbling aftershock might be the big one. One evening that was so stormy I decided to sleep right where I was at a friend's house, I was awakened in the dead of night by a deafening *whooosh*; the next morning, a large house on the corner was no more. At my apartment complex with its high percentage of foreigners, you could pretty much tell who'd been in Haiti on *twelve* and who'd come after. The former wouldn't sleep in their apartments. Each night, the courtyard metamorphosed into an open-air motel.

Homelessness played out in all kinds of ways, like the painful wince of an elderly market woman as she lowered a big pink bucket of papayas from her head. "Your back is hurting, huh?" I asked. "You know I sleep on the cement," she answered. Another effect was chronic sleep deprivation; Port-au-Prince had become a city of insomniacs. A filmmaker told me a few weeks out, "I still don't sleep. All I can think about is what I saw starting on the day after: bodies, bodies. Especially children, all laid out outside schools." If not from the inability to sleep on hard cement, the fear of another temblor, or the trauma, women and girls in public spaces lay awake to be vigilant against a possible attack. Or it was raining and they had to spend the night standing up as the water rose in their tents. Or there was so much noise and commotion in the camp that sleep was impossible.

In the Delmas neighborhood where I sometimes stayed, as in most neighborhoods, you heard the singing all night long. Those who couldn't sleep gathered and sat together and sang eerily beautiful, otherworldly hymns to God and dirges to the dead. They were unlike anything I'd ever heard, those pained voices rolling out into the night, filling the city, rising to heaven.

At least the elderly woman around the corner from my apartment finally got a tent. For weeks she had slept on a baby-blue sheet in the middle of the unlit road, with only a border of broken concrete blocks that she'd created to signal her presence. Twice, friends bringing me home late at night had almost run over her.

❈

"Haiti is surreal," Josette Pérard commented. She was right. Walking down a cement path one afternoon at dusk, I stepped on something, and looked down to see a black sleeve under my foot. The sleeve was attached to a suit, and the suit was attached to a skeleton. Months later I would go to a found-art sculpture exhibit and sale, spread across the lawn of a hotel favored by the foreign artist, journalist, and bohemian jet set. It would take me a moment to realize that the heads of several statues were in fact human skulls. It would take another minute to register that selling human skulls as art was unusual.

It was all part of the new normal.

The three domes atop the palace all pointed in different directions. Houses were converted into Escher paintings with phantasmagorical new shapes. On some, the walls and roofs rolled like curling skate ramps, while others reached and listed impossibly, like the drawings of children who hadn't yet learned about right angles. Corners of buildings were split into V's; unsupported walls tilted perilously. In the town of Léogâne, which along with the neighboring town of Gressier marked the disaster's epicenter, houses looked like another children's art project: sheared in half, the top layer sitting crookedly on the bottom, as though a little kid had cut a piece of paper in two and taped the pieces back together catawampus.

Broken cement beams, held together only by rebar, dangled over sidewalks. You walked down the street in switchbacks, crossing sides continually to guarantee your life. Electric wires dangled overhead, but at least you had pretty good assurance the wires weren't live—the one upside of scarce electricity.

Wilson Dumas took me around in his *taptap* on especially meeting-packed days. Most *taptap* are outfitted with elaborate plywood frames and extravagantly colored scenes of scantily clad women, Barack Obama, Samson wrestling a lion, and other sacred and profane images. Wilson's was adorned only with a Brazilian flag painted on the hood. One afternoon he drove me past the heap that used to be the Palace of Justice. Normally he offered an endless stream of politically reactionary opinions at no extra charge, but on this occasion I could relate to his comment. "You see this place? This was the Palace of Injustice. Before, you could buy anyone off and the court would let you go. God made it fall down."

Painted on one house was, "The artist didn't die, order your T-shirts 453 5789." And across Bourdon Road, a lingering banner, in English, served as a reminder of better days: "Tribute to Michael Jackson, Haitian musicians play."

8

Children of the Land

Small Farmers and Agriculture

April 2010

On a dry, lost stretch of land toward the northwest tip of the island is the village of Jean-Rabel. The surrounding region is mainly mountains with a little flatland, hard to farm, hard to irrigate. But there's no other way to survive besides farming—corn, sweet potatoes, beans, sorghum, plantains, peanuts—so that's what people there do. They've always been proud of working the earth with their hands, just as many generations did before them. And since they've always lived on and tended the land, they consider it theirs, just as their forebears did.

Today, most of the area is claimed by a couple of families who don't live in huts and who've never needed to work in a field. The *grandon*, big men, still refer to their "plantations"—though there's no big house anymore—and are just as committed to holding on to them as their fore-bears were. As far as the *grandon* are concerned, the peasants of Jean-Rabel are tenants and hired hands, and they make them pay either rent or half their produce for the privilege of living and growing food on the property.

Most Haitians don't grant much importance to the remote corner of Jean-Rabel, one of the poorest areas of the country. But the *grandon* do. Their family pride, their income, and their ideological hopes for the country's future are connected to that land. So when Duvalier fell and the farmers started calling themselves Heads Together Haitian Peasants and saying the land was rightfully theirs, the *grandon* knew what they had to lose, and they knew it couldn't be lost. One hot day in 1987, they gathered up some of the men they kept around to enforce their law and sent them to kill the peasants, whom they called communists. Not just the ones causing them trouble but their offspring, too: they tied nine young children together and sliced off their heads, one after another, with a machete. The ninth little head was spared just as the machete was coming down, because someone suddenly realized he was the son of the wrong guy. The killers took down 139 people on that long, bloody day.

Traveling down the upper arm of the nation brings us to Piatre. There, farmers hail from rebel slaves and maroons, like they do in Jean-Rabel. Though most village uprisings have been omitted from historical records, quite likely they plotted and killed the plantation owners during the revolution, and some of them were surely killed by those owners, too.

The people of Piatre felt the same way as those in Jean-Rabel: they made food come up from the soil with just a machete and a spit of water, the seeds they'd saved from the year before, and their hard labor. They had the right to feed their children from the land and call it their own. They started referring to themselves as Heads Together, too, and got more adamant about their claim to the land. So the local *grandon* hired some guys for cheap, and on an otherwise ordinary day in 1990 they went out to Piatre and nine other villages with guns and machetes. They eliminated eleven human beings from the earth, and their houses, crops, and animals along with them.

The people did what they've always done: buried their dead and stayed put. Hid their leaders in the rocks and the hills until the trouble calmed, shared what little food they had with them. Kept growing their crops and kept organizing. Claimed some of the land over time, just through their numbers and determination. The *grandon* still insist it's theirs, and still tyrannize the peasants from time to time. But the peasants are sure that history and God are on their side. So even though they don't have legal title to all the land, they believe that one day they will. And even though they don't have what they need to

Land reform activists and massacre survivors in the village of Piatre. Photograph by Roberto "Bear" Guerra.

grow enough food or sell it for a decent price, they believe that one day they will.

※

Haiti's people are among the most rural-based in the Western Hemisphere. Somewhere between 66 percent to 80 percent depend on small-scale agriculture.[1] "It's clear that you can't develop a country and build another Haiti where 80 percent of the people are excluded," said Chavannes Jean-Baptiste, the executive director of the Peasant Movement of Papaye and the spokesperson for the National Peasant Movement of the Papaye Congress (Mouvman Peyizan Nasyonal Kongre Papay, or MPNKP), a couple of weeks after the earthquake. "We have to take advantage of this catastrophe and say, 'The clock is set at zero.' We have to build another Haiti that doesn't have anything to do with the Haiti we had before. A Haiti that has political sovereignty and that has food sovereignty. It has to begin by building agriculture."

Rosnel Jean-Baptiste, member of the national coordinating committee of Heads Together, gave this opinion, "It's not houses which will rebuild Haiti, it's investing in the agriculture sector."

Regardless, state neglect of the farming sector has been extreme. As one data point, in 2009 and 2010 the government dedicated only 7 percent of its budget to agriculture. This was despite pleas from peasants that their urgent needs required more support, and despite international recommendations, like that of the Food and Agriculture Organization of the UN that no less than 12 percent of the budget be dedicated to agriculture.[2] The government's Post-Disaster Needs Assessment indicated that rebuilding agriculture and fisheries should get just 6.3 percent, over three years, of the total $11.5 billion it estimated to be necessary for recovery.[3] Most small farmers receive no support for production, like seeds and tools. No help in developing infrastructure like irrigation, storage, or transport. No credit or marketing support. No technical assistance, like information on how to combat blight or updated production methods. Recent administrations have given little discernible attention to combating the environmental destruction that has created floods and droughts and otherwise made growing almost impossible in many regions. Some nonprofits and foreign agencies help with reforestation and environmental management projects but can't come close to meeting the need.

Eighty-eight percent of the rural population lives in poverty, 67 percent in extreme poverty.[4] Rural communities are neglected, furthermore, in terms of basic survival services, like potable water, health care, schools, and roads. In rural areas one-quarter of births are attended by a skilled health professional, as opposed to 47 percent in urban areas. One hundred fourteen out of every thousand children die by the age of five in the countryside, whereas that number is seventy-eight in cities and towns.[5]

Dieudonné Charlemagne, a survivor of the Piatre massacre, said, "We love agriculture. We love to plant. We love to live as people who're recognized as citizens of this nation. Even if we're peasants, we deserve to live, too. It shouldn't be that because we're peasants we're condemned to death."

❋

How did the status of peasants and their farming drop to this abyss? Chavannes explained, "We peasants have been victims for more than two hundred years. The slaves who struggled to get their independence did so in part to get land from the colonialists. [But] from the moment of independence there's been division between rich and poor, between people of the city and people of the country. That gave us two countries inside one small country. Little by little, the state has abandoned the countryside, leaving the peasants as a marginalized class they just use when they need votes in an election."

Until recently, the two classes of citizenry were legally codified; birth certificates of those in the countryside actually bore the title "peasant," hand-scripted in the appropriate box. Rural families are still widely known as *moun andeyò*, people outside, meaning outside social value and outside the reach of economic benefits. *Moun anndan*, people inside, are those inside the Republic of Port-au-Prince.

The *grandon* claim ownership of most arable land. Only 5 percent of Haitian land is legally registered,[6] but it doesn't matter, since the *grandon* also frequently control the local courts, government, and the security apparatus—members of whom might be government employees or just paid thugs. The *grandon* usually control access to water, storage facilities for food and seed, and the local market, too, paying what they want since they have a monopoly. The urban elite holds the reins of the national food market through lucrative import-export businesses.

Making matters worse have been the economic policies that Washington and international trade and financial institutions have foisted since the 1980s on Haiti, as in most of the rest of the world. The unfair economic advantage of the Western nations who control these institutions has allowed them to pressure global South countries to eliminate policies that protect their agricultural markets, while the West protects its *own* markets through interventions like subsidies for wheat and rice. The IMF pushed Haiti so hard to open its borders to trade that by 1995, import tariffs on rice and flour had dropped from 50 percent to as low as 3 percent;[7] tariffs on sugar and other agricultural products plummeted similarly. By 1999, Haiti had reached the IMF's lowest category for trade restrictiveness, making it one of the easiest countries to which to export.[8] The resultant flood of cheap food from other countries has been a death knell for peasant agriculture.

Another blow to the well-being of the peasantry was the eradication of the Creole pig. The hardy animals foraged and ate scraps and required little to no investment. They served as a virtual piggy bank for those without savings or bank accounts; selling one off meant quick cash for tuition for a child or medical treatment for a spouse. In the early 1980s, several multinational agencies and the U.S., Canadian, and Mexican governments, in cooperation with the Duvalier regime, slaughtered every last pig they could find—an estimated four hundred thousand.

The declared reason was that African swine fever, with which some pigs were infected, might spread to the United States. A less touted reason, as stated in a U.S. Agency for International Development (USAID) project paper, was "to eradicate once and for all the Haitian model of swine raising, whose 'primitive' conditions may at all times be a source of nuisance for the modern swine industry of North America."[9] The loss caused rural families varying degrees of financial devastation, which many claim have repercussions to this day. On the profit side of the ledger, constituents of congressmen from the U.S. Midwest received contracts to export their breed of fat, pink pigs, along with the imported feed the pigs were said to need to survive. Once in Haiti, they were redistributed primarily to upper-class industrialists. Many of the U.S. pigs died over time because they couldn't adapt to the local conditions.

Given these political forces, today farmers are able to produce only about half of what is required to meet the country's food needs, causing a dire food crisis.[10] Haiti is the one of the hungriest countries in the world, with up to half of the population facing food insecurity.[11]

✖

Chavannes remarked, "The peasants have said, 'Let's develop an economy where we have control.' This could really develop the riches of the country while bringing Haiti back environmentally. One of our objectives in the Peasant Movement of Papaye has been to make the countryside into a paradise where people want to go live, instead of having to go to Port-au-Prince to work for potato skins."

Giving farmers and farming the funding, attention, and trade protections they require could help accomplish several vital goals. One is creating employment for the majority. Two is ameliorating the food crisis. Peasant groups assert that, with the necessary help, farmers could produce at least 80 percent of their country's food needs. Three is allowing rural people to stay on their land while getting the services they need to live, which is both their right as well as a way to prevent dangerous overcrowding in Port-au-Prince. Four is allowing those city-dwellers who wish to move out of the city to do so. In interviews with Port-au-Prince residents who took refuge in the Central Plateau shortly after the catastrophe, most said they would stay if they could find a way to sustain themselves there. They did not and had to return to the city, but the option remains.

Pre- and post-earthquake economic blueprints drawn up by the Haitian government and private sector, the World Bank, the IMF, and the UN all agree that the agricultural sector needs to be strengthened. The devil, as always, is in the details. For farmers and advocates of a justice-driven reconstruction, the first priority is food sovereignty. This is the belief that every people has the right to make decisions about, produce, and consume its own local, healthy, and culturally appropriate food. Based in farming practices, marketing systems, and policy choices, food sovereignty upholds the right of small growers to have control over their land and production. It also embraces ecological agriculture, which, as Chavannes said, "respects the environment, Mother Earth, as the mother of future generations." The approach is the counterpoint to the neoliberal agricultural model, which promotes agribusiness corporations while demoting government's and community's planning, investing in, and intervening in food and agricultural systems.

Other demands of the peasant movement include the following:

- Land reform, what the scores of peasants in Jean-Rabel and Piatre died for. This means the redistribution of large unused landholdings from the elite, the churches, and the state to farmers who have little or no land. Many farmers are currently trying to support themselves on what they call "a handkerchief of land," parcels sometimes no larger than fifteen-by-fifteen feet. The urgency for redistribution has swelled with population growth, as more and more people—nine million and counting—crowd onto a plot of earth the size of Maryland. Land reform cannot be just a onetime redistribution, because land ownership would quickly revert to its previous concentration as struggling farmers become forced to sell their small gardens again. Instead, it must offer secure legal tenure and the support systems mentioned below, so that peasants can keep their land for good.
- Government help for production, including development of water catchment and irrigation systems, food storage, agricultural research and development, and hands-on assistance from agronomists.
- Access to credit and aid for seeds, tools, and equipment.
- Assistance in marketing.

- Restrictions on food aid in the medium- to long-term. While farmers agree that aid has been critical in the catastrophe's wake, the blanket distribution of imports has been ruining their livelihood. Peasant organizations urge that foreign dollars go to procuring domestically grown emergency food aid and to improving agricultural production capacity. As the quantity of local food increases, imports should be phased down accordingly.
- The safeguarding of traditional, native seeds that Haitian farmers have cultivated for centuries, by barring imports of corporate-controlled and genetically modified (GM) seeds.
- A ban on biofuel crops—that is, plants that are grown to produce energy. For several years, farmers and alternative development networks have been lobbying the government to stop multinational and Haitian companies from growing the shrub jatropha. From it is made biofuel that is then exported to consumers in the industrialized world. Farmers insist that already insufficient arable land and water must be used to produce food for those desperate for it.
- Help in turning around Haiti's ecological crisis so peasants have the healthy soil and adequate water they need to cultivate. Farming would be greatly aided through programs of erosion control, reforestation, ecological agriculture, and protection of watersheds and biodiversity.

※

A statement of Haitian peasant and ally groups declared, "We . . . are motivated by the experiences and successes in Haiti that prove that food sovereignty is possible and we add our voices to save the planet, the earth, our environment and peasant livelihoods. We reaffirm our vision of transforming and improving the countryside . . . , protecting agricultural production and the peasant economy in the face of multinational agribusiness, and defending the people's right to food."[12]

Lacking political clout to get their needs and demands met, peasants have relied primarily on the tools they have at hand: the strength of their numbers, their collective will, and the power of grassroots organizing. Haiti's dry hamlets, terraced hills, and fertile plains are home to literally thousands of peasant associations. Heads Together, the oldest, was founded under Jean-Claude Duvalier, while many others emerged in the fecund days after the dictatorship's end. Many of the groups focus on mutual aid to help each other survive, sharing resources and labor and trying to develop collective solutions. Some are production and marketing cooperatives, in which people might compile what little cash they have to purchase a mobile irrigation pump so all their fields can get watered because a *grandon* controls parts of the river or a drought is bearing down, or might pool their grapefruit or pineapples to make jam, which brings in a better price than the fruit itself. Members might sell their corn or rice to the cooperative so it can be stored in the group's warehouse while they look for the highest-paying buyer. The bigger groups get outside funding and can offer technical support to their members, like help in setting up solar power and water cisterns and finding export markets for mangoes.

Some of the associations have the additional goal of increasing their power so they can win the policies and programs they need. Four of these, Heads Together, the National Peasant Movement of the Papaye Congress, the Peasant Movement of Papaye, and the Regional Coordination of Organizations of the Southwest (Coordination Régionale des Organisations du Sud-Est, or CROSE), have the size and force to lobby for their agenda at national and even international levels. They have teamed up with advocacy groups, other movements, and foreign friends to form strong, broad coalitions. Some belong to worldwide networks such as Via Campesina, the two-hundred-million-member-strong confederation of small farmers and landless people, and its Latin American cousin Cry of the Excluded (Grito de los Excluidos). They take part in global campaigns, like one against the corporate titan Monsanto and another to force the World Trade Organization out of agriculture.

Jean-Jacques Henrilus, one of the national coordinators of Heads Together, said, "We need to see how Haitian peasants, workers, street vendors, and everyone from the excluded sectors can put themselves together to create another Ayiti Cheri, Dear Haiti. Heads Together and popular organizations alone can't do this job. But we and other sectors— social, professional, all conscious people—can tie our strength together and get to our goal, constructing a Haiti where all Haitians feel like children of the land."

9

Grains and Guns

Foreign Aid and Reconstruction

May 2010

Patrick Elie put his life on the line to document and expose the collusion between the U.S. government, Haitian military leaders, and drug runners that allowed the illegal military regime to thrive from 1991 to 1994. As the National Coordinator against Drug Trafficking during Aristide's first term, Patrick possessed knowledge that made him a linchpin in exposés in U.S. congressional hearings, the *New York Times*, the *Washington Post*, and other forums,[1] which helped reverse the coup d'état. Others of us were involved, too, but Patrick was the front man and so took the flak. He was followed, threatened, and jailed for years for his troubles.

Once retired from his public career as intelligence czar and private career as chemist, Patrick began sharing his observations and analysis freely from the breezy veranda of a hotel where he spent many an afternoon seeing friends over a drink. After the earthquake, he began speaking of a more subtle form of external control: disaster aid and economic recovery. Here's what he told me on one of those afternoons:

The little bit of state that's left is almost irrelevant to the humanitarian aid and reconstruction. One thing to watch is a humanitarian coup d'état. We have to be careful. Especially in the early days [after the disaster], they overtook the goalie, which is the Haitian government. What's going to happen is that it's not Haitians who will decide what Haiti we want, it's people in other countries. This doesn't make sense from a moral perspective, and it also won't work. A people can't be developed from the outside. What's more, in Haiti we have a very strong culture. If you ask people if they want the U.S. to take over the country, even among those who say yes: come back in ten years and you'll see that the same people will have risen up against the occupation.

The Shock Doctrine, the book by Naomi Klein, shows that often imperialist countries shock another country and then, while it's on its knees, they impose their own political will while making economic profits from it. We're facing an instance of the shock doctrine at work, even though Haiti's earthquake wasn't caused by men. There are governments and sectors who want to exploit this shock to impose their own political and economic order.

The idea of our adopting the model of supposedly more advanced countries like the U.S., that's a choice, but it's a choice of death. I would rather see us break away and make another path for our own development.

After the earthquake, the United States, the UN, and others stepped in with expressions of grave concern and pledges of nearly $10 billion in long-term assistance, of which more than $5.3 billion (almost more than double the size of the Haitian budget) was to be disbursed over the next eighteen months.

Of the U.S. response, President Barack Obama said, "When we show not just our power, but also our compassion, the world looks to us with a mixture of awe and admiration. That advances our leadership."[2] From the ground, the "leadership" of which Obama spoke looked more than anything like a three-point program to impose control through militarism, material aid, and reconstruction.

※

U.S., Canadian, UN, Haitian, and French flags, in the traditional sign of conquest, atop a crushed hospital. Photograph by Beverly Bell.

Within days of the earthquake, twelve thousand UN troops (of whom nine thousand were already present) and twenty thousand U.S. troops were on the ground, in the sea, and in the air. According to embassy cables revealed later by WikiLeaks, President Préval did not list security among his immediate concerns during a January 14 meeting with the U.S. ambassador, and apparently hesitated in asking for U.S. military assistance.[3] The troops were deployed two days *before* Préval requested U.S. help in "augmenting security," in a communiqué issued jointly by him and Secretary of State Hillary Rodham Clinton.[4]

The U.S. military presence actually imperiled human life. During the first week following the earthquake, when so many lives hung by a thread, the United States took over the airport and repeatedly denied entry to planes carrying doctors, emergency medical equipment, food, and water. Tarmac space was limited, and the arrival of military personnel and supplies got preference. By day nine, while over one thousand people waited for surgery at the University Hospital, more than fourteen hundred flights of aid and relief workers awaited U.S. authorization to land.[5]

In only one instance, five Doctors Without Borders planes laden with eighty-five tons of supplies were diverted from the airport by the U.S. military over the course of five days. In a press release, Doctors Without Borders said that just one of those planes, "carrying 12 tons of medical equipment, including drugs, surgical supplies and two dialysis machines, was turned away three times . . . despite repeated assurances of its ability to land there." The dialysis machines were to treat crush syndrome, which occurs when damaged muscle tissue releases toxins into the blood, causing possible kidney failure and death. The Doctors Without Borders' press release went on to quote its emergency coordinator Loris de Filippi as saying, "We have had five patients in Martissant health center die for lack of the medical supplies that this plane was carrying. . . . I have never seen anything like this. . . . We were forced to buy a saw in the market to continue amputations."[6] In the absence of anesthesia and other essential medical supplies, some people had their limbs amputated with only Tylenol as a painkiller, while others had badly broken limbs set with cardboard splints.

Why was this war-size force necessary, its arrival so important that it trumped emergency flights? The U.S. military was helpful in setting up a handful of camps, extending the airport's runway, and repairing the port. Navy doctors on the ship USNS *Comfort*, which docked off the coast, treated more than 8,600 people and operated on almost 1,000.[7] While these actions were valuable, they do not explain the enormous, aggressive military and navy presence. Certainly many groups set up camps without guns. And as journalist Ansel Herz pointed out, a medical team sent by the Cuban government provided more than 341,000 patient consultations, more than 8,700 surgeries, more than 111,000 vaccinations, and many other forms of care to hundreds of thousands in the first six months,[8] all without soldiers or weapons.

No Haitian I spoke to believed that the military was there to provide security. The environment was largely peaceful, other than in some displaced persons camps where, ironically, the urgent calls of residents for more security went unheeded. The generally calm streets contrasted sharply with the rifle-toting foreign soldiers in their Humvees and trucks.

Leaked cables from the U.S. Embassy to Washington give more truthful insight into one rationale, which was to ensure that profits were not interrupted on export-bound goods from assembly plants. Embassy officials met with representatives of Haiti's business sector as early as five days after the earthquake and again a week later, and reported to Washington that the businessmen's main concern was "security at all levels, to include security of goods, at marketplaces, and for ports of entry."[9] Company owners subsequently requested UN troops "to provide security for reopened factories, and pledged to re-open in weeks."[10]

More insight can be found in a memo released only one day after the earthquake by the Heritage Foundation, which has long been one of the most influential conservative think tanks in Washington. The memo read in part, "Cuba and Venezuela, already intent on minimizing U.S. influence in the region, are likely to seize this opportunity to raise their profile and influence in a country that is already battling drugs and corruption. . . . The earthquake has both humanitarian and U.S. national security implications. . . . The U.S. also needs a strong and vigorous public diplomacy effort to counter negative propaganda emanating from the Castro-Chávez camp and demonstrate that U.S. leadership and involvement in the Caribbean remains a powerful force for good."[11]

A hint at a third motivation for the military escalation came from a State Department cable in 2008, on the subject of the UN military force, which had been deployed in part to quell popular unrest that threatened business interests. The cable indicated that a "premature departure of MINUSTAH [the UN military mission in Haiti] would leave the Préval government or his successor vulnerable to . . . resurgent populist and anti-market economy political forces."[12]

The U.S. response after the disaster drew criticism from French, Italian, and Brazilian officials.[13] The French cooperation minister urged the UN to "clarify" the U.S. role and said, "This is about helping Haiti, not about occupying Haiti."[14]

※

As for the material aid element of the U.S. response, Ambassador Kenneth Merten said at a February 12 State Department briefing, "In terms of humanitarian aid delivery . . . frankly, it's working really well, and I believe that this will be something that people will be able to look back on in the future as a model for how we've been able to sort ourselves out as donors on the ground and responding to an earthquake."[15] (It's hard not to recall President George W. Bush telling Federal Emergency Management Agency [FEMA] director Michael Brown, who oversaw the iconically botched crisis response at the time of the flood in New Orleans, "Brownie, you're doing a heck of a job!")

Merten's assessment would come as a surprise to people like Edèle Oscar, who lived with two children in a patchwork home of tin strips and frayed plastic, a little larger than most bathrooms in the United States. She told me, "Who is this urgent aid for? We're still in misery. We can't sleep. We hear that the schools are open but our children can't go. You're telling me there's $9.9 billion [the figure pledged at the time] in aid money? Is it for the rich?"

Some chaos and corruption are predictable following a mammoth crisis. But in Haiti, the disaster aid was an aid disaster.

In the first few weeks, U.S. soldiers threw sacks of rice down from cargo planes and helicopters, in what many survivors took as an offensive indicator of fear or distrust. Several people made the identical comment to me: "We're not dogs." For some ground-based rice distribution, U.S. and UN trucks showed up on streets haphazardly, forcing hungry people to drop what they were doing and run to line up, where they often waited for hours in the broiling sun. An elected spokesperson in one camp said, "Why can't they tell us when they're coming? We have schedules. Why can't they?" The troops kept automatic firearms and billy clubs at the ready while herding people into lines rimmed with razor-studded concertina wire. Usually soldiers spoke only foreign languages and so conveyed no information to those on queue.

Haitians across the board expressed strong resentment over the disjuncture between their needs and the militarized response. Marie Berthine Bonheur with the National Peasant Movement of the Papaye Congress said, "The soldiers have arms and batons in their hands; the Haitians have nothing. Our country is not at war. It's a provocation. Have you seen the soldiers bulldozing? No. We have a people who are stressed, they're traumatized. Is that a situation you respond to with arms and batons?"

Tania Felix with the community group Solidarity among Youth / Watch Out told me, "Our problem isn't insecurity. This is not how we should be helped. We need people helping us who won't humiliate us."

Preplanned distribution systems, like the one in which the UN doled out food aid in exchange for coupons that had been distributed in camps the day before, almost guaranteed favoritism and corruption. In a study later conducted by the UN High Commissioner for Refugees, 100 percent of the respondents said they had either been directly involved in or had witnessed transactional sex for food coupons, for direct access to aid distributions, or for spots in programs such as "cash-for-work."[16]

One leader of a feminist organization called the operations "an international parade." She said, "The aid has been given in total chaos. The way it's been run represents economic and political domination. It's being done in a context where the symbols of state power are gone, and the government is basically nonexistent."

※

Moreover, a yawning abyss existed between the promises of foreign dollars, heavily touted in an international PR blitz, and actual material assistance and services for the population in need. Two months after the quake, the UN revealed that only 56 percent of its target of 1.3 million people had received shelter supplies.[17] In one survey by human rights groups of ninety people living in camps in late February 2010, only 64 percent reported ever having received any aid.[18] Food would soon become even less available since large-scale distribution officially ended at the end of April, upon request by the Haitian government to protect local production, though nothing replaced it. As a U.S. military helicopter passed overhead, one woman announced, "That's the only thing they give."

So where have the billions of foreign dollars gone? As is often the case in crises, a sizable portion of the international pledges never moved beyond the promise stage.[19] Of every dollar that the U.S. government did pay out for initial relief efforts, thirty-three cents went to the U.S. military.[20] At least $160 million of USAID's post-catastrophe expenditures went to the Defense Department, FEMA, search and rescue teams, and USAID itself.[21] Corruption and poor planning redirected more funds away from desperate survivors.

Much of the aid financed by the U.S. public's tax dollars was never intended to leave U.S. borders in the first place. It went straight to U.S. corporations in high-stakes government contracts for damage assessments, military "mission support," long-term planning, food-security monitoring, and other projects that did not actually involve money moving to Haiti. When, two weeks after the earthquake, Ecuadoran president Rafael Correa said, "There is a lot of imperialism among the donors. They donate first, but most of it goes back to them," Préval, standing at his side, cracked a knowing smile.[22]

A small army of staff and consultants working for foreign governments and international agencies have sucked up exorbitant fees, too. One UN consultant told me he earned $30,000 a month. Additionally, he and his colleagues required personal expenses, plus an expansive and pricey secondary tier of support staff and infrastructure: drivers, translators, security teams, secretaries, accountants, offices, SUVs, computers, satellite connections, backup electricity systems, etc. Until mid-March 2010, many UN consultants and staff were lodged in a luxury cruise ship docked in the Port-au-Prince harbor, which featured minibars in the bedrooms, grand pianos, and sweeping crystal chandeliers. According to a consultant staying there, not one Haitian slept aboard. Dubbed the Love Boat, it reportedly cost the UN $112,500 a day.[23] Similar disbursement patterns, repeated by many nations, multilateral agencies, and foreign NGOs, siphoned money back to wealthy countries and away from the people in peril.

※

The third ring of the circus was reconstruction. In addition to the lucrative contracts it offered, reconstruction gave Western powers control in pushing a pro-business development model. Two weeks after the catastrophe, the organizations spearheading shelter had not begun distributing tents, and the lead agencies in food aid had yet to map the overall need,[24] but the world's major players had already assembled to recraft Haiti. In all, three donors' forums were held in Montreal (January 25), Santo Domingo (March 17), and New York (March 31), attended by as many as one hundred countries and international agencies. Préval and his government were there, too, though they asserted themselves weakly.

One Haitian alternative development advocate asked, "How can the government regain its leadership while being relegated to spectator status?"[25] But that was the point. The Haitian government *was* weak, but instead of trying to strengthen it, the international community fostered the weakness to make it easier to control the reconstruction process.

Secretary of State Clinton acknowledged at the New York donors' meeting, "It will be tempting to fall back on old habits—to work around the government rather than to work with them as partners."[26] Temptations die hard. The United States gave the Haitian government only one cent of every aid dollar.[27] It circumvented the government in decision making, too, in labyrinthine processes discussed below.

Helping to render the government functionally irrelevant, and therefore impotent in challenging the intervention, was the prevalent discourse of Haiti as a "failed state." The message had long been drummed, but the tempo picked up after the earthquake, pounded by foreign governments, academics, and media, such as *Time* magazine's piece "The Failed State That Keeps Failing."[28] Later, Haiti would even come in fifth in the 2011 Failed States Index of the think tank Fund for Peace, after Somalia, Chad, Sudan, and the Democratic Republic of the Congo.[29] A similar trope was that barriers to Haiti's development were "cultural." *New York Times* columnist David Brooks articulated a classic example on day three when he wrote about Haiti's "complex web of progress-resistant cultural influences." He informed his readers that "it's time to promote locally led paternalism. . . . It's time to find self-confident local leaders who will create No Excuses countercultures in places like Haiti, surrounding people— maybe just in a neighborhood or a school—with middle-class assumptions, an achievement ethos and tough, measurable demands."[30]

The colonial narrative that this black nation must be saved from its backwardness was unadorned. UN Secretary-General Ban Ki-moon stripped it naked at the New York donors meeting: "As we move from emergency aid to long-term reconstruction, what we envision is a wholesale national renewal, a sweeping exercise in nation-building on a scale and scope not seen in generations."[31] The message was repeated days after the earthquake in another blog from the Heritage Foundation, entitled "Amidst the Suffering, Crisis in Haiti Offers Opportunities to the U.S." It read, "In addition to providing immediate humanitarian assistance, the U.S. response to the tragic earthquake offers opportunities to re-shape Haiti's long-dysfunctional government and economy." When protests ensued, the blog disappeared off the site.

(The same news blog of the Heritage Foundation celebrated the inception of a steamroller drive to privatize education after the 2005 flooding in New Orleans, when nearly every public school employee was fired[32] and schools began being systematically defunded. The blog emphasized that "sometimes things get so bad that radical change can happen."[33] The father of neoliberalism, Milton Friedman, came out of retirement a few months after the flood on the same privatization mission. He wrote in the *Wall Street Journal*: "This is a tragedy. It is also an opportunity to radically reform the educational system."[34])

In an unguarded moment, the UN Assistant Secretary-General of Peacekeeping Operations in Haiti, Edward Mulet, confessed, "We complain because the government is not able to [lead], but we are partly responsible for that."[35]

The Post-Disaster Needs Assessment, launched one month after the earthquake, was supposedly a Haitian government process to evaluate the country's needs and create a ten-year development plan. The assessment's results were not unveiled to the Haitian people, but instead to foreign donors at the meeting in Santo Domingo on March 17. The blueprint that emerged from the assessment, the Action Plan for National Recovery and Development, was supposedly the government's own. In actuality it was, according to the World Bank, "assembled by experts from the United Nations, the European Union, the Inter-American Development Bank and the World Bank."[36] The action plan didn't receive its seal of approval in Haiti, but rather at the next donors' meeting, in New York two weeks later. Speaking about the action plan to the Haitian Senate, Prime Minister Jean-Max Bellerive said, "I hope you sense the dependency in this document. If you don't sense it, you should tear it up. I am optimistic that in 18 months, yes, we will be autonomous in our decisions. But right now I have to assume, as prime minister, that we are not."[37]

The action plan said that private investment would "form the backbone of the country's reconstruction" and called for the business sector's engagement in almost everything, right down to potable water. Should the plan work, it would effectively privatize many functions and services of the state, or semi-privatize them through "public-private partnerships." This would turn the country's development and service provision over to entities whose first priority was not collective well-being but private profit, and whose cost-cutting prerequisites ran counter to making the deep investments necessary to meet citizens' needs.

The action plan stated, "Among the commitments of donors, support will be given to the private sector to provide it with the capacity required to fulfill its role" in reconstruction; it called for "a series of measures to facilitate wealth creation by the private sector." In other words, companies were to be subsidized to make profit. Eschewing the basic principles of democracy, the plan also deemed it necessary that "the private sector has a bigger participation in decision-making."[38]

To direct the reconstruction envisaged in the action plan, the Haitian Parliament created a new body in April, the Interim Haiti Recovery Commission. Its mandate was to oversee rebuilding efforts through the billions in aid pledges, including approving policies, projects, and budgeting. In creating and investing this body with its broad power, the Parliament conducted a constitutional coup. Whereas the constitution mandates shared governance by an executive, a parliament, and a judiciary, the Parliament's ratification of the commission shifted it to the executive and the international community.

The commission's twenty-six board members were elected by no one and were accountable to no one. Half were foreign, including representatives of other governments, multilateral financial institutions, and NGOs. The foreign voting members literally bought their seat at the table through one of two criteria: pledging at least $100 million during two consecutive years from 2010 on, or canceling at least $200 million in the debt they claimed from Haiti.[39] The institutions chose their own representatives to serve on the body. The commission was co-chaired by UN Special Envoy Bill Clinton and the prime minister, and the World Bank managed the money. The only oversight measure left to the Haitian government was veto power by the president.[40]

For many months, the commission operated in total secrecy. It then began posting on its website reports, lists of published projects, meeting minutes, and an e-mail address and number for questions—in English and French, languages spoken by few Haitians. Web surfing was not an option for the majority of the population, about half of whom lack literacy and far more of whom lack computers and electricity. There remained no mechanism through which citizens could be informed or engaged. Speaking with the British solidarity organization Haiti Support Group, an international development consultant contracted by the commission said, "Look, you have to realize the IHRC [commission] was not intended to work as a structure or entity for Haiti or Haitians. It was simply designed as a vehicle for donors to funnel multinationals' and NGOs' project contracts."[41]

The commission was to dissolve on October 21, 2011. A note on its website at the time of this writing, June 2012, advised that, "Pending a decision of the Haitian Parliament regarding the future of the institution, a team is currently dealing with day-to-day business."[42]

Former factory worker Annie Joseph had an opinion much like those I heard most days from Haitians on the role of foreigners in their country. "We protest, they don't listen. We have a sit-in, they don't listen. We don't have a president, really; our president is the white foreigners. You guys are our president."

※

The vehicle for implementing the foreigners' plans has been almost as structurally undemocratic as the commission: foreign NGOs. The action plan explicitly stipulated that "the NGOs are the main operators for implementing [the plan]."[43] "Nongovernmental" is actually a misnomer, since many of the agencies, like Save the Children and Catholic Relief Services, get at least half their funding from the U.S. government.[44] They, plus CARE, World Vision, Mercy Corps, and others, annually receive hundreds of millions of dollars each from taxpayer-funded grants.[45] (Some receive no government funds.) Critics in different parts of the world call the big NGOs "BiNGOs," while disaster aid scholar Mark Schuller calls them "non-profiteers."

The NGO industry has received most foreign aid since the earthquake. It has largely replicated the practice of foreign governments, excluding the Haitian state from decisions about its own nation. "The NGOs don't tell us . . . where the money's coming from or how they are spending it," Prime Minister Bellerive said.[46]

Foreign donors and lenders have forced the government to privatize industry and services, and given money to NGOs to fill the gap in essential services and management in a de facto privatization. As the NGOs' reach and control expand, the Haitian government's retracts, thereby justifying the next round of international dollars to those NGOs. The problem long predates the earthquake. By 2006, only about 10 percent of Haitian schools and 30 percent of health facilities were run by the Haitian government; the rest were owned by NGOs or the private sector.[47]

Ronel Thelusmond gave rare insight into the process via his perch at the Ministry of Agriculture, Natural Resources, and Rural Development, where he serves as an official. He said the ministry no longer even develops its own program. "After many years, the ministry changed its vocation. Now it just works with [international] agencies. It plays a supervisory role." NGOs may rightly point out that currently the government does not have the capacity to coordinate or supervise, in what one insider termed the "chicken-and-egg" phenomenon.

But regardless of where the problem originated or who holds ultimate responsibility for the weakening of state capacities, since *twelve* the pace of NGO takeover of the public domain has become dizzying. Local control, decision making, and leadership have been cast aside, while NGO "experts" have stormed every field of the reconstruction with their own products, knowledge systems, and power. Services from sanitation to women's safety to agriculture function through UN "clusters," issue groups set up by the UN to coordinate NGOs and—theoretically, anyway—relevant government institutions. They operate without much or sometimes any engagement of those directly impacted by their work. Haitians without official titles are routinely barred from even entering the UN base where meetings take place, while foreigners can often enter just by flashing a passport. Cluster meetings are held in English or French, languages inaccessible to most community groups and camp representatives.

This is not to say that NGOs intentionally try to take over initiatives that should be the realm of government, or that NGO staff consciously undermine the possibility for a strong, autonomous state. Employees tend to work hard over long hours, are motivated by a deep commitment to a fairer future, and are able to do good in many individual cases. Yet they cannot alter the structural nonaccountability and power inequity between their employer, the government of their host country, and the people with whom they work. The agencies' foreign funding, largely foreign staff, and political relationship with Haiti dictate much about their effects in Haiti.

The Republic of Haiti, some say, has become the Republic of NGOs. Even before the earthquake, scholars and officials commonly stated that Haiti had more NGOs than any other nation. After the quake, Bill Clinton suggested that Haiti held ten thousand of them,[48] but no one actually knows. Foreign NGOs are legally obligated to register and submit annual plans to the Haitian Ministry of Planning and External Cooperation, but at last check, only 162 were listed.[49] (Some others have tried to apply, only to have had their applications lost in a maze of bureaucracy.)

As ineffectual as the Haitian government may be, its functions can't be outsourced. Haiti needs a government with responsibility to the citizens who elected it and with the ability to protect their rights. The public good requires a public sector that can guarantee basic services, physical infrastructure, and civil liberties. It requires more than unaccountable private business and foreign agencies that can and do pull out when they like.

NGOs could be useful in strengthening the government's capacity to function and provide services, and some do. Partners in Health, for example, works only in collaboration with the Ministry of Health, instead of creating parallel and competing health systems. NGOs could also help communities meet their own self-identified needs, and a notable few work toward this end. The Haitian-run Lambi Fund, for instance, provides small grants and training to citizens' groups so they can fulfill their own development priorities.

Haitian movements, organized communities, and other groups representative of the majority have further ideas on how foreign agencies can help, not harm. Some are described throughout this book. NGOs *can* work to break the cycle of which they are a part. They can open their ears to criticisms and suggestions for alternate approaches. They can advocate with their host countries for budgetary support for ministries and dedicate more of their own resources to supporting state capacities. They can work more closely with, and give more money to, Haitian-led and Haitian-staffed nonprofits. They can use their voices to push for better policies from their home government toward Haiti.

※

Patrick Elie said, "We know the Haitian government is weak, and we can't count on it alone to lead the battle. [But] I can't accept that there is no alternative. I see one, but it will take a lot of work. We all, organized Haitians and our friends, have to stomp our foot and say, 'No, this can't happen. Haitians have to develop their own country.' We need help and support from others, as they say here, to grow the plantains. But they're *our* plantains. Haitians have to be the ones to construct the country we need. We have to be in charge."

10

The Ones Who Must Decide

Social Movements in the Reconstruction

May 2010

If you had picked your way through the hills of debris on dead-end Gabriel Road, slid through a narrow opening in the metal gate, and cut
past tents, clotheslines, and chickens, you would have found yourself in
front of a wholly nondescript tan building. No matter the time of day, you
would have found its interior packed with people engaged in intensive
conversation on some element of the same dual themes: how to respond
to survivors' immediate needs and how to impact the country's future.
Eight nonprofit and community groups whose offices either no longer
existed or were uninhabitable were packed into three small rooms and a
front porch. Jammed into a kindergarten chair in the garden, you would
have seen that reporter who's heard all over the country. Sharing a desk
with two others, that economist who's often on TV. Tired and bedrag-
gled fellow travelers flowed steadily in and out, using the larger central
room and yard for work sessions and interviews.

Some local activists were so motivated to start organizing right after
the earthquake that they had to be told to wait so that others could first
attend to the immediacy of their survival and losses. But in passing days,

growing numbers braved recurring aftershocks to make their way across unidentifiable landscapes by foot, because many roads were impassable by vehicle. They arrived at the building on Gabriel Road and other borrowed spaces across town, where they triaged cell phones and laptops based on whose work was most pressing at the moment. When portable generators and routers were available, they passed Internet lines back and forth. Others went to tents in swelling displacement camps that had been designated as meeting sites.

By day eight in my little garret office in New Orleans, I had received e-mails proposing solutions and requesting solidarity from a workers' rights organization, a women's community group, a peasants' association, and an alternative development group. Within a couple of weeks, grassroots organizations were building coalitions to map out emergency responses and advocacy strategies. To consciousness-raise among their fellow countrymen and women, they began creating songs and street theater, and distributing Creole newsletters.

The circumstances under which this was happening could blow the limits of the human imagination. Activists had been killed, displaced, or disabled. Many were living in streets crammed in among strangers, with limited food and water. All were suffering deeply, and some were profoundly traumatized. Antonal Mortimé described the scenario at the Platform of Haitian Human Rights Organizations (La Plate-forme des Organisations Haïtiennes de Défense des Droits Humains, or POHDH), which was entirely typical: "Our office [was] destroyed along with almost everything that was inside it. One of our program managers was killed along with his family. The office administrator lost her sister and nephew, and five of us lost our homes."[1] One morning, I met a friend of three decades in that squat office on Gabriel Road; hollow-eyed, he told me he had come straight from the funeral of the mother of his son to draft a letter to international allies.

The first in a series of collective meetings, with representatives from eighty organizations and grassroots movements, took place exactly one month after the earthquake. From it emerged the first of many broadbrushstroke concept papers, which stated the need "to bring forth another vision of how to redevelop this country, a vision based on person-to-person solidarity and on people-to-people solidarity, based on strengthening national production, based on giving worth to the country's riches. . . . We [want] a reconstruction plan in which the fundamental issues of the majority of the people take first priority. These include: housing, environment, food, education, literacy, work, and health for all; a plan to wipe out exploitation, poverty, and social and economic inequality; and a plan to construct a society based on social justice."[2] Some weeks later, another collective meeting released a statement calling for "an alternative process which can define a new national project which incorporates strategies to counteract exclusion, political and economic dependence, and poverty."[3]

✳

Antonal Mortimé later explained the movements' strategies to activate public engagement in the reconstruction process.

> Social movements proposed, first, that the government host a national consultation process, including people in the refugee camps. We proposed, second, that there be a consultative body, including different sectors and different branches of power, to develop the construction plan, a plan that would allow us to address problems that have been structural to our society for more than two hundred years, that would address exclusion, lack of education, environmental degradation, poor urban planning and zoning, concentration of services, centralization of power, and lack of governmental accountability. We did a lot of advocacy work around this issue, talking to the government, to the press, and to our international partners so that they would put pressure on their governments.

Within the month, nonprofits were sending representatives to Washington and Santo Domingo to encourage colleagues to press their own governments for new policies toward Haiti. The coordinator of a two-hundred-church Protestant network in Haiti, part of the global Micah Challenge (Défi Michée), sent an open letter to advocacy organizations and policymakers in Washington, asking that the international community "hear the voice of the people of our nation. . . . We ask that no final approvals or definitive decisions be made . . . [until] after an inclusive national process is completed . . . with the participation of the Haitian people. We ask the international community to support a Haitian-led, broad-based consultation . . . in the recovery process."[4]

⚜

Josette Pérard, the Haiti director of the Lambi Fund, said, "A society that maintains so much exclusion simply can't achieve development. No way. Development has to involve everyone. Progressive ideas have to come forth. And there has to be space for participation by all citizens who've courageously begun the development of their communities with their own means, however modest. Change will come when the people are engaged right at the heart of things."

A statement by a coalition of grassroots groups said the same thing a different way. "Were all the money in the world to go to Haiti, the country would not be rebuilt if the people themselves do not mobilize for change."[5]

Having a vision and mobilizing were essential starting points. Getting anyone to pay attention, though, was something else altogether. (We saw similar hurdles in the stalwart but largely disregarded work of community organizations in New Orleans after the storm.) The grassroots was shut out from the moment the earth finished its trembling. The government communicated nothing. Publicly, that is. Who knew what officials were saying behind closed doors to international governments and other donors? Citizens didn't. They heard from Préval about his personal losses but about little else, least of all the substance of governmental plans for reconstruction.

The government granted just one week, March 13–20, for consultation with civil society and the private sector,[6] but even that week turned out to be PR. The government released its draft action plan halfway through, on March 17—and as mentioned, not even in Haiti. The doors to the donors' meetings, all of which took place outside Haiti, were slammed shut as well. A few carefully selected, polite civil society representatives were invited to Brussels, Santo Domingo, and New York to meet with influential foreigners and attend some of the conferences. Those meetings allowed the government to claim that its action plan was "based on a joint effort of reflection and consultation. . . . Key sectors of Haitian society were consulted."[7]

Besides the government itself, the Haitian business sector was the only one granted substantive participation in the donor meetings.

It developed its own Strategic Plan for National Salvation, whose priorities were to "reduce the deficit, encourage savings, control inflation, stimulate private investment, modernize state corporations and increase jobs." The plan noted that it was "important to limit the portion of aid that is strictly for charity."[8]

Civil society groups protested their exclusion, holding rallies and press conferences outside the donors' meetings in Santo Domingo and New York, and hosting radio spots back home. They demonstrated against Bill Clinton's visit to Haiti on February 5 and French president Nicolas Sarkozy's on February 17. They put out statements, like one signed by twenty-two citizens' organizations and progressive nonprofits denouncing the donors' forums as just the next in a cycle of international diktats "that bring together representatives from the highest echelons of imperialist governments, international financial institutions and the United Nations system, that have finally been nothing more than performances for the media. They have not resulted in the emergence of new paradigms for cooperation with Haiti, but instead have prolonged and reinforced relationships of domination over the Haitian state and society."[9]

Organized women decried the contents of the action plan, in whose fifty-five pages women—excepting the generic "Haitian men and women"—were referenced exactly six times, and in which solutions to their complicated problems were discussed only in the vaguest of terms. Calling themselves the Coalition of Haitian Women Citizens in Solidarity (La Plateforme Femmes Citoyennes Haïti Solidaire), fifty-three organizations published a highly detailed paper demanding that attention to women's status and rights be an essential focus in the reconstruction. They put forth careful analysis about the needs and rights of different sectors of women. They recommended steps the government should take toward equal access to education and the means of agricultural production, and equal representation at all levels of redevelopment planning, implementation, and evaluation.[10] A statement by the National Coordination for Advocacy on Women's Rights denounced the exclusivity of the Post-Disaster Needs Assessment and broader reconstruction process, and asserted that "the exploited and excluded strata, women dominated by the double system of capitalism and patriarchy, will be the principal protagonists of this qualitative change for a new Haiti, free, sovereign, equal, and prosperous."[11]

Yvette Michaud of the National Coalition of Peasant Women (Kowalisyon Nasyonal Fanm Peyizan, KONAFAP) was equally pointed. "It's true that we have a government without a plan. But if Haitians want Haiti to have a better future, we are the ones who must decide what that future is and construct it."

✳

The crisis has increased the urgency for citizens to have their needs met and their democratic rights respected, while at the same time making those prospects even harder. Beyond members' personal misfortune and the difficulty of the political conjuncture, organizations have been stressed and weakened. They lost organizing fundamentals such as their headquarters, computers, Internet, cell phones, supplies, and archives. Almost entirely bypassed by aid streams, most are flat broke. Schooled and skilled leaders have been hired away by foreign development and humanitarian agencies, with whose lofty salaries domestic nonprofits cannot compete. The influx of foreign NGOs into fragile political spaces has upset delicate balances. Differences of approach, partisan conflicts, and competition for scarce resources have aggravated factionalism and discord.

Yet at the same time, the political crossroads has offered hope, as Yannick Etienne of Workers' Struggle described: "We still have the remnants of an organized people; they didn't all die under the debris. We as a movement have the opportunity to unify the people to take change into their hands. This is an opportunity because some of the people didn't want to get involved in any political or social action before because they were so busy taking care of their children. Some people say Haiti has not been built, *now* it has to be built."

In private moments, I have seen people shake their heads and say variants of, "I can't see where this is going, or how it can end well." Then I have witnessed the same people get up the very next morning to gather cardboard boxes from which to make signs for a demonstration to demand better education, or work with neighbors to figure out how to start a cooperative business, or devise plans for protecting girls in their tent camp.

During Aristide's first term, part of the package of administrative reforms that the Clinton administration tried to shove down Haiti's throat included privatization of state-owned industries. At one point, as a high-level official from Washington announced a visit to Port-au-Prince to meet with the president, Aristide told me he hoped the population would organize large street demonstrations to protest the privatization. He said, "Then I could go to the meeting and say, 'You see, I can't sell state property because the people oppose it.'" Popular pressure, whether gratefully received or resented, could similarly impact every element of the reconstruction. We have seen how much the international community, foreign corporations, and national elite pressure the Haitian government to get what they want. If unified and strong enough, countervailing pressure from the grassroots could make it worthwhile for the government to support *their* agenda. The future dangles in the balance.

11

Our Bodies Are Shaking Now

Violence against Girls and Women

June 2010

"The way you saw the earth shake, that's how our bodies are shaking now."

The elderly speaker was a member of the Commission of Women Victim to Victim (Komisyon Fanm Viktim pou Viktim, or KOFAVIV), a group of rape survivors and former child slaves promoting women's and children's rights. About thirty Haitian women and I were packed together under a blue tarp in a camp that served as KOFAVIV's new headquarters since its office, and most of the members' homes, had been decimated.

On top of everything else that women and girls have suffered since the earthquake has been an increase in rape and other forms of gender-based violence. KOFAVIV community workers have told of hearing violence in the camps almost every night. In camps with gender-segregated outhouses, they have said, men sometimes hide in women's bathrooms after dark, awaiting a victim. Girls and women have spoken of being afraid while bathing outside, having no private place to do so, with male eyes watching keenly. A mother explained to me that she kept a machete

Commission of Women Victim to Victim members discuss support for rape survivors in a displaced persons camp. Photograph by Roberto "Bear" Guerra.

under her blanket for fear that someone might pounce on her eighteen-year-old girl as they slept in an open-air lean-to.

Sitting knee to knee in a tight circle with other KOFAVIV advocates and comparing notes on females they knew to be in danger, one woman said, "On the street, in the tent, there is no security. Only God."

KOFAVIV kept its own tally of violence, the single group to do for months after the quake. When, at the end of March, I asked about figures, outreach workers huddled and compiled notes and came up with 230 reports of rapes in fifteen camps—15.3 incidents per camp—in the ten weeks following the quake. So little documentation existed that even this tally—underrepresentative and not independently verified—circulated widely when I published in the United States. KOFAVIV lamented having no way to know actual numbers, since their findings came from a few camp-based advocates with sporadic access to transportation and cell phones and no additional research capacity. Mainly, members stumbled upon a case of violence because they knew the survivor or someone else who did.

The ages of those raped in that initial sample ranged from ten to sixty, the majority of them teenagers. In coming months, advocates began coming across rapes of young girls and even toddlers. Malya Villard-Appolon, KOFAVIV co-coordinator, informed me one day that she had just encountered a one-and-a-half-year-old in the hospital; the parents told Malya they had brought her in because she had been raped.

Men and boys have faced high levels of violence since *twelve*, too, according to COURAGE [KOURAJ], the only activist organization fighting sexual orientation–based discrimination. Yet they have rarely reported it for fear of the homophobic condemnation that usually results. The social backlash, on top of the violence itself, has caused a web of problems. For one thing, their silencing has kept the problem out of research and advocacy streams. Charlot Jeudy, COURAGE's president, wrote me, "The focus of gender-based violence solely on women and girls, combined with stigmatization of *masisi* [hate speech for "gay"] in Haitian society, has driven the problem out of sight, out of mind, out of the system."[1]

※

I could recount numerous stories of assault that I have heard from women and girls living in the camps and on the streets of the capital—the most typical settings for such crimes—but instead proffer one that occurred across the country in Jérémie. I chose it because I am close to the little four-year-old in question and to her grandmother, Suze Abraham, a women's and children's rights activist. I received from her real-time accounts of the violation and its aftermath on a near-daily basis. I chose this story, too, because it is demonstrative of the judicial apathy and the breakdown in community well-being in the post-catastrophe period.

The child, whom I will call Timafi, is shy and serious and speaks in a high little voice. She has full cheeks, round eyes, and—when her grandmother has time to fix her hair—a head full of colored barrettes. She likes to ride in the back of the *taptap* in which I sometimes show up, and to color when she has crayons.

At the time of the incident on March 14, Timafi was living just outside Jérémie with her mother, stepfather, and newborn baby sister. According to Suze, Timafi's mother sent her to a neighbor's house to buy a can of rice. As the child left the neighbor's yard, a seventeen-year-old boy offered to take her back home. Instead, he took her to the cemetery, where he covered her mouth with his hand and raped her. An elderly neighbor saw the incident and tried to grab the boy, who punched her and then ran. Timafi's mother went to the police and filed a warrant for the youth's arrest. The word on the streets was that he fled town.

Following the attack, Timafi bled heavily and ran a high fever for two days. She ate almost nothing for more than a week. "The first time

I heard of a case of a two-year-old raped, I couldn't stop crying," Suze told me, crying anew. "It never occurred to me that this would happen to my own granddaughter." Suze's youngest daughter, age fourteen, remains the single female in three generations who has not been raped.

※

KOFAVIV members have kept watch on girls and women in the camps, intervening when they suspect a beating or a rape to be underway. They have paid special attention to children who were orphaned or lost in the catastrophe, and who have been at risk of rape or, out of economic desperation, prostitution, and helped them reunite with relatives. They have taken the testimony of survivors and tried to get them medical and legal assistance. Members like Suze and Tibebe have also conducted "know your rights" training in the camps.

The women's advocacy has come with a price, or rather many prices. In the case of the co-coordinators, Malya and Eramithe Delva, the cost included four attacks. One of those became an unintended case study in government lethargy about gendered violence. On the evening of March 2, Eramithe told me, a man came under that aforementioned blue tarp where meetings took place, which also served as home to the two women, their thirteen combined children and grandchildren, and other family members. The man dragged Eramithe's seventeen-year-old daughter, whom I will rename Flory, outside and attempted to rape her. Flory beat him off. An hour or so later, the man returned with three others and a pistol, and beat Flory and three more of Eramithe and Malya's daughters.

Eramithe ran to the police station at the edge of the camp, but an officer told her that incidents like this were Préval's business and had nothing to do with them. He said that if Eramithe found the perpetrators, she should catch them and bring them to the police station. He directed her, furthermore, to go to the street at the edge of the camp to watch for a patrol car with a certain license plate number; if it should pass by, she should flag it down. The families quickly packed up their belongings and went out to the sidewalk to look for the patrol car. They sat there the whole night, but it never came. They spent the next day looking for a new location to live but, finding nothing, returned to their original tent site.

The incident became a second case study, this one of the lack of options for relocation. Following the aggression against Flory, more than a dozen phone calls were made to Haitian and foreign nonprofits, and others with spare space, to inquire about shelter. The request was turned down by all, for reasons underscoring that community response networks were overwhelmed, that the women's movement was factionalized, and that poor women were rarely taken seriously.

Malya, Eramithe, and their families suffered fifteen more weeks and three more assaults in their original camp locale, where assailants—of the four daughters and of other women whose cases KOFAVIV had reported to the police—knew just where to go for retribution. When the fourth aggression on June 14 appeared to forewarn a kidnapping plot, the families were welcomed onto the grounds of an ally organization, and subsequently got help resettling into homes of their own.

Post-rape health care has proved equally elusive. In one instance, two international advocates spent eight days unsuccessfully searching out testing and treatment for twelve- and eighteen-year-old rape survivors. The same has applied to legal support: for any woman in a camp willing to brave possible retribution from a perpetrator, finding a gender-conscious lawyer has been about as viable as finding funds to pay for his or her services.

❊

The security of girls and women has plunged perilously due to a deadly combination of factors. First has been the enfeebled and apathetic judicial system. KOFAVIV leaders have said they have received multiple reports of judges dropping cases for lack of a doctor's certificate of "proof " within seventy-two hours of the brutality, though no such legal requirement exists. KOFAVIV has also reported instances of accused perpetrators having bribed their way out of jail. Destitute, Creole-speaking women have an even harder time getting justice, since they have less credibility in the eyes of the law than middle-class or elite women. Malya said, "The government didn't respect our rights even before the Presidential Palace was destroyed, even before the Palace of Justice was destroyed."

Second, policing is lackadaisical even when it exists. Much more commonly, it doesn't. Women have complained they have never seen Haitian or UN forces in their camps at all, notwithstanding Secretary-General Ban Ki-moon's March 13 statement that the UN's first priority in Haiti was to protect women.[2]

A third factor has been access by perpetrators. A teenage rape survivor offered this insight: "I think the only thing separating how much men are raping women now from before is that now they can get at us more easily." Hundreds of thousands of unprotected women and girls have been sleeping inside nothing more secure than a piece of plastic, and any man can easily learn which shelters hold them.

Fourth, studies of gender-based violence in disasters all over the world reveal that for men, anger and desperation stemming from loss of power over their lives, and other effects of catastrophe, often manifest through exerting power over those they can control. While women in such circumstances tend to share emotional experiences of trauma with each other, men often suppress their emotions and resort to "auto-aggressive reactions" against others. The research suggests that, in the conditions of stress and aggravated sleep deprivation that characterize life in the camps and more broadly in post-earthquake Haiti, perpetrators may have subconsciously been finding momentary catharsis through terrorizing those more vulnerable.[3]

I am not seeking to justify the unjustifiable. The objective is zero incidence of violence. Yet it is important to understand the factors above so that Haitian men are not just typecast as "gang-raping monsters," as one U.S. American journalist labeled them.[4] An acquaintance in Haiti told me, "These are guys you know, Bev."

※

This brings us to how the story of rape has been covered. The issue has had more enduring international traction than most any element of the crisis. To fast forward: well past the first anniversary of the earthquake, my e-mail and voice mail were still flooded with requests for interviews, information, and contacts about the problem, while interest in all the other Haitian issues I have helped publicize had largely evaporated. To be sure, many of the messages came from women's rights and human rights organizations and conscientious media, expressing concern for the survivors and a corresponding desire to help. But a lot of the media inquiries, like the resulting coverage, either bordered on the salacious or suggested that the high incidence of rape was a view into the heart of darkness of a barbaric nation. An article in an East Coast paper was illustrative, reading, "Though the U.S. now seems to be committed to rebuilding Haiti, it is difficult to see how that is possible in a culture where an offense so heinous as rape is so commonplace, and basically accepted as part of daily life."[5] (To check just how accepted it is, I recommend starting up a conversation on rape, especially rape of children, with any group of Haitian women. Every time I have done this, they have expressed bewilderment or outrage over how or why anyone could engage in such actions.)

(As numerous analyses have documented, a similar media narrative played out after the 2005 flood in New Orleans, another locale where a low-income and black majority was subject to biased perceptions and reporting.[6] Gender-based violence was occurring as the disaster unfolded there, too.[7] As in Haiti, tensions were high, legal protection was low, and defensive resources that women normally had were unavailable. Thousands were crowded into shelters without adequate food, water, sanitation, or security. And as in Haiti, instead of highlighting the causes or possible solutions, a slew of media outlets hyped stories about babies being raped in the Superdome and a girl's throat being slit in the Convention Center. The stories were later proven false, but not before fueling the "black savage" myth.)[8]

In Haiti, the incidence of abuse is greater than in many places, and its effects on women worse, not because of cultural essentialism but for structural reasons. Extreme poverty means that a woman cannot pay for transportation, so has to walk at night. Political apathy to the needs of disaster survivors means that women must sleep under ripped plastic instead of in locked buildings. Lack of other social protections such as gender-sensitive health care and rehabilitation for survivors—owing to underresourced and overstressed social systems—aggravates the enduring trauma of the experience. Yet the underlying factors of patriarchy and judicial laxity are universal, and play out in many patterns that violate and terrorize women the world over, including in the United States.

Now let's go back in time for a moment, to a different component of violence against women. There is a history behind women's bodies being a terrain for negotiating violence, both in men acting the violence out upon them and in the discourse around it. Men have used rape as a weapon in state-sponsored, religious, and ethnic wars across time and space. It is documented as early as the First Crusade of 1096–1099, when knights and pilgrims perpetrated it on their way to Constantinople,[9] and has appeared more recently in wars in the Balkans, Rwanda, Liberia, and other places. Likewise in Haiti, during the three years after Aristide was deposed in 1991, death squads organized by the military regime and funded by the United States [10] made girls' and women's bodies targets in their terror campaign. In a survey by a women's rights group during that period, 37 percent of the women they surveyed said they had been raped or otherwise sexually abused or knew someone else who had been.[11] The National Truth and Justice Commission, which subsequently led an extensive investigation, called the rapes a prominent part of a "politically orchestrated campaign conducted in the context of intimidation and savage repression against opposition to the coup d'état."[12]

When we launched an international campaign of denunciation, the U.S. Embassy tried to discredit the evidence. In a leaked confidential cable, the embassy relayed to Washington, "The Haitian left, including President Aristide and his supporters in Washington and here, consistently manipulate or even fabricate human rights abuses as a propaganda tool. . . . A case in point is the sudden epidemic of rapes reported . . . by pro-Aristide human rights advocates."[13]

※

Many months after the attacks on Eramithe and Malya and their families, KOFAVIV got enough international funding and logistical help to set up a women's center. A steady stream of survivors of violence visit each day to give testimony, become trained in human rights monitoring, and get a little group counseling and encouragement. Demoralized women can drop by just to share a meal and a rousing song. KOFAVIV and committed friends set up rapid-response systems for post-violation health care. The Haitian-run International Lawyers' Office (Bureau des Avocats Internationaux) and the U.S.-run Institute for Justice and Democracy in Haiti have worked to build legal cases (though in neither instance can their capacities begin to cover the majority). Other women's groups have increased their support services for survivors and their advocacy for rights and protection. Notable among them are Haitian Women's Solidarity, the Women's House, and Women Victims Get Up Stand Up (Fanm Viktim Leve Kanpe, or FAVILEK), all of which have long histories of working to end violence against women.

Yet according to my queries of leading Haitian and foreign experts, the reported incidence of rape does not appear to have abated any as of this writing in June 2012. An urgent condition for stopping the violence is prevention, which in turn requires effective stigmatizing and a police force and justice system with the commitment and the resources to protect women. Another sine qua non is getting people out of the camps. Girls and women have the right to be free from violence, and to sleep, bathe, and use the toilet without terror, wherever they are. Housing will not end the violence, but it is an imperative toward keeping them out of harm's way. Ending the attacks will also necessitate more serious prosecution and penalization, though that should not mean just slapping perpetrators into Haiti's current inhumane, dysfunctional prison system. Ultimately, what is needed are new gender relations based on respect and equitable power.

In the meantime, back in Jérémie on March 22, 2010, police located and arrested the rapist of four-year-old Timafi. When I asked Suze what would happen from there, she made a clucking sound in her throat that signifies resignation and said, "We'll see."

Said Eramithe, "We did so much to advance women not being victims. We've taken a big step backwards, but we'll struggle from where we are and move forward."

12

The Creole Connection

People-to-People Aid and Solidarity across Borders

June 2010

"One thing about New Orleans: we understand about crisis." Someone told me that in the Big Easy, at a blues show at Tipitina's where I had gone a few evenings after the *event*, hoping to let down for a fleeting moment. Over the course of the evening, I heard of four separate benefits for earthquake survivors.

For us, it was personal.

It had all played out in our town five years prior, though of course on a different scale: not just the disaster but the disaster response. There as in Haiti, we saw the opening of a collective heart and we saw troubling exploitation. Both places received mammoth attention, which died out long before the problems were addressed. Both suffered under a lack of accountability in aid from government and agencies like the Red Cross. Volunteers and aid workers teemed into the two sites to offer some very sensitive and useful humanitarian assistance and community organizing support, as well as some very paternalistic and harmful charity.

I have heard U.S. Americans say about Haiti, "It's a different world." On the contrary, Haiti is very much the same world as the United States. We are two shores in the same ocean, two sides of the same coin. Our over-development exists at the cost of their underdevelopment, our material enrichment at the cost of their impoverishment.

There are positive elements in the interdependence of our lives and fates, too, of course, and some of them were on front-row display after the *event*. For all the horror of the period, it gave people in New Orleans and elsewhere the chance to see ourselves reflected in those normally portrayed as "other" and to express our shared humanity.

People outside Haiti reached deeply into their lives, communities, and piggy banks to do what they could. What most could offer was money, and they did so in record proportions, with more than one in two house-holds in the United States donating.[1] Throughout 2010, contributions from private individuals, churches, and other organizations were stu-pendous, rivaling what major foreign powers gave in their official capac-ity. Even Somali pirates wanted in on the action. Whatever you think of them, it is significant that they announced plans to donate some of their loot to Haitian relief. "The humanitarian aid to Haiti can not be con-trolled by the United States and European countries; they have no moral authority to do so. They are the ones pirating mankind for many years," a spokesman said.[2]

The Haitian diaspora rushed to send money and supplies back home through groups tied to specific communities in Haiti, called Hometown Associations, as well as through churches, places of employment, and other venues. In 2010, Haitians living abroad sent almost $1.5 billion in remittances, about 20 percent of the country's GDP.[3]

Among the bevy of nations who responded were not just the much-publicized high-income ones, but East Timor and Estonia, Mongolia and more. Senegal was one of twenty-two African nations extending support; it offered free land to all Haitians wishing to "return to their origin."[4] Cuba was among many Latin American and Caribbean coun-tries that pulled out the stops. Cuba organized and sponsored a team of thirteen hundred doctors from throughout the Americas, who joined the more than three hundred Cuban-sponsored medics already volunteering in Haiti. (Cuba had first organized the emergency-response brigade, the Henry Reeve Team of Medical Specialists in Disasters and Epidemics, to assist Katrina survivors, but the U.S. government had refused its help.)

The doctors would spend up to two years living in tents or other simple housing and earning a meager salary as they provided emergency and primary care. "We are internationalist doctors," a Colombian brigade member, Pedro Roa, told me. "When someone asks me where I'm from, today I say Haiti. Next week, I could be from Chile."

I heard repeatedly from Haitians what the evidence of so much care meant. Just one of them, Beethoven Cheri, a crisis responder working in several disaster-impacted towns, said, "We want to say how much we appreciate all the citizens of the world who've paid attention to Haiti and who've given whatever they could, whether assistance or solidarity. They make us know we're not alone in this fight to reclaim our lives and rebuild our country."

True, some responses reflected racist and colonialist narratives. Some set off to Haiti with their own brilliant schemes, ideas of "development," or belief in technology to save the world; they deployed without asking Haitians what they needed or wanted, or considering the possible ramifications of their power or money or cultural biases. The cursed-nation theory was big, the most famous expression of it being evangelist Pat Robertson's pronouncement not even twenty-four hours out: "They were under the heel of the French, you know Napoleon the third and whatever. And they got together and swore a pact to the devil. They said, 'We will serve you if you will get us free from the prince.' True story. And so the devil said, 'Okay, it's a deal.' And they kicked the French out. The Haitians revolted and got themselves free. But ever since they have been cursed by one thing after another." (Similarly, many evangelical leaders placed blame for Hurricane Katrina and the flood of New Orleans on that city's sinners.) I heard all kinds of things, like one man's enjoinder, "Bring us back a Haitian child." Ten people from an Idaho-based Baptist church tried to do just that, whisking away thirty-three babies and children with no authorization.[5]

As always, people looking to make a buck came out of the cracks. In the first four days, I recorded funding requests from some half-dozen religious, political, and corporate institutions, which seemed to have no experience in disaster relief or in Haiti.

But far more numerous were the selfless ones, who were everywhere hoping for the best. Like surely everyone from the island nation or one step removed, I was deluged with messages from long-lost friends and total strangers who were using whatever venue they could to offer sympathy and help to Haitians. I fielded them from every continent except Antarctica—from a professor in South Africa, an artist in Japan, an indigenous revolutionary in Colombia, a second grader in San Diego, and countless others.

My eighty-five-year-old mother called from the old New Orleans family home. Her voicemail said, "Honey, I've found forty-four baskets around the house and wonder if you can help get them to Haiti. They're so pretty, and I think they would be good for women to keep their belongings in." Her message was so touching that I hated to have to call her back and tell her that, actually, every inch of space not dedicated to transporting U.S. soldiers and guns to Haiti was needed to get in food, medical supplies, and tents.

Many of the offerings of love and care were as creative as they were heartfelt. Here is just one kind I witnessed from New Orleans: support through the universal language of music, which is also the blood running through that city's veins. Music benefits took place all over town, from swanky yoga studios and earthy community centers to churches of every persuasion. The announcement for one benefit urged: "Let's continue to show solidarity the way it works in New Orleans. MUSIC and DANCE." One late night between sets of traditional jazz, onto the stage of a juke joint came a group of youth who had paddled the Mississippi from its headwaters in Minnesota; sponsors had pledged money for every mile the team had paddled.

When New Orleans flooded and high school band programs lost their instruments, an all-out nationwide fund drive began replacing them, and they are still arriving today. Cycling the gift forward has been Jean Montès, a Haitian classical musician who directs orchestral studies at New Orleans's Loyola University. After the earthquake, he launched the Haitian Youth Music Relief, which has gathered more than fifteen hundred instruments and hand-delivered them to destroyed schools in Haiti. They have included, in a perfect circle, cellos going to the same school where Jean learned to play cello as a young boy. Jean said, "In terms of relief, there's what we think of as the primary needs—health, shelter, food. But what happens next? What makes us feel human again when we've lost everything? It's usually things like music."[6] He told me, "What we are lucky enough to be doing is connecting the world through music. That's what we do."

One of fifteen hundred instruments collected in New Orleans and donated to Haiti.
Photograph by Wadner Pierre.

The New Orleans Jazz and Heritage Festival agreed. In 2011, it would spotlight Haitian music. Eight bands from the island whipped the fest-goers into ecstatic frenzy—from the looks of it, no one more than the Haitians in attendance, who had driven in from as far as New York and Miami. A *rara* troupe snaked through the crowds. One woman from Port-au-Prince told me it was the happiest she had been since the earth-quake.

※

Some realized that the disaster was the time to centralize, not sideline, questions of Haitian power and self-determination, and set to work—immediately, even when bulldozers were still carting corpses. Those interested in offering the types of support Haitians were asking didn't need to guess about approaches; Haitians began posting messages right away. Camille Chalmers, economist and executive secretary of the Hai-tian Platform to Advocate Alternative Development, gets the prize for being the earliest; on day three, he got out an e-mail that zinged around the Internet, in which he laid out short- and long-term material and po-litical needs. A few weeks later, Camille recaptured some of the priorities for me:

> Haiti is a country that has been isolated since 1804, and now that it's back in the eyes of international public opinion, we have a chance to establish more real and permanent ties, beyond calls for charity. We call on people to . . . help us in the reconstruction task, but also to come out of our social crisis. We are talking of people-to-people solidarity, not of that solidarity that states use in order to dominate the people. We ask the U.S. people to work for a change in American policy toward Haiti, so they can truly leave space for Haitians to determine their own path. Come stand with us in what we're doing.

The responses of radical community groups from Lexington to Missoula, liberal Washington agencies, and organized Haitian immi-grants reflected the values Camille described. Small groups of activists, cultural workers, and students throughout the United States and else-where began public education about the racial, economic, and gender

underpinnings of the crisis. Researchers and journalists jumped on
the Internet, if not a plane, to explore and expose those using the crisis
for personal profit and power. Progressive foundations and individual
donors directed their funding to community-led groups. Lawyers jour-
neyed south to help document human rights abuses and violence against
women. Women's rights groups around the global North connected and
campaigned together. The preexistent Haiti Advocacy Working Group
and the brand-new Haiti Response Coalition, networks of Northern
NGOs and grassroots organizations, went into overdrive to try to wrest
more appropriate international policies. Advocacy from them and others won temporary protection for Haitian immigrants from deportation
from the United States, tried but failed to get U.S. aid to buy emergency
food supplies from farmers in Haiti, and got at least lip service from the
UN to prioritize women's needs and leadership.

Deepa Panchang is now my coworker at Other Worlds and a resident
of the Crescent City, but at the time of the earthquake she was a master's
student of public health in Boston. Her experience was one of many that
embraced what Camille and others were asking, in a response that went
beyond charity. Deepa had no prior connection to Haiti but, like so many
others, was moved by the immensity of the suffering she saw. She said,

> I felt that we weren't hearing Haitian voices about the reconstruc-
> tion from the high-profile U.S. groups providing relief. On the
> other hand, smaller organizations that had strong relationships with
> the Haitian grassroots informed us about an alternative perspec-
> tive that we could pass on. Through them, I got a chance to go to
> Haiti to meet some of the camp communities and groups that were
> shut out of the system. Those relationships were really vital, since
> I could go back to the university to help bridge the gap, raising
> money for the important groups that had no name in the media and
> supporting advocacy to pressure the UN system to take action on
> issues like Haitians' participation in decision making.

※

All over the world, people like my mother who wanted to help meet
needs and beautify life, and people like Deepa who wanted to be a useful
ally, were looking for guidance. Here are a few recommendations that

emerged from critiques of communities in Haiti and New Orleans about their encounters with aid and solidarity. They are based on two simple principles. First, do no harm. Second, follow the Golden Rule: do unto others as you would have them do unto you. People trying to work in Haiti should operate with the same respect that they would want someone coming into their community to show—with a heightened sensitivity to Haiti's history, continuing up to the present, of foreigners breezing in to do whatever they want.

- Support what Haitians are doing instead of starting your own initiative. If you really feel you must, test the idea with Haitians whom your intervention is intended to benefit before moving forward. Does it reflect their agenda and meet an expressed need? If not, your instincts or passions may not be aligned with their priorities. If you don't know any Haitian organizations to check with, or you are not certain they are interested, better to hang back. Sometimes doing nothing can be the wiser course of action. Note that even if you ask Haitians if they want what you are offering, they may not reject it straight up. Saying "yes" to people with more power is the standard; the "no" is usually more quietly embedded in what happens next. Be very attentive to ways, culturally different from your own, that a community may be conveying the message that it doesn't need or want that form of aid or service. The message might be encoded through "weapons of the weak": failing to show up, failing to fulfill a requested task, failing to make the project advance. You might then pause and ask some deeper questions, and listen very hard to what is said and what is left unsaid.
- At every step, promote mechanisms and opportunities for Haitians themselves—especially those whose voices go unheard and needs go unmet—to take the lead. Programs led by outsiders often fail as soon as the foreigners leave, and also perpetuate the sidelining of those directly impacted.
- Check your assumptions that Haitians need your technology, modernity, or other ideologically or socially biased approaches. Evan Hansen, editor of WIRED.com, offered this perspective: "Bad aid starts with ignorance and condescension. . . . I've been consciously and unconsciously framing the reconstruction in

terms of delivering telecom service over mesh networks, boot-strapping data mashups to bring a Web 3.0 layer to the relief, de-livering green tech and so on. Sexy. [But] here's what the Lambi Fund wants: Electric grain mills for grinding corn and millet, a portable irrigation pump, ox ploughs, a goat breeding program, a fishing boat and reforestation."[7]

- Act with deliberation instead of acting as quickly as possible. Haitians say that anything that happens fast doesn't last.

- Focus on assistance that may improve the life of, and deal fairly with, every Haitian it touches along the way, instead of trying to help as many people as possible. Bigger is not necessarily better.

- Avoid material aid unless you have a direct connection with a group that has asked for it—say, an eye clinic that can put the glasses you collect to good use. Cast-off clothes, shoes, and household items sent after the earthquake were generally not what people needed, and so fed booming sidewalk sales by those desperate for money to buy what they *did* need. The goods also undermined local businesses where they existed, like cobblers. Especially avoid sending food unless it has been requested by someone you trust to get it directly to those in need. This may seem counterintuitive, given levels of hunger and malnutrition, but imported food takes business away from Haitian farmers. Robert Naiman of Just Foreign Policy sent this suggestion: "If your aid dollar is used to purchase supplies produced in Haiti, it's doing double duty. And if it's being used to directly employ Haitians, it's doing triple duty. Push your aid dollar as close to the ground as you can."

- Give money, carefully. Cash is critical, and in the hands of a reli-able organization with deep roots in its community, it can go far in alleviating need. Unfortunately, most of the dollars given by global citizens after the disaster in Haiti, as in New Orleans and many other places, disappeared into the ether. There are two ways to increase the chances that your money will reach those in need and serve them well. First, before giving anywhere, ask lots of questions. Probe deeply into whether the soliciting group has a record of trustworthiness, how accountable it is to local communities, and exactly what it will do with the money. Second, make donations to organizations that support grassroots communities. A study by Grantmakers without Borders about the international response to the Indian Ocean tsunami of 2004 found what many have also found to be true in Haiti: grassroots organizations are by far the most effective in delivering aid and much-needed services.[8]

- Go beyond giving aid to assisting Haitians in resolving the systemic problems that they have identified. Use your voice to echo theirs as they seek to construct a democratic nation. Collaborate with advocacy groups to win fairer trade policies, labor rights, women's rights, environmental health, and food sovereignty. Call for reform of U.S. and UN policies to better reflect citizens' needs, while challenging the destructive elements of their political and economic interventions.

- To guide your and others' efforts, learn and share the priorities and analyses of social movements and organized communities.

I don't want to squelch good intentions and compassionate impulses. On the contrary, I celebrate them, and hope that justice will be served by what gifts are made, and how.

How can we learn as we go to improve the quality of our response? How can we listen carefully and engage in honest dialogue with survivors and community members? Keep in mind the difference between the leadership of those directly impacted and those just visiting? Be aware of power dynamics, for those of us with heavy footprints? Haitians still have dire needs for assistance and solidarity, so we have a wonderful opportunity to keep practicing.

13

We've Lost the Battle, but We Haven't Lost the War

(Tales from Six Months Out)

July 2010

Haiti during the World Cup operated under the same rule as New Orleans during the Super Bowl: don't make plans to do anything with anyone during a game. I knew this, but my mind was focused on other things, and I made the mistake of going to a cell phone store in downtown Port-au-Prince during a soccer match. Employees sat hypnotized in front of the big-screen TV, unwilling to have their attention distracted by customers.

When Argentina, favored among the finalists, lost its match, I could finally conduct my business and leave the store. Throngs of mourners danced through the streets, waving Argentine flags and palm fronds. A group of skinny men paraded in bikinis and wigs. Noontime drunks shouted nonsense at each other.

"Thank God it's almost over," my friend Maryse had said that morning. "Argentina's the last team in the competition that anyone here really cares about, so any day now all this madness will have to stop." Four Haitians had died in arguments after the loss of their preferred teams earlier that week.

"Soon," a young construction worker on break from hammering directly outside my window had said, "the demonstrations can resume." Political protests had stopped at the start of the World Cup because people suddenly had more important things to do. Another thing about the World Cup ending, Djab had assured me: the electricity that had been guaranteed during the past month to power the TVs would revert to its typical irregularity. "It's the same every four years," he had said. "We'll be back in a *blakawout*, blackout."

From the cell phone store, I caught a taxi to a women's community meeting. Collective taxicabs are identified in two ways: the red ribbon hanging from the rearview mirror, and their state of decrepitude. They are usually the oldest and crappiest cars on the road, and it's not uncommon for a key part to give out or a many-times-repatched tire to blow definitively en route. When that happens, customers simply climb out patiently, pay the driver for however far their journey reached, then catch another cab.

In this taxi, I established up front that I wasn't going to be ripped off. "Listen, I know it's one zone. I'm just paying a fare for one zone."

"It's two zones," the driver replied.

"No, *cheri*. To Bois Verna it's one zone, thirty gourdes. Don't give me the price you make up for *blan*, foreigners."

He gave me a circumspect look. "But aren't you a *blan*?"

In the cab as everywhere, it was all earthquake, all the time. You heard the word all day long—again like in New Orleans, where one friend said that all he wanted in life was to go one day without hearing "Katrina." In Haiti six months later, with a little distance and a lot of moxie, many of the horror stories had evolved into dramatic tales, complete with humor. The driver and the five other passengers who were wedged into this little Nissan were laughing loudly at one such account. I told them I was amazed they could laugh. The man against whom my thigh was jammed said, "If you stay traumatized all the time, it's not good for you. You have to find joy to diminish it."

The song "*Anba Dekonb*," Under the Rubble, by rapper DJ Tony Mix, came out in February and was one of the most popular in Haiti for months. The way you danced to it was to simulate an earthquake with your body, producing much hilarity in bars and nightclubs.

A feminist activist confused her catastrophes in a recent conversation, referring to the earthquake as "the coup d'état." When I smiled, she said, "Hey, if it's not a natural disaster around here, it's a political disaster."

A retired history teacher in whose family's house I sometimes stayed began each day by calling out: "*À la guerre!*" To war!

※

In some ways, everything had changed, while in many ways Haiti was the same as it ever was. The political class was, as always, apathetic in the face of desperate citizens' needs. One young man said to me, "The Haitian government is deaf, dumb, and mute." As they always had, grassroots organizations met continually to develop their strategies for political change. And as they always had—excepting, as mentioned, during the World Cup—demonstrators regularly took to the streets, the venue of advocacy for those not allowed into the halls of power.

Haiti was the same in much more plebian ways, too. No one in my block could breathe for two days because of the acrid smoke from wood charcoal being made up the ravine. Flies and mosquitoes changed shifts at sunset and sunrise, while sweat pulled twenty-four-hour shifts. Boys flew kites they'd fashioned from twigs and clear plastic bags, until the inevitable entanglement in power lines. Men shuffled by in shoes cracked down the middle of the soles that most anywhere else would have been thrown out long ago. Young women who were not carrying a bucket of water or a baby, and whose bodies were therefore free and light, flapped down the streets in backless sandals, swinging their behinds. To do a little commerce, older women pulled thin flowered handkerchiefs from their bras and slowly unwrapped them to produce crumpled gourde notes. For a few cents, you could buy a street lunch of cassava bread and peanut butter laced with chili pepper or, for a snack, a stick of sugarcane with its deep purple skin macheted off.

To pee, little boys faced out from the wall. Older boys and men faced into the wall. Salesmen stood at the front of buses and held up jars of dark liquid, which they told their audiences would cure impotence, fibroids, high blood pressure, and eczema. Pedestrians paused on the sidewalk to wipe thick dust off their shoes with a shred of newspaper, though they would become filthy again momentarily. Motorcycles zipped by with three or sometimes four passengers; I once saw five. Women walked through the streets, carrying on their heads straw baskets or plastic fan covers that they had repurposed, chanting in loud, nasal tones, "I've got peas, I've got carrots, I've got cabbage." Men got their faces and hairlines shaved in barber shops consisting of one chair, one pair of scissors, and one straight razor, right in the middle of high-traffic sidewalks.

People insisted on giving you a cup of coffee as though they had nothing else to do in the world. Folks disarmed hostile situations by making their voices supplicatory and calling each other *cheri*. They laughed easily and angered easily, engaged in gestures of touching tenderness and vile cruelty, showed impressive generosity and ripped off the most vulnerable.

✳

Back home from the women's meeting, I was struggling to wrap up a report when I heard a voice at my door. "*Onè!*" Honor. Normally I avoided the constant current of visitors while working, but this I couldn't resist. "*Respè!*" Respect, I called back, and ran to open the door. It's one of my favorite customs anywhere. One person—more often an elder or a person from the country, in these modernization-filled days of dying tradition—announces "*Onè*" as she or he approaches a courtyard or door. The neighbor answers "*Respè*," signifying her or his own intent. Trust established, the person may enter.

There in the courtyard stood two elderly women, both in ankle-length skirts and yellow-ribboned hats from another era. They politely introduced themselves as Jehovah's Witnesses. One was missing a foot, or perhaps a whole leg, and balanced on aluminum crutches—a big new import item. When I told them I was in the middle of something and couldn't talk just then, they left a handbook, in French, on as universal a focus point as you could get in this country today: *Quand la mort frappe un être aimé.* When Death Strikes a Loved One.

At dusk, I gave up on the writing project and went for a stroll around the neighborhood. A little boy danced by himself to nothing but the rhythm of a generator. Teenage boys played soccer after having taken the liberty of blocking either end of the street off with big rocks. They politely stopped their Concorde-speed ball to let me through.

Heading left up a sharp hill, I slowed and panted. On the other side of the road from me, a woman also slowed and panted, only she was balancing a five-gallon jug full of water on her head. When I told her I was sorry she had to carry that load, she slapped the back of one hand against the other palm in the gesture indicating acceptance in the face of no alternative, and said, "What are you going to do?" A boy walked by in the other direction, wearing nothing on his feet but thick orange socks. A man sat on a strip of grass beside the road, chopping down little trees that never stood a chance.

Now, it being Saturday night, neighbors did what they do everywhere that is short on funds: gather on stoops to talk. Mona, who used to cook for a friend of mine, appeared from down the road. We hadn't seen each other in several years, so we plopped down on the curb, tucked the edges of our skirts under the back of our knees in the Haitian gesture of modesty, and began with the only possible topic: the *event*. Mona told me,

I grabbed two of my grandchildren—I put the five-year-old on my back, the sixteen-month-old on my hip—and ran. None of us had sandals on, we just fled with what we had at that moment. Everyone was running to Champ de Mars, so that's where we went. A girl came and told us that the little boy who lived in the apartment below my daughter's was trapped, so we ran back to the house. The mother had died. Later we found out she was folding laundry and a piece of cement fell on her. It seems like she fell in the laundry basket and suffocated in the clothes. Anyway, the little three-year-old was stuck in there. He kept calling, "Zesus, save me. Zesus, save me." He was too young to even say Jesus.

We couldn't get him out, so we asked one of those thugs who was roaming around stealing all the money inside houses to help us. We couldn't go in there with all the fallen cement, but that guy didn't have a problem because there was money to be made. We had 250 [Haitian] dollars [US$6.25], but that thief said he wouldn't do it for less than 400 dollars [US$10]. So we went back to Champ de Mars and did a fund-raising marathon, and by three in the morning we had collected 150 more dollars that people had in their pockets when they ran. We cut a hole in the back of the apartment, and the man went in and got the child.

"We slept on Champ de Mars just like this." Mona reached out a foot and tapped it on the macadam. "We didn't have so much as a sheet. I didn't know about my other two children, but I said even if they'd died, I wasn't going to go to their house in the middle of the night to find them. Their bodies would have to wait till morning.

"The things I saw, oh. I had to step over so many corpses—children, old people—putting my foot down between them." Out came the foot again, pantomiming. "I didn't have a choice, they were everywhere. I said, 'Sorry, dead one. Sorry, dead one,' each time."

While we were talking, a couple of men who lived up the street came to join us. The conversation reverted to what just about every man wanted to talk about: Argentina in the World Cup. I offered them my condolences for that loss. One lifted his hands skyward and said, "We're resigned." Then he added, "We've lost the battle, but we haven't lost the war."

"Spoken like a true Haitian," I told him.

14

Social Fault Lines

Class and Catastrophe

July 2010

Champ de Mars was, until a few years ago, the chicest address in Haiti, a Caribbean-scale Champs-Élysées. On one side of the tree-lined square was the frost-white presidential palace, a relic from the U.S. occupation built to resemble the White House. Peacocks sauntered across its grounds. Spacious parks were lush with trees and grass, fountains flowed with water. Four movie theaters and upscale markets lined the remainder of the square.

Over the years, I have spent a lot of time at two addresses on Champ de Mars. The first was that palace.[1] The second, more recently, was a sprawling displacement camp that has taken over the parks and sidewalks like a successful Risk player. The new camp occupants delighted in making fun of the former palace occupant. From under their homes of scraps, they giggled as they repeated to each other Préval's comment: "I cannot live in the palace." They plucked out the collars of their only blouses and mimicked a statement they claimed he made, "I lost my shirts."

Haiti sits directly over a major fault system made up of multiple faults, one or more of which slipped on January 12.[2] Equally disastrous over time has been the socioeconomic fault line.

From outside Haiti, it might have appeared after *twelve* that the whole country was one deep, collective sufferance. True enough, land shifted under the rich and the poor with equal force. People of every class and skin shade lost loved ones, homes, businesses, and personal treasures.

For a few days the *event* had a democratizing effect. Common grief brought common cause, and people aided and sympathized with each other in mighty ways. Many—rich and poor and those somewhere along the axis—dreamed that a more unified Haiti might arise from the wreckage.

But a short passage of time revealed that the disaster's impact was as sharply delineated by class as the nation itself was. The degree of harm, whether physical or economic, roughly paralleled income. "The natural catastrophe just reproduced the preexistent one, with so much exclusion and exploitation," said Nixon Boumba, community and student organizer with the Democratic Popular Movement (Mouvman Demokratik Popilè, or MODEP). "It's the logical consequence of politics and the social system."

The imposing headquarters of the UN, the president's private residence, the high-end Hotel Montana . . . they and so many other establishments of the Haitian and foreign elite were on their knees, and thousands died within them. Two Haitian senators, the archbishop of the Catholic Church, the UN mission chief, and many other influential people passed away. Their lives were celebrated, their deaths publicly recognized.

Greatly disproportionate were the numbers of *defavorize* or *timalere*, the disfavored or little unfortunate ones, who died in poorly located buildings made of poor materials, which toppled like Legos. They passed away with the same public anonymity as they had lived. Some of their lives had never been formally recognized with so much as a birth certificate.

For months, people of all social stations slept outside. But middle- and upper-class people were able to sleep in courtyards or gardens on their own or their families' properties. Later on, if their homes needed extensive repairs, they could hire crews to do the job while moving in with friends or relatives with space to spare, or renting an apartment or hotel room, or even—once the airport reopened to passengers—relocating to other countries. Most of the rest landed in the streets or in displaced persons camps, where they remained for months or remain today.

Construction companies, earth-moving equipment, Internet and telecommunications businesses, vehicle rental agencies, and water delivery services were able to bounce back. Their owners stood an excellent chance both of full recovery and of making a killing from emergency relief and reconstruction business. The poor had no means through which to recover their losses, especially those on which they had depended for income; their personal catastrophes only cascaded with time.

Like the elderly woman who lived in a small maroon tent in the courtyard fronting my apartment. She spent her days sitting on a wooden stool under an almond tree, listening to a transistor radio. She never returned my greeting. Then one afternoon as I walked past, she suddenly informed me, "It's so hard. I used to work, I sewed for people, but my sewing machine got destroyed during the *event*. I'm old, I don't have any other way to make money.

"I rented a house before. It wasn't destroyed, but now the landlord took it back. I don't have any money to rent another one. I can tell the owner of this place doesn't like me being here. I used to bathe in the courtyard"—I had seen her washing from a pan of water behind the almond tree, trying to shield her bare top from public view—"but now I'm too ashamed." She whispered, "It's hard, it's hard."

"Sometimes my courage gives out, and I don't know what to do. This morning I went to church. I didn't have anything to say to God, so I just lifted my arms up"—she did this now, straight toward heaven—"and I said, 'God, I'm here. Please see me.' "

※

One Haitian expression goes, *Kote ou kanpe depann de kote ou chita.* Where you stand depends on where you sit. Another puts the matter a little more poetically: *Wòch nan dlo pa konn mizè wòch nan solèy.* Rocks in the water don't know the misery of rocks in the sun.

I was stupefied, after spending an entire day in camps with women who described their lives in terms approximating hell, to overhear a businessman give a status update to a faraway friend on his cell phone: "Well, things are getting back to normal here." For him, they were. Those in the upper strata were reclaiming their before-the-earthquake privileges. Jazz clubs, gyms, and gourmet restaurants were reopening. Lines were long in the capital's few supermarkets, where one could buy an array of imported goods without needing to sweat or sidestep piles of garbage. The streets in Pétionville, a town on the edge of Port-au-Prince where many of Haiti's tonier people reside, were largely cleared of rub-ble. Crumbled walls around the villas and grassy estates farther up the hill were rebuilt.

As for the rest, it was a koan: What does an even poorer Haiti look like? Haiti's destitution was already a marvel on the planet before Janu-ary 12. Besides rubble, the only thing in plentiful supply was scarcity.

No studies have quantified the difference between levels of material poverty before and after, and to an untrained eye it may have been hard to detect. However, survivors could tell you that the levels have been much, much higher since the earthquake. In a survey four human rights insti-tutions conducted of fifty-two camp-dwelling families in July 2010, 37 percent said they had no form of income whatsoever.[3] For many adults and youth of both genders in the camps, prostitution has offered the only means of income. The going price for intercourse has reportedly been anywhere from US$2.50 to US$5.00. Those engaging in transactional sex rarely have the negotiating power to protect themselves with con-doms, and pregnancy and sexually transmitted diseases have both esca-lated sharply.

Emergency food aid was rarely distributed after April 2010, and then what little food was handed out consisted mainly of raw rice. Some had no means to cook it because they had no stove, charcoal, or wood, but sold it for a pittance to buy edible food instead. Many just went perpetu-ally hungry. In the above-mentioned survey, 75 percent of families said that at least one member had not eaten for one full day during the preced-ing week; more than 50 percent said their children had not.[4]

Take Getro Nelio. As described earlier, his father's head was crushed in the quake. His home was, too. Getro became so emaciated that the contours of his face rose and sank over bones and hollows as dramati-cally as a mountain range. He had no income and survived through small gifts from friends. He gave me a tour of the national soccer stadium, the new home his family shared with seven hundred other families. Do they feed you? "They gave us a sack of rice, nine big cans, when we first got to the stadium. They haven't given us any more." They don't give you any food? "I think they don't want us to get too comfortable here, thinking we can get food and water and a tent. Well, once they gave us a card to get cans of Spam. But otherwise we have to find our own."

One week, Getro told me, "I'm hoping to find redemption from my tribulation. Do you think I will?"

For those who couldn't fly to Miami for treatment, medical care was another source of constant worry. Camps were full of illness, the result of lack of sanitation, poor nutrition, stress, and sleep deprivation. A few camp- or street-based clinics, like those organized by Partners in Health, Doctors Without Borders, and the Cuban government's medical team, were free, but I never met any camp residents who knew where these clinics were except those living in close proximity. Even when a clinic visit was gratis, the specialist to whom a patient might be referred, lab tests, drugs, and bus fare were not. Medical care remained a luxury.

Getro's mother, fifty-five-year-old Liliane Maconie, needed throat surgery. A doctor at the University Hospital scheduled her for the operation, but when she turned up on the appointed day, she was told that a necessary machine was broken. She was referred to another hospital, but there she would have had to pay for the procedure. A connection arranged for her admittance to yet a third hospital outside town and donated bus fare, and all our hopes soared. But once there, she learned she would have had to spend the night to complete the procedure. As she had nowhere to stay and no money for food, she returned home. Her malady remained intact.

I have heard other accounts of events that should never have transpired, such as from a young U.S. American nurse whom I encountered in the bathroom of a fancy hotel where I sneaked in to wash my face after a sweaty day in the camps. She had just come from a shift at the University Hospital. Wide-eyed, she told me about having delivered a baby with only a pair of plastic gloves she had provided herself and a cloth that had been used to deliver another baby minutes before. She had passed the previous night with a young boy who was dying from cerebral malaria, and had had nothing to give him the entire night except one bottle of water.

Many schools were reopening, but as a woman in a camp said, "It's only for the high-ups this year." Most couldn't afford the monthly fees, nor the new uniforms, shoes, notebooks, textbooks, or pencils to replace the ones lost under their falling houses.

※

There is no metric for misery. But if there were, it should reflect the distress level in cases like that of Guesner, a man who drove a rented *taptap* for about $12.50 a day. Guesner lost his eight-year-old daughter Gues-line, who was named for him. "She was playing in the yard and a house fell on her. I had to pull her out from under." Guesner reached under a swatch of gray carpet covering the dashboard and extracted a miniature Bible. He rifled through the pages to find a postage-stamp-sized portrait of a thin girl. "You know no morgues or hospitals were working. I wanted to bury her out in the country, but I didn't have money for transportation out there. I kept trying to get the money, but after three days she started to rot. I couldn't wait anymore, I had to put her beside the road. The tractors came with their buckets in front. But I couldn't stand for them to scoop her up, so I wrapped her up tightly in a sheet—two sheets, in fact—and placed her in the scoop myself."

Do you know where they took her? "They dumped her." Guesner flicked his hand: *away.* "I think about her every second." His stoicism gave way and his face crumpled like a balloon when the air rushes out.

Alina "Tibebe" Cajuste should be included in the study, too. Tibebe has become, inconceivably, even skinnier than before. Cement blocks fell on her during the earthquake, breaking her toe and injuring her back, but she never got proper medical attention. She didn't get it, either, for her ankle, which was injured after she fell while trying to protect her twenty-something daughter from a rapist's assault; she now walks with a limp. She mentioned in passing one day that she was spitting up blood. Hoping to sound nonchalant, I asked if she had thought of checking that out. Of course I knew the answer, which reflected her financial status.

She used to live in a fifteen-by-fifteen-foot house on the noisy, pol-luted Carrefour Road. After that house was shaken to bits, Tibebe, one of her daughters, and two other families—eight people in all—took to sleeping on the slab. One family got hold of a Coleman tent and the other a thin single mattress, but Tibebe and her daughter continued passing the nights on the cement. The two salvaged from the wreckage of their home one suitcase of clothes and the book *Walking on Fire*, where Ti-bebe's poetry was first published. That's all they possessed.

Tibebe said, "It's only the heat of the sun keeping us alive."

15

Monsanto Seeds, Miami Rice

The Politics of Food Aid and Trade

August 2010

On June 4, 2010, thousands of peasant producers marched down kilometers of dirt road in the Central Plateau farm belt, kicking up dust. Wearing matching straw hats and carrying banners reading "Monsanto GM [genetically modified] and hybrid seeds: Violent poison for peasant agriculture," they were simultaneously celebrating World Environment Day and protesting a recent donation of Monsanto seeds. At their destination in the remote town of Hinche, they set fire to a pile of those seeds, which they called their "declaration of war."

A few months prior, the Ministry of Agriculture had given Monsanto permission to donate 505 tons of hybrid corn and vegetable seeds. Some were treated with a chemical fungicide so toxic that the EPA banned its purchase for home use in the United States.[1]

Why would the hungriest people and the poorest farmers in the hemisphere demand an end to handouts? First, the peasant movement is strongly committed to its Creole seed stock, and considers the imports an assault on food sovereignty and on biodiversity. Doudou Pierre, a coordinator of the Haitian National Network for Food Sovereignty and

Security (Réseau National Haïtien de Sécurité et Souveraineté Alimentaire, or RENHASSA), explained: "We're for seeds that have never been touched by multinationals. We say that seeds are the patrimony of humanity. No one can control them."

Second, they view the hybrid seeds—the result of breeding different varieties of plants to improve the next generation—as a Trojan horse, rolling in a potential dependency that could put peasants out of business. This is because the seeds from hybrid plants can't be easily saved and planted the next season since, unlike traditional seeds, the traits of subsequent generations aren't predictable. While hybrids have worked well for farmers in the United States and elsewhere who can afford to buy a new stock each year, many Haitian farmers don't have that luxury. So, like their counterparts all over the world, they religiously save their traditional seed stock for each season's planting. However, low-cost and easily accessible Monsanto seeds, available for purchase for one year through rural stores run by USAID-subsidized farmers' associations, could entice peasants to make the switch, hooking them in a way that would profit Monsanto down the line. Not for nothing did Elizabeth Vancil, Monsanto's director of development initiatives, tell the Haitian Ministry of Agriculture that the ministry's approval of the donation was "a fabulous Easter gift."[2]

Agronomist Bazelais Jean-Baptiste, director of the Bassin Zim Education and Development Fund, said that importing seeds "creates a devastating level of dependency and is a complete departure from the reality of Haiti's peasants. Haitian peasants already have locally adapted seeds that have been developed over generations. What we need is support for peasants to access the traditional seeds that are already available."[3]

Monsanto claimed the $4 million delivery was "to support recovery efforts" because farmers "otherwise may not have had sufficient seeds to plant this season in their earthquake-ravaged country."[4] That justification was undermined by several surveys conducted shortly after the catastrophe by organizations with strong knowledge of Haitian agriculture. One was Catholic Relief Services, whose assessment in March found that farmers did have enough seeds to plant. They broadly circulated a report to development and relief organizations in Haiti urging that external seed not be introduced during the emergency period.[5] A study by the Peasant Movement of Papaye, the National Peasant Movement of the Papaye Congress, and Foundation Hand-in-Hand

Demonstration against Monsanto seeds. Banner reads "Defend Food Sovereignty in Our Country and the Planet." Photograph by Alice Speri.

(Fondasyon Men nan Men, or FONDAMA), a coalition of farmer groups from the Central Plateau and international allies, also found adequate, good-quality seeds available on the local market. "What they *don't* have is money to buy them," said Stephen Bartlett of FONDAMA and Agricultural Missions. FONDAMA was one group that jumped in to address that problem, raising funds in the United States so that thousands of peasant families could purchase locally the Creole seeds they needed for the post-earthquake planting season.

The international small-farmer movement Via Campesina has called Monsanto one of the "principal enemies of peasant sustainable agriculture and food sovereignty for all peoples."[6] The producer of Agent Orange used by the United States during the war in Vietnam, Monsanto is now one of the leading manufacturers of genetically modified seeds and holds more than 650 biotechnology patents.[7] Together with Syngenta, Dupont's Pioneer, and Bayer CropScience, Monsanto controls 50 percent of the world's commercial seed market.[8] Monsanto has amassed its empire in part by buying up major seed companies to stifle competition. According to a report by the Center for Food Safety, it has sued hundreds of farmers throughout the United States, even small ones, for alleged contract violations, and investigates an estimated five hundred more a year.[9]

U.S. taxpayers subsidized the distribution of the seeds in Haiti. They were dispensed by the Watershed Initiative for National Natural Environmental Resources (WINNER), a five-year, $126 million Haiti-based USAID project.[10] WINNER's chief-of-party in Haiti is Jean-Robert Estimé, a former member of Jean-Claude Duvalier's cabinet and one of his closest associates.

WINNER is run by Chemonics International, one of the biggest Beltway bandits. Ninety percent of the funding for this self-described "international development consulting firm" comes from USAID, including for war-related work in Iraq and Afghanistan.[11] In 2009 alone, Chemonics earned more than $256 million in taxpayer-funded contracts and ranked seventieth on the list of top U.S. government contractors.[12] Chemonics has a history of corruption in obtaining contracts in South Africa, poorly done or abandoned work in Afghanistan and Poland, and strong ties to the U.S. government that often give the company a free pass despite past failings.[13] The former majority owner of Chemonics stock was a senior USAID official with a record of substantial personal contributions to the Republican Party, raising questions of influence buying.[14]

※

Another import that has debilitated Haiti's chance for food sovereignty is rice. The country that was once nearly self-sufficient in rice production now imports almost all the staple from the United States—90 percent, according to the USA Rice Federation.[15] Worldwide, Haiti is the third-largest importer of U.S. rice.[16]

Rice is among the five most heavily subsidized crops in the United States. Its growers received $12.9 billion in government subsidies between 1995 and 2010.[17] The combination of subsidized and industrial-scale production and lowered import tariffs for goods entering Haiti has yielded this bizarre outcome: beginning in the early 1980s, rice grown in such places as Arkansas and California and shipped by boat to Haiti could be sold cheaper than rice actually grown *in* Haiti. As a result, Haiti's domestically produced rice supply fell from 47 percent in 1998 to 15 percent in 2008.[18] "Miami" being interchangeable with "United States" to many a Haitian, the import was quickly nicknamed "Miami rice." Its name had a second derivation: the show *Miami Vice*, which was blaring on many a Haitian TV at the time.

An estimated 90,000 to 110,000 metric tons of rice was sent to Haiti as emergency assistance in 2010, much of it from the United States.[19] Food aid in response to a crisis is a logical and moral response, and there are ways to furnish it without sacrificing domestic production. In the short term, they involve using international aid dollars to procure available domestically grown food, importing food only to fill the gap. In the medium to long term, foreign aid could invest in programs to strengthen small-farmer production.

Instead, the dumping of U.S. agribusiness rice has devastated local production and risks making Haiti more, not less, hungry. Yet where Haitians sit—on a scale from well-fed to hungry to malnourished to starving—appears to be a small consideration in foreign aid decisions. USAID's own documents lay bare another, seemingly far more significant, part of the rationale: Food donations benefit U.S. corporations in a couple of ways. First, about 80 percent of the funds ostensibly given as food aid never leaves the United States but instead goes straight into the pockets of companies that produce, process, package, and transport the commodities. Second, as USAID's own documents state: "Aid leads to trade, from which Americans stand to benefit directly."[20] In a perfect exposé of how dependency is built into the aid system, nations that are recipients of today's handouts overwhelmingly become purchasers tomorrow. According to USAID, of the fifty highest-purchasing nations of U.S. agricultural products in 2002, forty-three were former recipients of food aid.[21]

One of those hurt was Jonas Deronzil, who has been farming in the fertile Artibonite Valley since 1974. When I spoke with him in April 2010, his entire spring rice harvest had been languishing for a month in burlap sacks inside a collectively owned cinder-block warehouse. Sitting barefoot on a sack of beans on his shady front porch, Jonas said,

> Since foreign rice has invaded Haiti, we plant our rice but we can't
> sell it. The foreigners have all the possibilities: they have water,

they have machinery, they have easy access to fertilizer and other inputs. They can grow their rice in quantity. The peasants, poor devils, we spend a lot to grow it, but we can't sell it. Sometimes we have to go to the loan sharks just to get enough money to survive. We were already in a black misery by the time all the cast-off rice came here after the earthquake. But with the rice they're dumping on us, it's competing with ours and soon we're going to fall in an even deeper hole.

Here's what Jonas Deronzil has to say to the American government: your policies are bad. Help us produce, don't give us food. We have to be able to work. We're not lazy. We have water. We have land. What we need from the aid is agricultural machinery, is the means to collect water, ways to clean out our irrigation systems, fertilizer, technicians to help us, outlets to sell our produce, cheap places to buy seeds. Don't give us rice, we don't need it. Our country can produce rice. If we're short, we'll let you know.

Rony Charles is a member of the coordinating committee of the Cooperative Farming Production Network of the Lower Artibonite (Rezo Asosyasyon Koòperatif pou Komès ak Pwodwi Agrikòl Ba Latibonit, or RACPABA). RACPABA comprises seven marketing cooperatives with two thousand members, Jonas among them. In April, Rony reported that since the disaster aid started arriving in Haiti, the cooperative hadn't been able to sell any of the crops it had purchased before the earthquake. Without being able to recuperate its capital, he said, it couldn't buy the new harvest from producers, either.

⌘

On March 10, speaking to the Senate Foreign Relations Committee, Bill Clinton said of U.S. rice exports to Haiti, "It may have been good for some of my farmers in Arkansas, but it has not worked. It was a mistake. . . . I had to live everyday with the consequences of the loss of capacity to produce a rice crop in Haiti to feed those people because of what I did; nobody else."[22] Mea culpa notwithstanding, nothing has changed in the foreign aid and trade policies of the U.S. government. A bill in the U.S. Senate would have encouraged purchasing from Haitian farmers in a vague way, "to the extent possible," but it died in late 2010.

As for the March rice harvest grown by Jonas Deronzil, Rony Charles, and other members of the cooperative in the Artibonite, it sat in the warehouse until June. The farmers said that having their investment in that crop tied up for three months, with no income in the interim, was a bitter blow to their families. When the rice finally sold, Rony told me, it brought in only two-thirds of what it would have brought in before the earthquake: US$13.27 a sack versus US$20.77.

Jonas had a few more comments to make:

> I would like to tell the [U.S.] leaders the way things should be done, but they don't pay any attention to the peasants. They're thinking about the well-off, not the bad-off. They're just watching their own backs. But the poor class is dying of hunger, and we need people thinking of us. The [earthquake] victims are getting a few grains, but what about the rest of us? Plus, the rice they're sending won't be forever. They might start having problems back home, and then what? When they don't give anymore, are we all going to die? If we keep going like this, there's one chance for the future of this country: to perish.
>
> There're a lot of things I'd like to tell the American government, but I don't know where to find them. If I could find them, I'd tell them that.

16

Home

From Tent Camp to Community

August 2010

An out-of-business Hyundai dealership.

A field next to mass graves.

An eight-foot-wide median between four lanes of whizzing traffic, in a perennial thick gray haze of exhaust.

A scalding savanna of white shale at the foot of a denuded mountain.

A shared feature of these locales was that homeless earthquake survivors had taken up lodging on them. In a city choked with pulverized concrete and other detritus, where no one in charge had provided a better option, these were the best spaces to be found.

One of the estimated 1.5 million homeless people[1] who had been left to fend for herself was emaciated, seventy-year-old Marievierge Youyoute. I met her at a rally in front of the prime minister's office one Wednesday afternoon. This rally, one in a growing number of protests against government inaction on the housing and displacement crisis, was wholly typical. It featured a couple hundred fed-up people; a staticky bullhorn; handwritten posters saying things like, "If there's land for factories, there's land for housing"; a momentary surge westward to

surround a camp resident and a lawyer as they entered the prime minister's office to deliver a letter with their demands; and a minor confronta-
tion with a police car that tried to push its way into the mass of bodies.

On a short break from chanting, Marievierge was pressed against a
wall seeking the thin sliver of shade it offered. When she spied my tape
recorder, she asked if she could say something into it. What she said was:
"Misery is killing me. I'm old, I'm going to die, but I don't want it to be
from hunger. I don't have a husband. I don't have children. I've been
sleeping in the street since my house in Martissant fell flat. I came to
protest so we can find a solution."

Thirteen hundred recognized camps, and many more unrecognized
ones, dotted virtually every open space in Port-au-Prince. Some com-
prised no more than a few shaky lean-tos colonizing a sidewalk, while
others held tens of thousands. Where streets had been cleared of rubble,
some more enterprising individuals had taken them over; several times a
day you drove down a side road to find it dead-ended by a passel of tarps.
The camps stretched as far as a two-hour drive out of town, a megalopo-
lis of tent cities.

Shelter materials would take first place in any competition for impro-
visation. A U.S. flag. A Muslim prayer rug. Cardboard boxes. Strips of
foam. A plastic banner advertising Nivea skin care products, featuring
a racially diverse crew of stunning models with perfect skin smiling out
across a camp. Mostly during the first few months, it was a bed sheet for
a ceiling held up by saplings, no floors, no walls.

"In the U.S.," said one elected camp leader, "homes like these
wouldn't be considered suitable for the pets they keep."

There was a scramble for humanitarian aid tents among some middle-
and high-income people who were sleeping outside. Being better net-
worked than most, they came out pretty well. Others without the big
connections could buy one in the black market that had sprung up
around the commodity. Torine Champs took me down a narrow path
through a camp maze to show off her new octagonal blue-and-white tent.
"I got this for [US]$110." A Belgian man she met had donated the money
for the purchase. "Pretty good, huh?"

In the strange land that Haiti had become, tents were luxury living.

The camps were a spot-on portrait of social neglect. Hunger, illness,
and sleep deprivation were the norm. People were wedged in among
strangers, often no more than an arm's length away. Residents spoke

regularly about feeling violated by the overcrowding and the all-night noise. Rarely did they have safe or private places to bathe, wash clothes, relax, or—in the case of kids—play. The risks of violence and abuse were constant. (I tried to imagine that seven months after Hurricane Katrina, New Orleanians were still trapped in the Superdome and the Arena, without access to sanitation, food, health care, or even drinking water.)

By mid-April, aid agencies had installed fewer than fifty-five hundred latrines in camps,[2] and most were unusably filthy. Seven months after the earthquake, a team of researchers found that the number of camp residents without access to water was 40 percent, while only 30 percent of camps had toilets.[3] According to one research project by four human rights and legal groups, in July more than one in four had to resort to "bathroom" procedures involving plastic bags or buckets,[4] which they then dumped in trash heaps, ditches, or the edges of camps. Sometimes camp residents could get wash water provided in giant nylon bags by NGOs; other times, they could capture water in buckets at public spigots; other times, they were just out of luck. Rats, flies, and mosquitoes posed additional health risks.

Drenching rains, which came every few nights and crashed for hours with gale force, began a few months after the earthquake; then they started coming nightly. Hundreds of thousands of people watched rain seep into their tents and passed the night standing up, holding their children away from rising water. When hurricane season started in June, the improvised, rickety housing posed a threat to life.

"Aren't we all Haitians? Is any one of us more a person than anyone else?" inquired one woman. Several others asked me an identical question: "Do they think we're animals?"

Many expressed the suspicion that they would be left to languish in those conditions permanently. "They'll just become the new slums," observed one UNICEF consultant.

⌘

Then came the *abse sou klou*, abscess on a sore. Beginning in late March, armed police, sometimes aided by private security guards, began demolishing shelters and their meager contents.

Getro is one of those who underwent this insult to injury. He lost his home twice in three months, the first time to the earthquake and the second time to the government. "Everything we owned got smashed. We lost everything," he said. On April 9 or 10 of 2010, Getro said (he was unsure, and press accounts differed), the director of the camp in the national soccer stadium told everyone they had to evacuate the next day so soccer teams could recommence their practices and games there. "They had said they were going to give every family one thousand gourdes [$25] and a little three-person tent, so people organized a demonstration to demand the aid they promised us. They sent in CIMO [anti-riot squads] to crush our houses and beat us with sticks like we were dogs. They destroyed our little house. One CIMO officer beat me on the head, cutting it open. He beat me on the chest and the back, he pushed me, he pulled his machine gun on me. People were shouting for help. My mother was crying. I told her to relax." Getro told me that at least some were given small tents on their way out. Receiving nothing, his close-knit, nine-member family had to split up around town since they couldn't find a single space big enough to hold them all.

The scenario was repeated regularly across the city. The UN and advocacy groups tried to negotiate a three-month moratorium on evictions with the Haitian government in April, but the government only agreed to hold off for three weeks.[5] Even then, evictions continued.

⚜

Rare public statements by the government evidenced conflicting strategies for limited, short-term initiatives. The government's action plan, released in March, asserted that it would settle at least one hundred thousand people in temporary shelters in five locales, which would gradually be replaced by long-term housing "with sustainable infrastructure and basic services."[6] However, by July, fewer than six thousand "semi-permanent" shelters had actually been erected,[7] and those were usually just one step up from the original improvised lodging.

Haitian officials suggested that people should resume residence in their former homes, many of which they said were still habitable. Survivors, some of whom had watched the walls of their cracked houses lean more with each major aftershock or tropical downpour, demurred. Regardless of the buildings' condition, though, in the majority of cases people were renters instead of owners, and did not have the option to return to their prior home, regardless of its conditions.

From Washington, Cheryl Mills, chief of staff for Secretary of State Clinton, said on May 10, "People seek to remain in the temporary communities because, as surprising as that might seem outside of Haiti, life is better for many of them now."[8] (It's hard to miss the parallel between Mills's comment and that of former first lady Barbara Bush when she visited evacuees from Hurricane Katrina in the Houston Astrodome; just substitute "camps" for "Texas." She said, "What I'm hearing, which is sort of scary, is that they all want to stay in Texas. Everybody is so overwhelmed by the hospitality. And so many of the people in the arena here, you know, were underprivileged anyway so this—this is working very well for them.")

Decent housing is a human right guaranteed under both the Haitian constitution and the Universal Declaration of Human Rights to which Haiti is a signatory. The Guiding Principles on Internal Displacement of the UN Office for Coordination of Humanitarian Affairs, moreover, mandate the government to provide internally displaced people with an "adequate" standard of living and shelter. Regardless, the government has offered no viable solution.

So as to build a social force that could catalyze pressure on the government, dozens of camp committees, community groups, and nonprofits came together in April 2010 to form the coalition Force for Reflection and Action on Housing (Fòs Refleksyon ak Aksyon sou Koze Kay, or FRAKKA). Its short-term mission has been social and economic rights for those residing in camps, including safety from eviction. Its long-term mission has been secure, quality homes for all.

Political organizing has increased consistently, despite repeated attacks on demonstrations by government and UN troops. After learning of planned evictions, camp residents have spontaneously launched *bat tenèb*, beat back the darkness, banging on pots and pans to alert the community to the impending danger and let the authorities know of their defiance. In cases of evictions, too, those directly affected by the assaults and those standing with them have held press conferences and tried to negotiate with the owners of the land in question. Activists have hosted public discussions and know-your-rights trainings in camps. The public-interest law firm International Lawyers' Office has aggressively pursued a legal resolution, armed with forceful rulings from complaints it and others brought to the Inter-American Commission on Human Rights of the Organization of American States. Some groups like Other Worlds have run campaigns with housing rights coalitions around the world.

The movement's first priority has been to get the government to develop a national housing policy for all citizens, not just earthquake survivors. Substandard housing collapsing on people was the number one cause of death from the earthquake, exposing the breadth of the crisis. Reyneld Sanon of FRAKKA said, "The government owes the poor the right to housing. That's a responsibility it's never taken, and that's what caused so many people to die. If you look at the slums before January 12, those weren't houses that anyone should have been living in. As the proverb says, *Kay koule twonpe solèy men li pa twonpe lapli*. Leaky houses can fool the sun, but they can't fool the rain. And the problem isn't just in Port-au-Prince; it's a national problem. If you travel around the country, you can see the status of peasants' housing. You can see that everyone in the country needs better housing."

Colette Lespinasse, director of the Support Group for Refugees and the Repatriated (Groupe d'Appui aux Réfugiés et Repatriés, or GARR), pointed out, "We can't just re-create what we had before. Houses are vulnerable, space is overcrowded, conditions don't encourage people to live well together and instead generate conflict, there's no space for children to play or for the elderly, no space to hang out."

The vision for a national housing policy includes the following:

- A law guaranteeing the right to housing. While the constitution recognizes the right to decent housing, it does not make the government responsible for ensuring it.
- Enforcement of existing rent control legislation, in response to rents rising many times over since the earthquake. Similarly, prohibition of housing speculation through regulating the price of house purchases.
- Equal access to women in housing and land ownership, with enforcement of their legally protected right to own and inherit land, and with their names consistently included on titles.
- Public housing on state land. Proponents say the residences must be safe and dignified; have access to roads; provide water, electricity, and sewage; offer community and recreational spaces; and be accessible to people with disabilities.

- Where the government doesn't provide public housing, provision of small grants and credit to help people repair or build their own houses. The movement is asking foreign NGOs to do the same.

Another prerequisite for housing for all is a national land use policy. The movement is advocating a holistic policy in which the government would:

- Make use of space outside Port-au-Prince to begin the process of decentralization.
- Enact an urban land redistribution program, because cities and towns are plagued by the same unequal distribution of land as rural areas.
- Invoke eminent domain, meaning claiming private property for social purposes. A Decree on the Recognition of Public Interest from 1921 gives the government the right to use eminent domain, and the constitution says that private property cannot oppose public good. "The law is perfectly clear. There is a problem of political will and a problem of exclusion," said Mario Joseph, human rights attorney and director of the International Lawyers' Office. He called on the government and international community to immediately "verify land ownership titles and nationalize by decree all empty and idle lands in the hands of purported landowners."[9]

As with every other element of the reconstruction, people are insisting that they have input in developing policies and programs. Reyneld Sanon said that people have to be part of reconstructing "their neighborhoods, their cities, their country, and their dignity." He said, "People have needs and they have ideas. Go into a camp, and ask any child to make a drawing that shows what kind of house they want to live in. And you'll see. You'll see. Even children have ideas and ideals."

※

The right-to-housing network's alternative vision goes further to include an integrated vision of "home." In public forums and in interviews, women in camps have said they want to move beyond simple residences to new paradigms of housing and environment. While lodging would provide a roof over their heads, they have said, they also want living conditions where there is no violence, where the community is foundational, and where power dynamics between men and women can shift. They want healthy interdependence, proximity to essential services like education and health care, and dignity.

Today, instead, Colette Lespinasse said, "What we are seeing in terms of housing plans have come largely from foreigners, with proposals for prefabricated houses that respond more to the interests and needs of businessmen. In general, the proposals don't correspond to Haitian culture or our climate, and also don't give people a chance to learn techniques that they can use to continue building on their own.

"But you can't just denounce what you don't want," she said. "We're meeting with others and drawing inspiration from housing movements and cooperatives in other countries. We want to propose alternatives that our country's leaders could use as models." GARR and other nonprofits have stepped out of their normal missions to create pilots. One is a small-scale model program of land and housing co-ops that GARR has begun near the Dominican border. Members pool their resources and land and run their own intentional community, making democratic decisions about planning and governance. Their long-term dream is to evolve "villages of life," which would offer on-site or nearby services like clinics and schools, and provide job opportunities in agriculture and small business. The vision springs from a forty-year-old experiment in Uruguay, where twenty-five thousand families live in land and housing cooperatives that they manage communally, and is reminiscent of the land reform settlements of the Landless Workers' Movement in Brazil and elsewhere, where small farmers collectively run democratic communities on redistributed land.

The peasant support group Institute of Technology and Animation (Institut de Technologie et Animation, or ITECA), has initiated another small program in Gressier. ITECA has begun building houses that offer water and electricity, almost unheard of in rural parts. Furthermore, they do so in environmentally low-impact ways, through rainwater collection systems and solar panels. The homes are earthquake- and hurricane-resistant, and use local building materials, like stones, to the degree possible. Another feature is that the homeowners themselves do the work that doesn't require specialized skills, like transporting materials. ITECA has been working with the mayor to ensure that each owner receives proper land and housing titles.

⌘

Many displaced people have just swelled up with *move van*, bad wind. This is a popular health diagnosis for all manner of malady—in this case, despair. From the camp where he moved after his home in the stadium was razed, Getro said, "I've been abandoned without any help. The Haitian state isn't doing anything for anyone. I have nothing. I just sit here with my two arms crossed."

Others, like Marievierge, whom we met in front of the prime minister's office, have thrown themselves into the fight for housing rights. "The government has to do something," Marievierge concluded her interview with me. Then she returned to the street to join with gusto in a call-and-response chant. "Tighten our belts, we can't take it anymore," was the first line. But that was no metaphor; "tighten our belts" is a reference to the literal belts or ropes that people bind tightly around their waists in an attempt to dull hunger pangs.

And on she sang with the crowd:

> Heat under the tarps, we can't take it anymore;
> We have fever, we can't take it anymore;
> We're being raped, we can't take it anymore;
> We have no water, we can't take it anymore.

17

For Want of Twenty Cents

Children's Rights and Protection

September 2010

Jean-Jean, six, was part of a pack of kids that raced to meet me each time I arrived at their camp in Port-au-Prince. Jean-Jean was usually at the front, all flashing eyes and big toothy grin, out-shouting the others or engaging in some ridiculous antic for my attention. On one visit, Jean-Jean's mother appeared dragging a very different little boy, slow and sad, by the arm. Jean-Jean feebly raised his eyes to mine; the whites were just a few shades this side of French's mustard. Hepatitis.

"How long has he been like this?" I asked, trying to mask my panic.

"Five days."

"What have you given him?"

"Nothing. I know he's supposed to be drinking a lot of water, but we don't have any money just now." Of course, that also meant no medication and little food. Or perhaps, on some days, no food.

"Have you taken him to a doctor?"

I knew the answer before I asked. "No, but I will," she said. I rousted up some small sacks of water; asked Jean-Jean's neighbor, a friend of mine, to help keep an eye on him; and finished my business at the camp. Three days later, I returned. Jean-Jean had still not gone for care. An all-too-familiar look on the mother's face—some combination of shame and desperation—let me know that that had not been an option. This time we worked together and devised a way to get him medical help.

This story had a happy ending: Jean-Jean got well and went back to being a heart-stealing mischief-maker. But I've known it to go the other way, many times over. Decades ago when I was living on Millet Mountain, an unofficial part of my job description was transporting to the Léogâne hospital babies and young children who were in the final stages of starvation—dying, effectively, from poverty. I made additional trips to the hospital—more precisely, its morgue—to collect the bodies of some of those patients, whom we wrapped in a sheet when we had one, or folded into a cardboard box when we didn't.

Late one night, someone knocked on my door. It was a woman I didn't know, clutching a baby to her chest. The infant's barely conscious state, wizened face, loose skin, and distended stomach made it clear that she was in the last round of a match with hunger, diarrhea, and dehydration. Not having a car to drive her to Léogâne, I gave the woman a note to the hospital staff, many of whom I knew from repeated visits.

The next morning, a neighbor came to tell me the baby had died. "Died?" Her admission had been good to go and the treatment was free. "Didn't they connect her to an IV?"

"No," the neighbor said. "The mother didn't go to the hospital. She couldn't come up with the gourde"—at that time, twenty cents—"to take the bus there."

In Haiti, an estimated sixty-three children out of each thousand die in the first year of life, and eighty-three of those one thousand never make it to age five.[1] Chronic malnutrition of those under five is about 30 percent, with one of those children dying every hour from hunger.[2] The former UN special rapporteur on the right to food, Jean Ziegler, pointed out that each of these deaths—those of any child, anywhere—could have been prevented, because there exists enough food to feed twelve billion people, almost double the world's population. Therefore, said Ziegler, "every child who dies from hunger is assassinated."[3]

Different policy choices could yield socioeconomic well-being for Haiti's children. Photograph by Jocelyne Joseph Mesilien.

The death of that baby, like almost all the little ones from Millet Mountain that I collected from the morgue, was the result of structural violence. Children carry its consequences disproportionately.

❋

Another way that structural violence impacts Haitian children is this: desperate parents, usually from the countryside, regularly pass their children on to better-off relatives, acquaintances, or strangers who promise to provide good care and schooling. A large subset of the children end up in forced servitude as *restavèk*—anywhere from ninety thousand to three hundred thousand—with one report by the U.S. Department of State suggesting that girls between six and fourteen years old make up 65 percent of this population.[4] Many work every day from before sunup to after sundown. They are often sexually and physically abused. There is some dispute among researchers about what percentage go to school, but a large number do not. They usually eat table scraps or have to scavenge in the streets for food, sleep on the floor, and wear cast-off rags. Though no one has gathered hard data since the earthquake, advocates suspect that the numbers have risen, because hundreds of thousands of children either became separated from their parents or were orphaned.

The children are not chained or locked up. One reason they stay is the very real threat of severe punishment, often in the form of beatings, if they are caught trying to escape. Another reason is that they have no other source of food and shelter. Some *restavèk* flee to live on the streets, but there their survival and safety options are not good. Guerda Lexima-Constant, a child rights advocate with the Light of Life Foundation (Fondasyon Limyè Lavi), said that adults who were once *restavèk* "have another chain which is worse, which is in their spirit, and that one's hard to break. They've integrated the idea that they're not human. I see that in my work all the time."

Guerda went on, "I have yet to meet anyone who wanted to send their kid to be a *restavèk*. Parents are forced to because of a lot of national and international givens. The means they used to have, they don't anymore. People who had Creole pigs, they could sell one to send their kids to school, but the pigs have been eliminated. The invasion of foreign rice, eggs, and other things on the market by big business, destroying the peasant economy . . . there's been a whole chain of events that makes some people have to send their child away."

Guerda, Suze, and Tibebe are all engaged in eradicating the *restavèk* system. All three have traveled as far as Washington, DC, to speak out about it. In discussing the topic, which inevitably brings her to tears, Suze said, "I'm struggling to end slavery because I know how I suffered."

One strategy national antiservitude groups use is educating and promoting children's rights at all levels of the *restavèk* chain. This starts at the source, letting parents know exactly what may happen to the children they give up. Suze described one tactic of the Commission of Women Victim to Victim (KOFAVIV), which is encouraging parents in the countryside to do everything possible to keep their child.

Rights education continues at the level of the families keeping *restavèk*. The Restavèk Freedom Foundation hosts meetings with families to challenge assumptions about what kids need and deserve. At KOFAVIV,

Suze said, "We tell them, 'Look on that child as though it's your own.' We tell them, 'This is a human being and you need to treat them well.'" She said that they are starting to see families change the way they treat others' children.

At the community level, advocates are encouraging neighbors to share responsibility for children's well-being. Light of Life and its sister organization, the U.S.-based Beyond Borders, does this through radio programs and classes. At KOFAVIV, Suze recounted, "We tell people, 'If you hear someone beating a child in their home, go tell them to stop.'" At the national level, the Restavèk Freedom Foundation hosted an "I am Haiti Too" conference in 2009, which brought together more than five hundred people to discuss the problem and how to change norms. That same year, KOFAVIV held two major protests. Thousands of women wore T-shirts saying, "I oppose the *restavèk* system. And you, what are you waiting for?" as they marched down the streets of the capital, holding signs and singing.

Beyond rights advocacy, another strategy is to try to retrieve children from the system. Beyond Borders and Light of Life run trainings for nonprofits and the Haitian government to help reunify children with their birth families. The Friends of Children Foundation (Fondasyon Zanmi Timoun) has established a foster care network to provide interim care for children while the group tries to track down their biological families. The Maurice Sixto Home (Fwaye Maurice Sixto) provides safe haven while helping restavèk children reintegrate into society, and the Ecumenical Foundation for Peace and Justice (Fondation Oecuménique Pour la Paix et la Justice) tries to support the *restavèk*'s families in the countryside so they can take their children back.

A third strategy is to reverse tacit government approval of the abuse. A 2003 law prohibits children under twelve from serving as "domestic workers," but the law remains unimplemented, as do the protections in the UN Convention on the Rights of the Child which the government signed onto in 1994. Guerda said, "To stop this practice requires political will. The government has to make a political decision; it's their responsibility."

A fourth strategy, were it to succeed, would have more impact than all the others. That is to address the root cause of child servitude, which is poverty. Improving the economy, especially through government support for the rural population, would undermine parents' incentive to give children up. So, too, would providing health care and more and better schools.

Changing the national system is a painfully slow process. "We now have more people who consider child servitude a crime," said Guerda. "But at the same time it's like there are so many children and there are so many things we [advocates] have to do, sometimes you don't feel like anything is happening."

Suze holds a long-term view. She said, "Just like I've learned and am speaking out, everyone will become aware this system has to end. We're going to keep struggling to do away with it completely. It will end; that's certain."

⌘

I have thought hundreds of times throughout my life about the baby girl that died that night on Millet Mountain. I have always wondered about the woman she might have become. I like to imagine that she would be fighting so that no child dies for lack of twenty cents or is put into bondage as an alternative to starvation. Today, I like to think, she would be working for a world order that allows all children to be safe and well.

18

The Super Bowl of Disasters

Profiting from Crisis

September 2010

"THE GOLD RUSH IS ON!" was the headline of Ambassador Merten's February 1, 2010, cable to Washington. "As Haiti digs out from the earthquake, different [U.S.] companies are moving in to sell their concepts, products and services."[1]

Many a corporation, lobbyist, and consultant have seen Haiti's losses as their gain, leveraging humanitarianism for profit. Plenty of the $1.1 billion in U.S. disaster relief has gone not to desperate Haitians but to inside-the-Beltway contractors. In the first year, the U.S. government awarded more than fifteen hundred contracts, worth $267 million. All went to U.S. firms except twenty, worth $4.3 million, which went to Haitian businesses.[2]

"The Super Bowl of disasters," one contractor called it.[3]

Among those who have gotten deals, we have seen everything: many millions going to U.S. corporations that had previous contracts canceled for bad practices, that paid out as much as eight-figure legal settlements for violence happening under their watch, that were investigated by Congress for gaming the system, and that were the subject of federal reports for wasting funds.[4] We have seen corporate executives and members of Congress going through a revolving door and leveraging both sides for money. We have seen public funds given without any competition or transparency, in quite a few instances to well-placed insiders like friends of the Clintons.

Two months out, companies gathered in a luxury hotel in Miami for a Haiti Summit to discuss post-earthquake contracting possibilities. The meeting was sponsored by the International Peace Operations Association, but these were no peaceniks. Their members are predominantly private mercenary companies that enforce "security" in war and disaster zones and which, unlike government, can completely avoid public scrutiny and accountability. They included groups such as Triple Canopy, who took over Blackwater's contract in Iraq.[5] One of the corporate reps at the summit described the outlook: "[Haiti's] infrastructure is pretty much destroyed, communications are destroyed, there's a lot of opportunities there for companies, particularly US countries [sic] because of the close proximity."[6] The meeting was apparently worthwhile, as the U.S. government paid out more than $10 million to the industry for "guard services" and riot suits and shields.[7]

Similar deals have been cut over Haiti before, particularly during periods of political instability. Some of the same corporations wrested financial and political gain from the wars in Iraq and Afghanistan, the countries hit by the 2004 tsunami in the Indian Ocean, the Gulf Coast after Hurricane Katrina and New Orleans after the ensuing flood of 2005, and lots of other places.

Below are a few examples of post-earthquake contracts and grants, selected to show just some of the problems at play. They offer a small glimpse into a much larger, secretive world of disaster deals. They demonstrate a fundamental flaw of the foreign business–led redevelopment model: the targets of the projects are objects, not subjects. The Haitian citizenry factors into the system no more than as a component of a business deal. Only rarely do the contractors involve Haitians in planning, designing, or implementing. Even local labor and production, elements critical to economic recovery, have been disregarded in favor of U.S. business profits. According to federal procurement data, among contracts that provided products (as opposed to services), 77 percent have been for products manufactured in the United States; they don't list which, if any, of the remaining 23 percent have involved Haitian labor or materials.[8]

A related core defect is that the arrangement is entirely unaccountable to the Haitian government or people. The foreign business interests have no inherent commitment to Haiti, and Haitians have no oversight of them.

※

The story of housing shows what can happen when foreign corporations are put in charge of essential needs. One of the first proposals passed by the Interim Haiti Recovery Commission, a $2.4 million effort called Highlight Best Practices for Housing, was illustrative. Public and private funding sources included the Clinton Foundation, the Inter-American Development Bank, the telephone company Digicel, the large investment bank Deutsche Bank, and a Canadian NGO called OneX1. The planners allocated the majority of funding to a housing exposition in which participants were to "test and demonstrate innovative housing ideas." According to news reports and our interviews, there was never a plan for how destitute people would be helped or even how designs would be chosen. The default assumption was that families would purchase their own housing, probably with subsidized bank loans. In the country with the lowest per capita income in the hemisphere, the homes were to sell for an average of $21,000, with prices going up to $69,000.[9] An official from the Clinton Foundation said, "This is a private sector exposition, you're seeing people here who are hopeful to make some money."[10]

A government engineer estimated that fully half of the model homes at the expo were not resistant to earthquakes and hurricanes. A salesman from one participating enterprise said they did not have to be tested for resistance to strong winds.[11]

The expo itself only transpired after Haitians had spent half a year under tarps waiting for homes or even temporary shelters. Actual shelter for homeless people would have come many steps, and many months or years, down the line. In the end, it didn't matter anyway, because no houses were ever built except the demonstration models. As of this writing in June 2012, the sixty-odd units remain, abandoned, on the site.[12]

A second component of the Highlight Best Practices for Housing project was to create a model "exemplar" community with 125 units and a community center in Zoranje, on the outskirts of Port-au-Prince. In addition to providing funding for the project, Deutsche Bank assisted in developing "new mortgage instruments" for future housing via "experts from the Bank's residential mortgage backed securities group." Essentially, Deutsche Bank was developing strategies to make it easier for Haitian banks to offer loans to potential home-buyers. Even with low interest rates, this would guarantee most a life of debt. The prospect sounded eerily similar to the predatory lending that took place in the United States in the lead-up to the subprime mortgage crisis of the late 2000s, when low-income families were trapped by housing loans they could never pay back and were set up for foreclosure. Deutsche Bank was a key player there, too, popularly dubbed "America's Foreclosure King" because of its position as a major financier of the corporations that pushed high-risk mortgages. The bank is currently being sued by the Federal Housing Finance Agency for selling the misvalued mortgage-backed securities that helped precipitate the financial crisis in the United States.[13]

Another building project approved by the commission in 2010 was the Clinton Foundation's purchase of twenty trailers from Clayton Homes. At the time, the company was facing a lawsuit in the United States for having sold trailers containing poisonous levels of formaldehyde to FEMA for Hurricane Katrina survivors. Whether the Clinton Foundation went through a bidding process before deciding on the contract is disputed, but a Clayton Homes press release noted that a company director had called the foundation after Clinton was named cohead of the relief effort to see if they could "help."[14] Clayton Homes's owner, the corporation Berkshire Hathaway, is one of the Clinton Global Initiative's private sector members. Its CEO, Warren Buffett, was a major contributor and fund-raiser during Hillary Clinton's 2008 presidential bid.

The twenty trailers were to serve as hurricane shelters and schools in the town of Léogâne. These were the same structures that residents are advised to *evacuate* during hurricane risk in the United States. The Clinton Foundation promised that the trailers, which were to be equipped with water and sanitation facilities, would provide a suitable venue for schoolchildren. According to a subsequent investigation by the *Nation* magazine, the results turned out quite differently. One trailer contained two and a half times the level of carcinogenic formaldehyde as that which the Center for Disease Control warns can cause adverse health effects. Children and staff using the buildings suffered from headaches and eye irritation, symptoms similar to those experienced by some Hurricane Katrina evacuees living in FEMA trailers. Inadequate venting made the trailers unbearably hot, and two of the schools had to cut the school year short because of the heat. One school never opened at all owing to lack of sanitation and water. After less than a year of use, the shoddy buildings were already deteriorating.[15]

⁂

"American corporations and their stakeholders must understand how helping Haiti over the long term also helps them," wrote a trustee of the nonprofit CHF International in *Philanthropy News Digest*. "By contributing to Haiti's reconstruction in a lasting, meaningful way, companies will be helping to build a new, more vibrant Caribbean market for their own goods and services."[16]

CHF's involvement demonstrates how "development" is often just a guise for propping up U.S. business interests on the backs of poor Haitians while purporting to lift them from poverty, even when the actor is a not-for-profit. What CHF referred to as "helping Haiti" meant using U.S. tax dollars to underwrite sweatshops, making it easier and more profitable to score the cheapest source of labor in the Americas. In 2006, USAID gave CHF a $104 million, four-year contract to help "existing industries to increase their capacity, efficiency and reach new markets," primarily through the export textile industry. The money subsidized a CHF project to plan and fund infrastructure such as roads around industrial plants, and to train factory laborers in skills like "how to work in a formal work environment."[17] This project was bolstered by additional USAID funding after the earthquake.

CHF received another USAID contract in 2010, this one for $20.9 million for clean-up projects, including cash-for-work.[18] Cash-for-work means camp residents engaging in hired-hand projects such as digging drainage ditches and clearing debris, for a stint of a few weeks at a time. The scheme came under fire by camp residents and human rights groups, with even a USAID evaluation raising serious critiques.[19] The jobs are unpredictable, workers said, and while they can palliate personal crisis for a brief duration, the program quickly returns the worker's family to its desperate state. Those hired are paid officially at the unlivable minimum daily wage of two hundred gourdes, or US$5, though unofficially they often earn less. A Haiti Grassroots Watch exposé found, furthermore, that cash-for-work hiring is often based on corruption, with many workers having to negotiate sex, pay a kickback, or affiliate with a certain political party or candidate for a job.[20] USAID also noted that cash-for-work programs it funded carried risks of "serious and avoidable" accidents on the job "by failing to develop and enforce consistent workplace safety rules and accident procedures."[21]

CHF's factory jobs and cash-for-work programs have neither provided livable incomes to employees nor offered development opportunities to the nation. Meanwhile, CHF has gained humanitarian clout and an influx of funding, and its garment industry partners sit happily with the perks.

⁂

It's one thing to privatize government services. But after the earthquake, U.S. firms were actually involved in privatizing governance. Corporations with little to no knowledge of Haiti were brought in as volunteers to plan, kick off, and even staff the Interim Haiti Recovery Commission, the actor with the single greatest operational influence over shaping the reconstruction model after the quake.

McKinsey and Company came in to help "design" and "launch" the commission.[22] Our background interview with an official close to the process revealed the Haitian government to be at the beck and call of McKinsey as that company structured the commission and determined membership and decision-making processes, aspects that later received vehement criticism from Haitian civil society. At the very first meeting, according to official minutes, it was McKinsey's lead consultants who "made a presentation to the Board regarding the mission, mandate, structure, and operations of the IHRC [commission]." The consultants sat in on subsequent meetings, as well.[23]

McKinsey performed its services pro bono. Whether paid or not, the post was a lucrative one; it positioned the firm to influence future contracts and to shape a climate favorable to business.

McKinsey was well placed to get the job because of its former managing director's longtime personal and political ties to Bill Clinton. The firm was also a prime candidate because it has served governments around the world in advancing what it called the "government as business" paradigm.[24] As one example, McKinsey played a key role in designing and setting up the reconstruction commissions in Indonesia and

Sri Lanka after the Indian Ocean tsunami. As with the Interim Haiti Recovery Commission, those bodies entrenched foreign private sector individuals into policymaking. And as in Haiti, Indonesian civil society groups denounced their own Rehabilitation and Reconstruction Agency for being extremely centralized and discounting the opinions of the local population.[25]

Controversy surrounded McKinsey again after Hurricane Katrina. Prior to the storm, it had helped major insurance companies develop tactics that stalled court proceedings and allowed them to avoid paying out to their clients who had suffered natural disasters or accidents. Lawsuits and investigations later proved that McKinsey's pre-Katrina advice, particularly to Allstate, effectively helped insurers cheat their customers whose homes were damaged or destroyed.[26]

Another U.S. firm, Korn/Ferry International, came on board to headhunt the executive director of the Interim Haiti Recovery Commission. This was to replace the initial staffing that had been provided by the Clinton Foundation, the Inter-American Development Bank, and the governments of the United States and Canada. Korn/Ferry circulated a job announcement, in English, through politically connected circles in the United States and Haiti, as though it were hiring for any business instead of for a team that was making major decisions in the name of a nation. The announcement noted that "leadership experience in highly efficient and structured organizations, such as the military, is an advantage."[27]

※

What we were unable to uncover was at least as alarming as what we did. In the case of a few other contracts that we knew to be operating in Haiti, two hound-dog researchers on our team spent hour after hour on the scent. They trailed Internet resources, news articles, and company websites. Nothing. Not even a mention, sometimes, in the one-hundred-plus-page 2010 annual reports.

We wondered whether the U.S. government has had any more knowledge or oversight of the actions of the corporations they have funded than investors have. As for the people of the United States, they have no way to know how their money has been spent or what has been done in their names. The lack of transparency has also empowered opportunists to disregard standards, quality, and honesty.

There is one group for whom the secrecy, foul play, taking of power that should never be taken, and giving away and selling off what should never be given away or sold off matters most of all: Haitians, whose country is being treated like a Monopoly game. They alone will have to live with the long-term effects of what foreign companies disrupt, coopt, or steal.

19

The Commonplace amid the Catastrophic

(Tales from Nine Months Out)

October 2010

Luc showed up at the open door of the office where I was working. He was looking for his chicken. Luc was two years old and, at least to the casual eye, seemed to have survived both the quake and its aftermath unscathed. He normally wore a hundred-watt grin and spent most of his time scooting in and out of the courtyard and up and down neighbors' steps, looking for bugs and for people who would play with him.

We found Luc's chicken, which had installed itself on the Internet router.

Amid the pall of suffering, Haiti was still full of the commonplace, the sweet, and the funny. It was still a place where people fell in love, relaxed in the shade, got bored, and took pride in their homeland. They still hung out in the courtyard come evening, talking about the goings-on in the neighborhood or village, the latest government scandal, and the price of this year's school tuitions or crops. Lots still attended Catholic baptisms or Vodou celebrations together. They still had epic feuds and fooled around with each other's spouses and stayed out way too late dancing in a buddy's front yard. The *griyo*, the storyteller who shared community history, still opened tales with *"Krik!"* and those ready to listen still responded with *"Krak!"*

In the countryside, where the earth and life were less impacted, you could especially forget for a while the effects of those thirty-five long seconds in January. Routines went on like this: a certain repeated, sharp sound signified dominoes being slapped down hard on a table; you rounded a hut and saw some dejected guy whose skinny face was pulled tightly by many clothespins clamped on his forehead, cheeks, and chin. In the absence of money to gamble, a clothespin was the cost of a game lost. Two boys carefully rolled between them a bicycle to which a squealing pig was lashed. A flag flew over a Vodou temple, which was adorned with bright murals of *lwa*, spirits: La Sirène, the mermaid that rules over the seas; Erzulie Dantor, the goddess of love, depicted as a black Virgin Mary holding baby Jesus; or Ogou, painted as Saint James astride a white horse. Oxen strained to pull their wooden-wheeled cart across a river. Signs on the sides of buildings put to use the English learned from foreign missionaries and troops: "Black honor barber shop for ever." "Here for eat, sleep, drink." "Big soldiers excellence."

Opportunities to kick back, celebrate life, and just go about daily business existed throughout disaster-struck areas, as well. Late one night, Marco and I hopped a truck back from Léogâne, which meant driving through Carrefour. The name of the sprawling shantytown means "crossroads," but to outsiders it might mean only raw poverty. The population is so dense you can't believe everyone fits, and in fact they don't: folks sleep in shifts in the small houses because there isn't enough room for everyone to lie down at once. One result is that the streets are packed at all hours. As always, that night the smell was thick, as was the gray slime covering the road because it didn't drain and no one with power or resources had ever bothered to fix it. At that moment, the electricity was out, and the only light came from the glow of kerosene lamps made from Famosa tomato paste cans, which were set on tables on the side of the road as there were no sidewalks. Crowds packed around each table spinning yarns, arguing, and laughing, arms draped over shoulders. In the candlelight, their sweat-covered faces glistened. "Look at all this community," Marco mused as we drove through. "Beautiful, huh?"

Random observations from a Sunday in Port-au-Prince included this: Proud parents returning from church with their young kids, some of whom were dressed in somber black pants and button-down white shirts, or shiny Cinderella frocks with layer upon layer of tulle and lace. The air vibrating with sounds of clapping and singing from hundreds of Protestant churches, a soccer match narrated by a hysterical sportscaster, a rhythmic *squish* of wet laundry being rubbed between a woman's palms, Steely Dan from a journalist's computer, a metal lid clanging on a pot as food was stirred.

On busy Nazon Road, cars veered around a wedding vehicle that was deserted in the middle of the road. The red pickup, decorated with lavender and white bows, tilted over a missing wheel. So much for the bride and groom's charmed day.

The setting sun relieved the day's oppressive heat, and it being Sunday, I forewent the rest of my work for a walk in the neighborhood. I swung left with the road and suddenly found myself in the middle of a camp. Lean-tos of wood, tin, and cloth lined both sides of the road. But this camp was different from most; it was positively festive. Someone had put on loud compas, Haiti's catchy, up-tempo musical mainstay. One woman wanted to make sure I saw her son, but two-year-olds rarely get past me; we had already waved energetically at each other when I was still back a ways. His name was Jesley, and he was elated to practice his high-five on me. His four-year-old sister tried out her French, asking, "*Tu t'en vas?*" Are you going? Two older women sat on a smashed refrigerator turned on its side, braiding each other's hair. A young girl spun a long piece of black tape in a circle, arcing it high into the air.

The boys, as usual, dominated the scene with volume and motion. One shrieking youngster took running leaps back and forth over a pile of burning garbage. Others played soccer on the steeply sloped road with a ball that more resembled a filthy round of yarn. Each time it went flying down the hill, a poor little kid with no bargaining power was sent to retrieve it.

Four teenage boys bathed in their shorts with gallon jugs of water, clearly relishing the chance to show off their sleek bodies to the crowd. As I approached, one shouted, "*Blan*, foreigner, come shower with us."

"Oh, thanks," I startled them by replying in Creole. "But I'm not really dirty right now."

Five more teenage boys were using a tall bamboo pole to liberate mangoes from high in a tree behind a garden wall. Soon they came marching to the center of the camp, holding the pole above their heads with their right hands and their stolen treasure aloft in their left, loudly singing a victory song.

The residents were old neighbors, if not dear friends. They'd come together from their nearby shattered houses to re-create community and help each other make the best of a calamity.

Returning to my own street, I turned sideways to squeeze between two sheets of corrugated tin to enter my local market, which was one Igloo cooler and a rickety table under an almond tree in a family's courtyard. Sometimes the table held nothing at all, but this day it was stacked with the basics: long yellow sticks of tallow soap, an open twenty-five-kilo USA Rice Federation sack, hard white bread rolls, candles, matches, cardboard rounds of Laughing Cow cheese, gum balls. I requested the usual: three phone cards and three tall bottles of water. The vendor reminded me again to return the two beer bottles I'd bought last week, and I got a bubbly gurgle from the roly-poly baby who always made me laugh.

Waiting outside my apartment were Marco and Djab, come to take me to our hangout that we called Base Camp. It was a nameless, open-air speakeasy that had informally privatized a corner of Babiole Road. A couple had put up three tables and a makeshift shelf lined with a few liquor bottles, rimmed the whole thing with broken cement blocks, blasted Creole rap out of a tape deck, and voilà! Not that Haiti had ever been what you might call over-officiated, but everything was especially jerry-built in those days. You didn't ever want to lean on the tabletops at Base Camp; they were all unsecured and would flip. You were lucky if you got a rare chair, as your only other option was to gingerly perch against the rim of one of the old seatless bar stools.

The clientele that night was the standard smattering: guys with a few gourdes and hours to spare, drinking out some of their outrage and misery over life since the *event*; a couple of street kids, eyes drugged-up and scary, trying to cadge money from customers for a box of red wine; *blan* who pulled up in their SUVs to buy a case of Prestige. Marco and Djab, inveterate politicos, as usual espoused their analyses to anyone who would listen—just then, about Haiti's worthless political parties. Normally gentle men, they became bellicose about politics once they'd gotten a beer into them. I'd seen them almost come to shouting over how to understand contemporary socialism in France. That evening, Marco had had a few and got into such a furious debate with a former UN soldier from Brazil who waxed on about how Haiti needed others to govern it that I was sure he was going to pop the man. I put my arm around Marco, and Djab instructed him to stand down, and together we got him out of the man's face. The night ended peaceably.

※

At the end of a long day, after the last in a series of meetings that all presented more challenges than solutions, I waited in the street for a taxi to pass. A water truck pulled up, advertising itself with an endlessly repeating, tinny, full-volume version of "Happy Birthday." As the teeth-gritting song drilled into my throbbing headache, I registered an aged man coming down the street, carefully maneuvering a wheelbarrow laden with cement bricks through piles of rubble. He was dressed in nothing but flip-flops and cutoffs, and his emaciated frame spoke of chronic hunger. I wondered where he got the strength to push his load. The thought bubble that arose each time I saw an elder doing hard physical labor in the hot Haitian sun came up again: this man should be at home relaxing. If he had a home, that is. And if he didn't, he should. Someone should be bringing him tea while his grandchildren amused him.

As he drew closer, I realized he was singing along to the water truck's song, with gusto, in English. "Happy birthday to you-houuuuu . . ." As he passed me, he gave a happy little shake of his head and said, "*Bèl bagay.*" It's a lovely thing.

20

Beyond Medical Care

The Health of the Nation

October 2010

The measure of Haiti's health care after the earthquake could be taken by the state of its Ministry of Public Health. Not just the output, but the actual ministry. Until the building was bulldozed to the ground, its outer walls were nonexistent. The floors rolled like a wave. The cement pillars tilted. The roof was carved into geometrical slices. The quake also destroyed eight major hospitals and seriously damaged twenty-two more, plus medical and nursing schools. It killed hundreds of doctors, nurses, and other health care workers.

The calamity simultaneously wiped out caregivers and facilities and created a greater need for them, not only because of the innumerable injuries, but also because of the illness and malnutrition of those living with inadequate sanitation and food in displacement camps. The seven thousand women who gave birth within one month of the disaster and their infants faced even more extreme health and nutritional risks.[1]

Public health and medical care are only two arenas in which the earthquake amplified preexisting social catastrophes. Survival was already so dicey that life expectancy only hit sixty a few years ago.[2] Before the earthquake, the country had about twenty-five physicians and eleven nurses for every one hundred thousand people.[3] On average, that is— many rural areas have never had any health care services other than traditional leaf medicine. Eighty-three percent of people had no access to sanitation, and 37 percent had no improved water source. In rural areas, these statistics were 90 percent and 45 percent, respectively,[4] and "no improved water source" almost certainly meant drinking out of a highly contaminated river or stream. According to the World Health Organization, access to sanitation actually *worsened* between 1990 and 2008.[5]

For most, when health care has been available at all, it has all too often treated only the immediate problem. Given the conditions under which most Haitians live, the next grave infection (diarrhea that won't stop, malaria, tuberculosis, HIV/AIDS, meningitis, typhoid, etc.) lurks just around the corner.

The World Health Organization's Commission on the Social Determinants of Health has recognized "social injustice" as a force "killing people on a grand scale." The commission attributes the fact that the majority of the world's inhabitants don't have the good health that is "biologically possible" to "a toxic combination of bad policies, economics, and politics."[6] These factors determine essentials like the kind of housing people live in, their exposure to violence, their ability to feed their families, and the contaminants running in that river they drink from. Economic, political, and environmental conditions—and the structural forces that cause them—are known as the social determinants of health.

In Haiti, the social determinants have been displayed in the stubborn negligence of government toward its subjects' health. Under the Duvaliers and subsequent military regimes, for example, the University Hospital was medieval, with dead bodies and those waiting to die—who received no food or medicine unless family could bring it—scattered randomly on the floor throughout the wards. Subsequently, the ability of the Aristide and Préval administrations to improve the miserable state of health was curtailed by foreign debt payments that shrank the pool of available funding. Payments often exceeded the entire health care budget for the country. By the middle of Préval's first term, the government budget allocated, per year, $4 per person on health, and $5 on debt payments. In 2001, the debt service was $38.5 million, compared to the health budget of $34.5 million. And things got even worse: in 2003, during Aristide's second term, $57.4 million of the budget went to the debt, while $39.2 million went to health, education, and environment *combined*.[7]

Physicians and social scientists, including Partners in Health's founder Dr. Paul Farmer, a leading proponent of the right to health, have also documented the impact of aid embargoes—as Haiti experienced from 1991 to 1994 and again from 2001 to 2004—and trade policies. Both have worsened already low life expectancy, access to potable water, and levels of sickness.

The links between politics and health were dramatically exposed in October 2010, when the Ministry of Public Health announced an outbreak of cholera. A disease of poverty that infects those without safe drinking water, cholera can kill a malnourished or otherwise weakened body within four to six hours. We have known since 1854—when the physician John Snow discovered the source of a London cholera epidemic and halted its spread—that clean water is all it takes to sever the fecal-oral route on which the bacteria depends. And yet, in an attempt to destabilize Aristide's administration, the U.S. government held hostage funds that would have provided clean water to parts of Haiti, including where cholera first broke out. The story played out this way: In 1998, the Inter-American Development Bank (IDB), in collaboration with the Haitian government, approved funding to improve water and sanitation infrastructure. But in 2000, the U.S. government became alarmed when Aristide's party won an overwhelming majority in parliamentary elections. The bank's articles of agreement explicitly prohibit "interfer[ing] in the political affairs" and being "influenced in their decisions by the political character" of recipient countries, and yet that was exactly what the United States, a majority voting stakeholder in the development bank, did. Internal e-mail traffic from the Treasury Department, obtained by human rights organizations through the Freedom of Information Act, revealed that, in exchange for the Haitian government manipulating the voting results, "the U.S. would adopt a helpful posture in the IDB on the release of some of the resources pending in that institution." Alternatively, if Haiti would not comply, the United States "believes it is inappropriate for pending resources to be released."[8] Because the Aristide government did not meet the illegal ultimatum, the IDB concocted more and more excuses for delaying disbursement of the loan. When cholera arrived in Haiti, work on the clean water project had still not begun. On October 26, 2010, the week after disease was announced,

Partners in Health's Dr. Evan Lyon commented that it was "reasonable to draw a straight line from these loans being slowed down and cut off to the epidemic."[9]

The international community is culpable for the cholera epidemic in a second, more immediate way. Scientists have proven that the cholera pathogen came to Haiti via foreign UN troops who carried the bacteria in their bodies, and whose military base in the town of Mirebelais was dumping its sewage into a nearby river.[10] The UN has yet to acknowledge any responsibility.

Despite billions in post-earthquake aid dollars and hundreds of humanitarian NGOs, the country still faces a dearth of water and sanitation services, which fuels the disease. This is especially true in displaced persons camps. As of this writing in June 2012, the disease has claimed more than 7,000 lives and infected almost 550,000 people.[11]

⁂

Improving health care requires tackling the root causes of bad health. Improving the social determinants can allow all people to have the health care that is their right. The Haitian branch of Partners in Health (Zanmi Lasante) has, since its 1983 launch, achieved unparalleled success by taking a social determinants approach. Its rates in getting people to follow HIV/AIDS treatment programs in Haiti, for example, have exceeded even those of the United States.[12] Partners in Health has achieved other markers of progress in Rwanda, Russia, Peru, the United States, and elsewhere. Its pioneering model has both changed the status of health for some low-income countries and let other countries know that change is within reach.

Partners in Health's mission is medical, moral, and political. Its record comes, first, from its philosophies, including a belief in the power and dignity of the patient, a commitment to health care as a human right, and an understanding that true health for the material poor can only come through challenging the poverty that underlies so much illness. The group's record is due, secondly, to the zeal with which it pursues hands-on, community-based, medical and social care. As discussed earlier, Partners in Health is also unique in the vehemence with which it reinforces Haitian government programs in everything it does, as opposed to just building its own nongovernmental empire. As Paul Farmer said, "It's hard to imagine public health without a public sector."[13]

Loune Viaud is the director of operations and strategic planning for Partners in Health in Haiti. She has been with the group since 1989.

When you start working here, you enter a vocation. You have to love it to do it, because it doesn't pay very much. You do it because you truly believe in the human being. We treat every person as though it were our own sister, brother, mother, child.

When we started in Haiti, we realized right away that you can't talk about health without talking about the social aspects of health: justice and rights. When a patient is sick, we don't see the sick person only, we see the environment and community they come from. After they leave the hospital and go back home, will they have water to drink? Will they have a place to live? Will they have food to eat? Can they send their children to school? Do they have work? We try to touch on all of it: job, home, malnutrition, agriculture. That's why we don't just consider ourselves a health organization, although we have a big medical team, with doctors, nurses, pharmacists, lab technicians, etc. We also have community health workers, outreach agents, and agricultural agents who live right in the communities [four thousand total staff].

I think what makes us successful is our accompaniment program. Take tuberculosis, a disease of poverty. When a person comes in and tests positive for tuberculosis, what we do is send a community health worker, what we call an "accompanier," to visit his or her home to see the social conditions they're living in. If that person sees they need a new house, we work with the community to get them one. In terms of water, we set up filters or other catchment and treatment systems so they don't have to keep on drinking from the river. The accompanier goes to visit the sick person every day and makes sure that person takes their medications. If the patient has a problem the accompanier can't solve, he or she will go talk to the supervisor in the hospital. The accompanier becomes an advocate for the sick.

I can't say that we change the lives of the people completely, but we've seen improvement. But I don't want to start rejoicing about success, because we still have a lot of work to do. It's forward, forward, forward. Matter of fact, every time we see the numbers [in illness and disease] going down, we make more effort to see if we can get them to zero.

What Haitians need for good health is access to care. One of the things that really makes me mad is to find someone who's walked eight or ten hours to get to our hospital in [the village of] Cange, sometimes in terrible pain. For that person to go through what it takes to get there, you can imagine how advanced the sickness must be. Sometimes it's almost too late. If that person could go to the clinic or dispensary where they live without having to go far from the community, they could get care early on.

It's access, access, access. But I'm not just talking about access through proximity. It's not just about building a hospital or a health clinic nearby and then asking people to pay. If the care or the medication is expensive, the people won't get it. It's the right of people to get heath care when they need it, just like drinking water and sanitation. They have the right to have their needs met quantitatively and qualitatively.

But the state is the one who's in place, legally, to respond to the needs of the people. What Partners in Health tries to do is to collaborate with the state to reinforce its efforts, so down the road it can better meet its responsibility. We always say the Ministry of Public Health is our most important partner. Partners in Health provides a lot of staff. We pay for salaries and equipment. We're really part of managing the hospital with the ministry. But we ensure that everything we do supports and reinforces the Ministry of Public Health, the Ministry of Education, and the Ministry of Agriculture. If there were a Ministry of Housing or Water, we'd support them, too. We don't invest in separate efforts. We realized a long time ago that it doesn't make sense for us to do our own small effort apart, to build our own hospital or clinic or even separate schools.

Beyond our own hospital in Cange, we work with ten public hospitals. And then we've started building what's going to be one of Haiti's best hospitals, in Mirebalais. It will have a training program for residents in a partnership with the national medical school. That's twelve hospitals where we're working in all. Then January 12 came on us without warning. We started clinics in four displaced peoples' camps; we've hired almost four hundred new medical staff to provide services in these camps. Another thing we did right away was start supporting the government in the largest hospital, the University Hospital. That falls into our line of work, supporting what the ministry is doing there so people can get the care they need in a hospital, with dignity. We've provided and coordinated volunteers; we've come with medications and equipment. Also, with other partners we're creating a foundation, Friends of the University Hospital, to really rebuild the hospital and make it into what it should be. We're working with the national medical school, too, so students can get training there.

I always avoid saying that our services are free. Health care is expensive. Someone pays. We look for partners, as our name implies, as long as they share the philosophy. We're always looking for people to help cover expenses so the poor don't have to, because they can't afford it. People pay with what they have. Sometimes they carry bananas on their heads, fruits they grow, they bring a chicken, you understand. They bring what they can. But we don't ever want the poor to say, "I don't have money, so I'm not going to the doctor."

�֍

The Association for the Promotion of Integrated Family Health provides medical service, urges structural change, and promotes the Haitian government's strong and central role in public health, all at once. The association runs a multifaceted program in the Carrefour-Feuilles section of Port-au-Prince. Launched in 1983 with the support of Partners in Health, the program is based on a social-determinants framework and stretches traditional definitions of health care. Rose Anne Auguste, founder and nurse, told about the work:

> At first, we operated in the classic public health schema: you have a clinic, you provide contraception, you do vaccinations, you teach protection against AIDS, etc. But we realized that's not what health is. When you address the health of a neighborhood, you have to identify the social programs that underlie the state of health. We had to reflect with the people to better understand what health really means. They've taught us to question the dominant model of health provision.

Health is not just medical care. It depends on many factors. It's about people becoming responsible actors, questioning what's happening in their neighborhood, improving the community. But health is something larger still. Health is the right of people to eat, to have a place to live, to love—yes, love, because love is part of people's physical and emotional equilibrium—and to have a clean, healthy environment to live in.

From the beginning we gave priority to those who were most in need: women, youth, and children. Over eighteen years, more than three hundred thousand people have passed through [the association]. We've closely accompanied about six hundred to seven hundred kids from the cradle on. When babies and little children come into the clinic, we weigh them. If they're underweight, we put them into our program for six months. We embrace that child and help their mother out. They get enriched milk two or three times a day and a bowl of hot food in the afternoon. As soon as a child is better, we let them go and take in another. We do literacy classes with the mothers, though we've had to pause since the earthquake. We also do workshops with them about sexual and reproductive rights, violence against women, and all issues related to women's health. We give them a bit of financial support so they can run a little business, but we don't do micro-credit because we don't believe in it.

We see about two hundred people each day in the clinic. We have forty staff, some in the clinic and some doing outreach in the region. We struggle to provide services that respect the dignity of the people. But we refuse to become a big organization with a lot of funding and bureaucracy. What we do, we do with very little money.

Our clinic is always open, but our social programs on the ground, we reevaluate and renew them every two years to reflect developments in the neighborhood. For example, there's been a lot of violence around here in the past couple of years so we've worked hard with youth for violence prevention. There aren't any recreation centers in the area and the kids have nothing to do. We started an art program for them so they can transform themselves into responsible actors. People say, "You're a clinic. Why are you involved in painting, sculpture, photography, videography?" These people in conventional public health, they don't know the relationship between painting or sculpture and health. They don't know that when someone has a paintbrush in their hands, when they're involved in something meaningful, they can free their mental state from being constantly burdened with problems. Plus they can make some money and change the conditions of their life. We've seen good results from the youth we work with. We're proud of them.

But it's not just to teach the kids and then send them away; we're here to help them reflect on social issues. We have a crafts program for children with recycled garbage, for example. Those kids start thinking, "I shouldn't just throw my water sack or empty spaghetti bag on the street. In fact, I could reuse it, sell what I make, and help out my mother."

But we don't delude ourselves: we're just a neighborhood association. We are neither an NGO nor the state. We're not the ones who are going to change the social conditions of people's lives. I'd like to tell the international agencies that they have to work in alliance with the state.

21

Hold Strong

The Pros and Pitfalls of Resilience

November 2010

Yolette Etienne didn't even mention that her mother had been killed and her house turned to powder. It was exactly one week after the earthquake, and Yolette, then director of Oxfam Great Britain in Haiti, was standing in the wind at the top of a hill telling a journalist from Channel 4 in the UK about the work ahead. Only when he inquired did she say yes, we buried my mother in the garden the morning after, just before I had to go to a staff meeting. She concluded by saying, "We only can maintain hope, and we can transmit hope."

In the same broadcast, deputy mayor of Port-au-Prince Guercy Mouscardy appeared like all other government officials: utterly overwhelmed, without any training or resources to manage a scale-topping catastrophe. He said, "We don't have any money, but we have the will."

Haiti serves as a reminder of the lesson we in New Orleans got after the levees broke: the capacity of humanity to survive, create positive change, sustain culture, and hold joy is fierce. Except in the most extreme, sustained cases of oppression, it is unsinkable, like a cork that won't stay underwater.

Courage, resistance, and survivability are among the most valued traits in Haiti, both in the personal and the political. The highest compliment you can pay a woman in the movement is to call her a *fanm vanyan*, a strong woman. An expression used often and with great pride is *Nou se wozo, nou pliye nou pa kase.* We are bamboo, we bend but we don't break. When you are taking leave of someone at a party or a meeting or a street corner, the standard exhortation is *kenbe fèm*, hold strong. That's how most sign off from phone calls and e-mail, too.

Getro Nelio told me, "Each day when I think of the earthquake, I feel like crying, I want to scream. I don't know if I'm going to get psychologically sick later on or what. But don't forget, I'm a man. I'm not a coward. I do what I do with all my courage and my heart."

My neighbor's wife was killed, and now he is raising his three sons in a two-person tent wedged into an alleyway. He told me, "Well, I can't complain about it. Everyone lost someone. No matter how bad off anyone might feel they are, a lot of other people are worse."

A longtime friend, the administrator of a community nonprofit, shared this private analysis over cups of coffee in her kitchen. "This country is no good. Really, it's no good. But what can you do? We're just going to keep throwing everything we have into making it better."

As Wilson negotiated his *taptap* through traffic, dodging kindergarteners on their way home from school and scrawny dogs, he said, "We do so much with so little. People here can take anything and make it work. Just give us a little bit and we'll fix this country."

Haitians are extravagantly proud of turning something meager into a great resource. *Degaje* is a verb that roughly translates as deploying ingenuity and creativity. I have heard mothers who gave their children a glass of salt water before bed boast of having *degaje*-ed so the kids didn't go to sleep on empty stomachs. Many a down-time conversation is occupied by tales of *degaje*-ing, like someone getting the medicines she needed for her twins' diarrhea though not even a small coin had crossed her palm in the past week, or someone finishing up a taxi run in first gear after the brakes gave out, to earn the day's fare.

You see the resourcefulness in one of Haiti's most popularly selling crafts: sculptures of breasty mermaids or bird-filled trees or Jesus on a cross, cut from discarded fifty-gallon oil drums. A whole new industry has sprung up from the rebar jutting from demolished buildings, which men saw off and reshape into the base of tables and chairs to sell on the street. The number of items held together with a bit of string that people have found on the side of the road could fill a catalog. Finding utility and beauty in refuse, when that's all you've got, is both science and high art.

⁂

Lenz Jean-François, whom we met at the BelAir community shelter and who heads the psychology department at the State University of Haiti, analyzed resilience:

> Haitians' humanity is threatened today. If there is one battle that Haitians don't want to lose, it's their humanity. Conserving it is their point of resistance.
>
> In families, the way they socialize their kids, they give a lot of importance to the capacity for endurance. They teach kids to always be ready for a tough situation, to struggle to hold on to their dignity. In this adversity we've been living under since January 12, a lot of people have been having the experience of realizing, "I didn't know I had all this strength. I thought I would crack. I thought I would collapse." When people realize that they have a government which is extremely weak, and that they have together—with their fingers, with their little hammers, their machetes, their sticks—saved so many neighbors, so many family members, they realize just what strength they have, individually and collectively.
>
> There are some organizations that live off victims, they have to have victims to survive. We say instead, "Reinforce Haitians' capacity, build up their self-confidence. Let them see their own worth. Let them know they're agents." It helps them have control over their lives, over their environment. What's positive within the population, build on that.
>
> Gandhi said that certain things have to be done by Indians. When they do something with their own hands, they come to believe in themselves. The Haitian people have to do things with our own hands. Then we can say, "This was our dream."
>
> We say we're not only rebuilding ourselves, we're rebuilding our nation. We're promoting collective resilience and tying it to a political vision. We in social psychology are saying: "Believe in your strength and in your capacity to rebuild this country." They prove

that capacity each day, the way they're surviving.

The difficult situation that Haitians are going through today makes them more fragile. But it can also be a force.

�֍

Resilience cuts different ways, though. Foreigners often praise Haitians for it, as if they can handle more, as if their endurance for pain is somehow greater. Does the uncanny toughness they have been forced to develop make their suffering a bit less shocking in the eyes of the world? Does it become a subconscious way of absolving one's conscience while living with unjustifiable levels of inequality and violence?

Even Prime Minister Bellerive, in discussing the failure of the international community to come forth with more aid, said, "Everyone is talking about the resilience of the Haitian people, and everyone is taking advantage of that resilience."[1]

Suze Abraham is a poster child for it. She grew up a *restavèk*. The trials she suffered could fill a book of their own, but here are a few:

> One day I was coming back from delivering food to the child of the house, that I had to carry on my head to her school every day. There was a man holding a school under a thatched roof. He called to me, "Come be part of this school." I said, "No, I can't, because when I go home my aunt [the common term for a *restavèk* keeper] will beat me." He said, "You should come." I went. Now when I got home, I said, "There was a man holding school, so I attended today." The woman said, "What? You went to school?" I said, "Yes, and could you please give me a little pencil and a notebook?" She asked me what I thought I was doing, and started beating me. Poverty and misery made me not know how to read and write, or count in my head, until I was a grown-up.

Still today, she can only read or write a few words.

Suze escaped three times and went to different homes, four in all. "But each time I suffered as bad or worse than before. I was abused so much. Misery was killing me." She finally broke free with the help of a loving man with whom she partnered and bore five children. One night during a period of political upheaval in 2004, men broke into their home, killed her husband, and raped her and her eldest daughter. Suze was left to raise the children alone, without help from nearby relatives or income from a job. When she ran out of ways to feed her offspring and was scared that they would starve to death, she gave away four of them, the youngest just three years old; they all became *restavèk*. She kept only her baby, who hadn't yet cut his teeth. Later, she went to a children's rights training. She said, "That gave me consciousness, and I went and got my kids back. I said to myself, no matter what, I'm going to keep them." Since then, she has taken in her granddaughter, Timafi, too, to raise and feed. Suze has also had to face Timafi's rape, as related earlier.

Suze's eldest son, Michel, twenty years old, and her sister both died in the disaster. "Michel used to come see me every few days," she said. "No one had heard from him. They kept trying to tell me that he went traveling and that he'd come back. But I wouldn't believe them. I knew he was dead." She sifted through the pages of a notebook and found the only photo she had of Michel, which was not much larger than a thumbprint. In it, her son's face was the width of a pencil eraser, indecipherable. Suze's eyes were already perpetually red from crying, and now she started again.

She lost her home, too, a small cement box with no windows or kitchen or bathroom or lights or running water, a short stone's throw away from a wide sewer of unmoving gunk. The quake had shifted the house's walls to an arresting slant; when they would fall was just a matter of time. Suze wouldn't set foot inside, there or any other cement building. She moved herself and her children to a concrete yard inside church gates, where they slept next to about seven hundred strangers in one of many sardine-like lines. They had no sheet under them and no protection over them. "Here's where we go when it rains," she told me on a tour of her new residence, pointing to an exterior wall of the church without any awning. "Here's where I keep my stuff. This neighbor watches it for me." She gestured to a woman sitting beside a pile of bundles wrapped in sheets. "And here's where we wash," indicating a rivulet of water as wide as a finger, running down a crack in the sidewalk. "Yes, really. Me and the kids. Where else are we going to get water?" She used to have a small wooden chair, but someone stole it.

One late night, Marco and I were working on laptops when we heard a giant crack and then the din of rain on the tin roof. We both looked up with the same alarmed faces. I know he was thinking what I was, of the

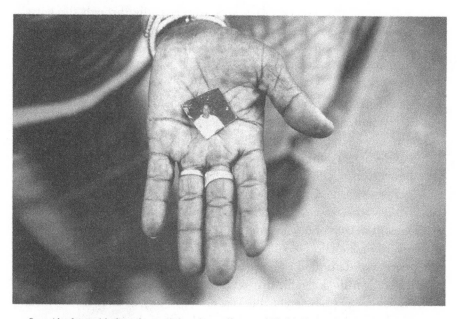

Suze Abraham with the only remaining photo of her son, killed in the earthquake. Photograph by Roberto "Bear" Guerra.

million-plus people living out-of-doors. Within minutes, the phone rang. It was Suze. "We're standing on the sidewalk. We'll be here all night. I don't even have a plastic bag to put over my head."

The location of her daily calls was like a compass on suffering. One morning she relayed, "I'm sleeping in front of my old house. Some man in the churchyard shouted at Ghislene"—her fourteen-year-old daughter— "last night while she was getting ready to lie down; he threatened her. I don't know why." The neighborhood containing Suze's ruined house had largely been deserted after *twelve*, so she and her children faced high danger in sleeping outside, alone and exposed. Another morning she reported: "I'm calling you from the clinic. Two of the kids are sick. You know, they spent the last two nights in the rain." One call was to tell me that Ghislene had developed an illness that doctors couldn't diagnose. She was barely eating and freaked out at loud noises.

One morning after a rain, Suze called with a rare piece of good news. "Guess what? I have a tarp. A neighbor saw my kids trying to spend the night lying on the mud and gave me a tarp. I cut down a few little trees and made a shelter." But after a couple more torrents, Suze called to inform me that her new tarp was leaking badly through the holes where she had nailed it to the sticks. I tapped all my connections and she tapped all hers, and we went off on several maddening goose chases to find a tent. We never did succeed, and she and her children continued to pass the nights wet.

A benefactor helped her move to an apartment, but Suze soon learned that it was in a high-rape area, so they moved back once again to the homemade shelter in front of the open sewer. Ghislene has repeatedly been hospitalized for mysterious and grave symptoms, which appeared to lie at least partially in anxiety. Suze herself has suffered from very high blood pressure, and can't always get the medicine she needs.

Suze's experiences are a testament to the fact that poverty is not just the result of lack of money, but of lack of power over even the smallest elements of one's life.

Suze has dedicated a considerable amount of energy to helping out other women and kids: identifying those who have been attacked, taking their testimony (the literate Ghislene taking notes), accompanying them to the hospital, and connecting them with one of the two women's support groups she works with. Her cell phone is a de facto hotline. She has engaged in other kinds of solidarity with her neighbors and friends, like taking up a contribution to claim from a morgue the body of an eight-year-old who had simply, she said, dropped dead. She used her own money to buy underwear and socks for the girl's burial. She took in a neighbor's child even though her own were hungry because "the mother needed help." I've seen her offer many a kiss or an encouraging word to a distraught acquaintance, when that was all she had to give.

In visits to my apartment—rare moments when she has no child to watch and no chores to do—she sits and stares blankly, her brows pulled together and her mouth a tight line. "There are so many times I don't have anything to give the kids to eat. In the evening, we just all get up on the bed and fast together," she confessed once. Also anguishing to Suze is her inability to keep all of her kids in school. She is determined her kids won't share her fate of illiteracy. But only Timafi and one other child are in school now. She puts them in, as many as she can, and the school pulls them out, in a rhythm matching the rising and falling of her finances. She said, "You don't know what it costs us to try to get our kids educated. We have a right to education. I know that. I don't know how to read, but I know my rights. I know what's in the constitution. The government knows that. I'm going to find someone to write a letter to the president and tell him that free education is my right."

One afternoon, Ghislene made a little speech to me to please take her mother out of Haiti because she was suffering too much. And once Suze admitted that she had contemplated drinking bleach, the poor person's route to suicide. "But then I thought, 'What would happen to all these kids?'"

On another occasion, she fixed her sad eyes on me and said in her soft voice, "I have no mother, I have no father. Suffering is trying to crush me, but what can I do? I have to resist." Day after day she goes on because she has no choice. Like most, she doesn't have the luxury of despair. Some do give up or cope destructively, but when one has to find a way to feed one's children tomorrow no matter what, burning out or copping out are rarely options.

Suze has told me repeatedly that only her courage keeps her and her children alive. One morning she said, "I can't suffer anything else that I haven't already suffered, so I still have hope."

❈

"People are surviving because they're survivors," a doctor friend told me. While that may be true, why should it all come down to their internal defenses, bolstered by solidarity from similarly strapped members of their community? To quote a woman from New Orleans in the aftermath of the flood: "I'm tired of being resilient."

A taxi driver laid it out as he gave me, together with many more people than were ever meant to fit into his compact Toyota, a ride across town. "Hello, *blan*, foreigner," he said as I got in. "Hello, Haitian," I replied. "How are you?"

"My tarp is torn. The other night I was completely wet in the rain. We're children of God. But still, really, we need some help."

22

Mrs. Clinton Will Never See Me Working There

The Offshore Assembly Industry

November 2010

"Haiti offers a marvelous opportunity for American investment. The run-of-the-mill Haitian is handy, easily directed, and gives a hard day's labor for 20 cents, while in Panama the same day's work costs $3," wrote *Financial America* in 1926.[1] That may be the most honest portrayal of offshore industry in Haiti to date. Today, the United States, the UN, multilateral lending institutions, corporate investors, and others are more creative in their characterizations. They spin the high-profit labor as being in the interest of the laborer, and as a major vehicle for what they call "development."

In the export assembly sector (factories owned by Haitian and foreign companies, making a host of consumer products that are then sold around the world), the minimum wage is 125 gourdes, or US$3.13 a day. According to the Associated Press in February 2010, 125 gourdes is "approximately the same as the minimum wage in 1984 and worth less than half its previous purchasing power."[2] Two studies done by the Solidarity Center of the AFL-CIO showed that a living wage (what would be required for workers to cover basic expenses) is at least US$29 a day

in Port-au-Prince and US$12.50 a day in the border town of Ouana-
minthe, home to one free-trade zone.[3] (Free-trade zones are groupings
of export-producing factories that enjoy tax exemptions; fewer safety,
health, and environment regulations; and other benefits to owners.) Even
a study commissioned by a World Bank–sponsored pro-garment assembly group, Nathan Associates Inc., acknowledged that for factory workers, "the costs of transportation to and from work and food purchased
away from home eat up a substantial share of that minimum wage."[4] For
the typical worker, who is a single mother with three to four children,[5]
this leaves less than nothing with which to keep her family healthy, fed,
housed, and schooled.

In a minority of cases, workers don't necessarily even earn the legal income. Factories establish weekly production quotas (number of bra cups
or pajama legs produced) that are sometimes set so high that employees
have to put in extra hours—what should be paid as overtime—and forgo
their forty-five minutes of daily break just to try to meet the quota, but
still they cannot always sew fast enough to do so. Even with the extra
hours, a worker may end her or his week at well below minimum wage.

"They're always struggling to see how they're going to make ends
meet. When they get paid each payday, they already owe all of it. Their
problems weigh them down so heavy they don't know what to do,"
Nadine Deloné told me. Now a health care assistant in a clinic frequented
by many factory workers, Nadine sewed in a plant herself for eleven years
until, she said, she just gave out. Like many other workers I have met,
she did not want her real name used or her photo published, for fear of
retribution from management.

In dozens of interviews I have conducted over twenty-five years,
workers have consistently stated the same outcome of trying to support
an entire family on this wage: they grow *poorer* over the course of their
employment. For the opportunity to keep stitching at the plant, survival
can involve desperation credit from the neighborhood loan shark at interest rates as high as 25 percent per month.

Why would anyone take such a job? People in urgent need of cash
rarely have the luxury of performing cost-benefit analyses. In interviews,
women said they worked in factories simply because they needed jobs. In
a country with about 40 percent unemployment,[6] any amount of money
on payday might stave off starvation, even though the worker loses over
the long term.

In 2009, as mentioned, thousands of workers joined students and others in the streets to demand an increase in the minimum wage from seventy gourdes (US$1.75) a day. During the "two hundred gourdes movement," protests paralyzed Port-au-Prince's industrial sector for more than a week. According to one organizer, Nixon Boumba of the Democratic Popular Movement, factory bosses cracked down, forbidding phone usage and changing workers' shifts to keep them away from fellow organizers and demonstrations. Those they couldn't stop, they laid off. Police lent management a hand, arresting dozens of protestors, including the dean of the State University's School of Social Sciences. Parliament responded to the popular pressure nevertheless, and passed an across-the-board wage raise for workers in all sectors to two hundred gourdes (US$5.00) per day. However, when Haitian factory owners complained to Préval, he vetoed the law. According to U.S. Embassy cables later released by WikiLeaks, Washington became actively involved in keeping wages low at export assembly factories. USAID funded studies to show that the demanded increase in minimum wage would "make the sector economically unviable and consequently force factories to shut down." Subcontractors for Fruit of the Loom, Hanes, and Levi's held numerous meetings with Préval and members of Parliament, using the USAID studies to argue for a lower wage.[7] Parliament gave in and worked out a compromise with Préval, creating a special wage category for export assembly workers only, at just 125 gourdes (US$3.13) a day.

⌘

Women in the assembly plants are often compelled to sleep with supervisors, once or many times, in order to get or keep their jobs. Health and safety protections in the workplace rarely exist, and those that do are habitually violated, with repetitive motion injuries and failing eyesight only two of the more common occupational hazards. Workers have no job security and paltry opportunities for pay raises or professional advancement. Employment connotes few rights, least of all the right to unionize. Though protected in the constitution, unions are prohibited in practice by the standard management response of firing those who attempt to organize.

Mirlène Joanis, director of communications for the Center for the Promotion of Women Workers (Centre de Promotion des Femmes Ouvrières, or CPFO), reflected,

It's not just money. The workers have to have social advantages, like the right to housing, the right to health care, the right to hygiene, to transportation, to food. The totality of these social rights would add a lot to the value of minimum wage, but not one of them is respected. They don't even give people potable water. They just buy tanks of untreated water in trucks; people have to buy their own little plastic sacks of water out of their 125 gourdes. I give this as an example of the most basic of rights, the right to drink water, and they don't even offer that.

When the worker goes to ask for her rights to be respected, that means nothing. She can organize a union, but the boss will fire her immediately and then there's no more union. The boss has money, he can call the minister [of social affairs and labor]. If union rights aren't protected, there's no way this sector will improve. People have to be able to raise their demands and say, "Respect my rights." That doesn't exist. Even the movement for the minimum wage to be raised . . . people took to the streets to demand it, but it ended badly for them. A lot of people lost their job as a result.

Some groups are considered human beings, some aren't. Some have rights, others don't. Without the principle of rights, nothing's going to change. It's just going from bad to worse, with no relief of the workers' misery in sight.

In telling how they survive on factory jobs, workers use a standard refrain: *sou fòs kouray*, on the strength of my courage.

Whether in a whispered conversation under a pseudonym or through unabashed declarations by labor rights organizations like Workers' Struggle and Workers' Antenna (Antèn Ouvriye), laborers and their advocates all state basically the same conditions for fair employment. They include

- a living wage;
- overtime and severance pay;
- protection from sexual aggression by supervisors;
- physically safe working conditions;
- coverage of medical costs in the event of work-related injury or illness;
- at least one break a day, plus the time necessary to eat lunch and go to the bathroom;

- provision of drinking water and decent bathrooms;
- the right to organize; and
- protection from arbitrary or retaliatory firing.

�֎

In 2005, the World Bank wrote about post-conflict zones that "employment is likely to be scarce, and almost any kind of job opportunity will therefore be welcome."[8] This suggests that no matter the pay or conditions, sweatshop jobs are the best that Haiti should expect, given its "comparative advantage." According to the rules of the global economy, that advantage is its cheap labor and proximity to U.S. markets. The model creates a race to the bottom in which the lowest wages, the fewest health and safety standards, and the worst possibilities for unionizing are actually considered advantages. The Haitian government's Action Plan for National Recovery and Development explicitly uses the "comparative advantage" language.[9]

The UN places the expansion of free-trade zones for offshore assembly toward the center of its development road map for Haiti. A 2009 report it commissioned and has promoted said of expanding the garment industry, "It is truly important that this opportunity should be taken." According to the paper's author, Oxford University economics professor Paul Collier, Haiti's duty-free, quota-free preferential access to the U.S. market (created by the Caribbean Basin Initiative in the 1980s), combined with low labor costs and a lack of protectionist policies, makes the country "the world's safest production location for garments."[10] Weeks after the earthquake, Collier likened the catastrophic moment to nineteenth-century development of the U.S. West, with its "investment booms, financed by enthusiastic outsiders. The earthquake could usher in such a boom in Haiti."[11]

Apparently sharing this view, four months after the earthquake the U.S. Congress passed a new free-trade law that was touted as a relief measure, the Haiti Economic Lift Program (HELP). It nearly tripled the quota on fabrics that were eligible to be imported duty-free into the United States. Also since the earthquake, the Inter-American Development Bank joined the U.S. government in coming up with $224 million to subsidize development of a new free-trade zone for garment assembly in northern Haiti.[12]

Yannick Etienne of Workers' Struggle gave this characterization of the trade preferences: "Actually, what you have is U.S. companies benefiting by getting stuff assembled at a very low price for the U.S. market without paying taxes or customs. But the workers who are making those factories' profits are not getting anything. They're sweating hard and working hard and they don't get anything. No one even remembers them."

⌘

For all the funding and attention the sector has received, the nineteen factories currently making garments for export employ very few people: 23,300, or approximately 0.4 percent of the working-age population as of June 2010.[13] Even in its heyday in the 1980s, the industry employed only around one hundred thousand people. No matter the numbers, the industry's contribution to the national economy is false development, said economist Camille Chalmers with the Haitian Platform to Advocate Alternative Development:

> It doesn't serve the economic engine of the country. These industries have no forward or backward linkages to the national economy. They contribute little toward making the economy more productive. They work on behalf of the external market, and almost all of the primary materials used in manufacturing come from outside. When they say that Haiti exports hundreds of millions of dollars in products [US$370 million in apparel exports to the United States alone, just for the first three quarters of 2010[14]], a lot of that goes to [foreign companies to] pay for the inputs like cloth and equipment. Once assembled, the goods aren't consumed in Haiti but are shipped abroad. The government doesn't even benefit from taxes or tariffs. Haiti's only role is as a stopover in the production process, where cheap labor keeps profit margins high.
>
> The sector is based on volatile capital. It's very unstable and it's very easy for this capital to go elsewhere without any obstacles; there are none. When the companies find lower production costs, they leave.

Businesses rely on a network of low-wage labor supply, and can circle the globe to find the cheapest wages and lowest costs for health and safety. They do up and leave countries regularly, and not just for lower production costs. The Canadian apparel manufacturer Gildan Active-wear, for instance, decided to move some of its operations out of Haiti within one day of the earthquake, shifting them to the Dominican Re-public, Nicaragua, and Honduras. The company hastened to assure its retail customers in the United States that they would not be affected.[15]

In discussions among foreigners about working conditions and wages in the assembly industry, I've often heard, "But Haitians need jobs. Wouldn't things be worse without them?" The question creates a false choice between no job and a grinding, exploitative job. As a counterex-ample, plants across the border in the Dominican Republic often pay more than US$10 per day, thanks to a strong union movement, and they employ roughly twice as many workers as in Haiti. One of those Domini-can factories, Alta Gracia Apparel, pays three times the average industry wage in that country and has a unionized workforce and still, according to its owner, makes a profit.[16]

The wouldn't-things-be-worse question also discounts the role that Western governments and their international financial institution part-ners have played in creating this dearth of options among Haitians, and the possibilities that could be opened if they changed their policies to enable higher incomes. Even Bill Clinton, as mentioned earlier, felt com-pelled to apologize publicly for ruining the farming sector's shot at earn-ing an income their families could live off.

Haiti needs work opportunities, as any cash-desperate person there will tell you. But not at any price or under any conditions. The former factory worker Nadine Deloné said, "It can't be based on the exploita-tion of people. We need to be treated like human beings." And Camille Chalmers said, "When we speak of employment, we have to talk about the quality of employment. [This sector] doesn't create work that can develop our human resources or reduce poverty. These comparative ad-vantages just reproduce misery."

Another, more appropriate question is how to ensure good jobs, based on the requirements the laborers and their advocates outline above and as required by the International Labour Organisation. Here is where we come in. There is no reason to consent to a system wherein both the maker and the wearer of the product are degraded. There is no reason for us to docilely buy clothing that is made under rules that mean that the seamstresses can't send their children to school. We can engage in campaigns for labor and human rights called for by the workers affected, like boycotts against corporations with bad records of payment, worker treatment, and union busting.[17] Working together with unions in the countries in question, university campuses around the country have succeeded with this tack on apparel made by Nike, Russell Athletics, Reebok, and others.

It is often still the case that when companies are pressured, they just relocate operations. This gets to the heart of the problem: As factories move to the next country, they *create* dirt-poor workers from the vulnerability and powerlessness of unemployed farmers from Millet Mountain and single mothers from Cité Soleil. This doesn't mean that we should stop the campaigns, but rather that we should redouble our efforts to raise the floor everywhere. We can help stop the race to the bottom so that all workers within the world economic system can support their families and live with dignity. Another way for consumers in the North to exercise good global citizenship is to pressure our government and the international financial institutions to make enforceable labor rights and living wages standard policy in all trade agreements and so-called development programs. We can also strengthen alternative sources of employment that provide more power and economic advantage to workers, their families, and the domestic economy, like worker-owned businesses, cooperatives, fair-trade enterprises, and smallholder agricultural production.

Meanwhile, Misericord St. Anne asked me to publish her opinion. Misericord ran an embroidery machine in a clothes factory from 2005 to 2008. She said the experience made her so sick and weak that still, at the end of 2010, she was not able to work. "Me, if I had a message I could send to the higher-ups: Factories have always existed, crushing the poor. I don't speak for other people, but me, I will never go to whatever factory Mrs. Bill Clinton has opened. Mrs. Clinton can have her factories. But she'll never see me working there."

23

The Central Pillar

Peasant Women

December 2010

After decades of working underground, in 1987 about eleven hundred people gathered in an airless auditorium on a dusty field for the First National Congress of Democratic Movements. For three days they listened, debated, and strategized about the creation of what they hoped would be a just and democratic society. Family farmers, people of faith, students, human rights activists, progressive academics . . . they were all there. We heard about their struggles, and we committed ourselves to their causes.

With one exception. No issue specifically related to women appeared on the program. Aside from one established leader, no woman did, either. Except, that is, at the very end of the forum, when a man at the podium called for applause for the women's group that had made all the meals. We turned our heads back toward the kitchen and saw unnamed women peeping through a diminutive serving window. We clapped for their fine cooking.

One decade later I returned to that same cinder-block auditorium, only this time for a gathering of peasant women. The several hundred participants had traveled from distant regions to talk about the urgencies their families and communities face, compare notes of their pasts and visions for their future, and develop plans to convert their dreams into reality. When I told them of my last experience at that venue, they were scandalized.

In fact, rural women are still frequently confined to the kitchen—literally and proverbially—in their home, grassroots organizations, and society. It is still the case that they and their children are by far the most marginalized group in the country.

However, as the two conferences indicate, peasant women are challenging and changing their lot. Below, three peasant leaders recount what they and other women are doing to be seen, heard, and respected, and to guarantee their political and economic rights.

❋

Gerta Louisama sits on the Executive Committee and the Women's Commission of Heads Together Haitian Peasants.

My father was a member of Heads Together, and I chose to follow him. I've gotten all my knowledge through Heads Together. If it wasn't for them, I wouldn't have any value in this society. Even spelling my name and writing a little: I'm illiterate, but thanks to the organization, I could do that after women helped me for three months.

In this country we have plenty of laws, and men and women have the same rights. They're on paper, they've just been set aside. Part of our movement is to get these laws respected. Now it's like the peasants have no rights because they don't have access to clean water, no access to roads, no access to health care, no access to free schooling. And if we protest for our rights, they'll send in the police or the UN troops and they'll spray tear gas, arrest people and beat them up. We don't even have the right to protest. When we peasants ask for our basic necessities, especially our right to land, they just slaughter us.

We Haitian women, we have a lot of challenges, but as peasant women we have even more. We truly carry the burden of society. We're the ones who hustle to feed the household and send the sick to the hospital if need be. We women, we work the land, we raise cattle, we transport merchandise like plantains, yams, and black beans to the capital. If we don't work, no goods move.

What the women in Heads Together do is group ourselves in teams of ten to fifteen. We work the fields together, we do laundry together. We do personal development training to remind peasant women that we're human, too, and part of society. The Women's Commission helps us understand our strength in society and understand that, as for those services we're entitled to, the government's not doing us favors: they're our rights. And we're addressing economic and social problems, like processing the foods we produce [which fetches a higher price than the raw product] and getting help from the courts for women who've been victims of domestic abuse.

We're showing that this isn't a movement of women against men, but rather a movement against society which has isolated women. You find there are men who really misunderstand women, who assume we're increasing our strength against them, but the fight to change the conditions of women is coming from men in Heads Together, too.

We in the Women's Commission are asking the government to do a thorough agrarian reform so the peasants own the land we work. Land needs to be taken away from people who aren't using it, and the state needs to let go of land it's holding. We need other resources to farm, too; otherwise, it's like asking us to wash our hands and dry them in the dirt. The problem is even worse for women because both the family and the society keep us from owning land or other big assets. If the land isn't in the hands of the government or the church, it's mostly for the sons. Say my father died. If he owned three hectares of land and he had two sons and me, he'd never say that each of us could have one hectare. Me, I'd only get one-quarter hectare or so, and the extra would be divided among my brothers. And if I was living in common-law marriage with a man and he died, I'd need to race to get myself off the land even if I didn't have anywhere else to sleep. I wouldn't have any right to stay on the premises.

The lack of respect for peasants is also why today cholera is spreading throughout the country. There was no [government] plan from early on, and that's why it's killed so many, especially the poorest who can't get medical care. They talked about sending Clorox [to purify our water], but we haven't gotten any. They've told peasants to use soap to wash their hands, but some of them don't have the money to buy any, because it costs twelve gourdes [thirty cents]. In remote areas, people might need to carry some-one with cholera four or five hours [long enough to die from infec-tion] on planks of wood to make it to the hospital. Cholera is an even bigger burden on peasant women because we're the ones that have borne the children and that are responsible for the household.

Based on how things are going, we can almost say we're losing the battle fast. So far, we haven't seen any positive outcome. In fact, we're slowly but surely going backwards. But as long as we're breathing, we can't get discouraged. We're responsible for chang-ing the conditions of our country, so we'll keep fighting. I'll be en-gaged till the day I die. And even if we don't see the changes, our kids will. I have one daughter, and I'm trying to give her everything society has refused to give me.

✳

Iderle Brénus Gerbier works with many peasant organizations to sup-port women's rights and food sovereignty. She is a trainer with women's groups, a member of the Haitian National Network for Food Sovereignty and Security, and an adviser to the National Coalition of Peasant Women.

Some well-off women from Port-au-Prince and other cities are also involved in the struggle, but we're not always on the same side. Even within the women's struggle, there are a lot of contempt-ible practices that have yet to be overcome. Right now there are two kinds of women: women with a capital *W* and women with a small *w*. Most of the urban well-off women look down on the poor country women, calling them *tèt mare*, kerchief heads. They forget that peasant communities constitute the greatest part of the country. We need to redefine the concept of feminism in Haiti. We have to reshuffle the cards and reduce the differences between our women.

Peasant women are always present in activities to win human rights, respect for life, and food sovereignty. October 15 was declared Day of the Haitian Peasant Woman, but unfortunately this day has never been commemorated. But they'll never get discouraged. They'll always be involved in all kinds of constructive activities and keep supporting their country.

⚒

Yvette Michaud cofounded the National Coalition of Peasant Women in 2008. This is the first effort to unite the voices and interests of this group at a national level, though to date only a couple of organizations are actively engaged.

> We peasant women have a lot to say about the elections. We have things to say about the reconstruction plan. We're ready to do everything possible to get our rights respected from the home to the society. We're ready to hold demonstrations, do sit-ins, circulate petitions, and do advocacy, to demand services from the state. For example, for International Women's Day, we had a big demonstration that left Papaye and went to Hinche. Women came from everywhere.
>
> We saw that all the [formal] activities focusing on women always happened in Port-au-Prince. So we in the [fifty-six member organizations of the] Haitian National Network for Food Sovereignty and Security passed a resolution to say we were going to establish a national women's peasant organization. If we could organize ourselves together to form a bloc, we could accomplish a lot of things. What women do, we don't say that men can't, but they can't do the things that are necessary for survival without us.
>
> One thing that happens in mixed-gender groups is that women don't get to participate. You don't hear women's voices. They have to bring the water, make the food, clean the rooms. They're almost there for service instead of as members, more like slaves.
>
> There are some violent men who prevent women from attending women's meetings because they know women can speak freely and badly about them. But it's much less these days. There's been an improvement in violence in the past ten years or so, but that doesn't mean it's gone away. But now that men know that women

can denounce them, they temper themselves a little. That's another reason why we've started to organize as women, apart. In a mixed-gender group, if a woman's husband is beating her at home, she can't say anything about it. But in all-women's groups, she can get support and advice from others.

Why a women's group like this one is important is that we're more comfortable to speak. We participate freely. We want to create more of these spaces so we can think about ourselves and our future.

24

Elections

(In the Time of Cholera)

December 2010

The purple-black thumb on the white hand was arresting. Indelible ink could be seen on the right thumbs of Haitians all over the country, showing that they had voted in the first round of national elections on November 28, but my neighbor was *French*. When I inquired, she said that she and a fellow Frenchwoman had applied for electoral cards on a dare. They had cast ballots without anyone questioning them.

As fraud went, that was trifling. Local authorities intimidated, committed violence, stuffed voting urns, and faked ballots. Boxes full of votes became balls in soccer matches. Ballots wound up in toilets and canals. Gangs burned down stations entirely. The portion of the electorate who voted and had it counted was a mere 22.8 percent.[1]

People referred to the elections as "selections."

The campaign itself had been farcical. The singer Wyclef Jean—who had lived in the United States for the prior three decades—had declared his candidacy for the presidency on *Larry King Live*. The electoral council found a way to bar Aristide's political party, Lavalas Family (Fanmi Lavalas, *lavalas* being a cleaning flood that comes following a deluge,

washing away debris): having excluded it from participating in the previous year's senate elections because of technicalities, the council main-
tained the exclusion during this election. It eliminated at least thirteen
additional candidates.

Many people, like Tibebe, reported that they weren't able to vote
because they had never gotten an electoral card to replace the one lost
within their obliterated homes. Still more said that they had been turned
away from polling stations, told their names weren't listed. The population was full of plausible theories of how deleting those registered names
was schemed to throw the vote. At least some of the instances were surely
due to the chaotic state of records, given the government's loss of offices,
archives, and infrastructure; that is why some human rights and democracy institutions had urged that the elections be postponed.

The grand bulk of the electorate hadn't bothered to turn out in the
first place because they didn't believe any of the nineteen candidates
would produce a president sympathetic to their cause. Since *twelve*, not
one of the candidates had been outspoken or active on behalf of those
languishing in camps, or of a reconstruction process that gave more than
a token nod to the most vulnerable. Manès Souffrance, a young database
technician, told me, "People would be interested in the elections if they
saw that the outcome would have an impact on their needs. But the candidates are all *gran manjè*, big eaters, from the same group of people who
always exploit us. Most of them have been in the system, benefiting from
it, for a long time. They're not going to do anything for us poor people."

Some camp residents boycotted. Janine Leclerc, a lead organizer in
one boycott involving ten camps, told me, "We will resist as long as we're
living under tarps in the rain and the mud. We'll participate once they
respond to our demands, once they address the problems of people living in tents and getting evicted from them, once they stop forcing women
to sleep with men who control humanitarian aid to get any of it."

※

Unlike the earthquake, the crisis over the initial election results came
with ample warning. The population anxiously awaited word of the
two candidates who would be sent to a second round, as it seemed clear
that no candidate was popular enough to have gotten the required abso-
lute majority. According to general belief, those two should have been

Campaigning in wrecked national elections before a wrecked National Palace. Photograph by Joris Willems.

Mirlande Manigat and Michel Martelly. Martelly was notorious as a compas musician and carouser who favored such distinctly nonpresidential behavior as baring his butt on stage. But he wasn't just a harmless buffoon; he had been public in his support for Duvalier and the death squad–friendly regimes that had reigned after coups d'état against Aristide, and had recently made on-camera statements such as, "I would kill Aristide to stick a dick up his ass. Fuck your mother."[2]

Street conversations were full of boisterous speculation about how the outcomes would be manipulated, with many suspecting that Préval would insert his heir-apparent, Jude Célestin, into the runoffs. There was less speculation about whether violence or chaos would ensue after the council's announcement; just about everyone was convinced of it. When the appointed day, Tuesday, December 7, rolled around, most Port-au-Prince residents scurried to their homes for safety. Sure enough, Célestin was declared one of the two finalists, along with Mirlande Manigat. Because the corruption was too thick for definitive results to be seen, a Center for Economic and Policy Research recount found that it was impossible to determine the real winners. (In their estimation, no single candidate received more than 6.4 percent of the vote, showing the electorates' disdain for the contenders and the process.)[3] The National Human Rights Defense Network (Réseau National de Défense des Droits Humains, or RNDDH) and other experts denounced the initial results, too.[4]

The electoral theft threw the country into a rage. Beginning at nightfall and lasting for five days, gunfire ricocheted around the capital and other towns. Radio Metropole reported five deaths over the first two days alone. The rabble-rousers were a mix of ordinary folks fed up with the political class, people who had been paid by the candidates, and thugs who controlled various neighborhoods. Small crowds rampaged through towns, destroying government offices, electoral headquarters, shops, and even a school, and setting fire to cars. The acrid stink of smoke from burning-tire barricades mixed with that of tear gas thrown liberally by the Haitian police and UN soldiers.

Outside the safety in numbers of the ramparts, few stirred in the streets. In my apartment complex, the black-thumbed Frenchwoman, who was normally gone by dawn to offer eye care in a low-income clinic, dropped by each morning for a leisurely cup of coffee. The normally busy journalists, development workers, and service providers strolled between each other's flats to borrow what they had run out of: Barbancourt rum, condensed milk, toilet paper, whatever. They exchanged political gossip and climbed to the roof to see where the newest fires were. Our e-mails were full of concern from friends in other countries inquiring if we were safe amid the "riots."

As always, the poor paid the highest price. For starters, the week provided the perfect conditions for a spike in cholera in the camps. Much of the humanitarian coordination effort was in lock-down, a cholera-focused government employee told me. One sanitation worker described toilets and garbage overflowing to extremes, and the port-o-potties, moreover, "overturned and used as roadblocks."[5] A health agent sent out an urgent call for anyone who could travel to ten camps to deliver cholera-prevention essentials. The sporadic rains throughout the week spread the vector stew of contaminated water and sewage.

In areas where much of the violence was concentrated, many couldn't leave their homes out of fear. Those under tarps or tents couldn't even lock themselves in. Several friends in those settings who call me whenever they have the funds for cell phone minutes gave grim accounts: their meager supplies of food and water had given out after a day or two, and they were running to neighbors' homes in calmer moments in hopes of gifts to sustain their children. One morning, Suze called to say that she had just returned from two days in the hospital, where she had been watching over her cholera-infected father-in-law. I asked how she had been making out. "It's been hard, hard, hard, I tell you. There's been so much shooting in my neighborhood, there's been nowhere to run. I haven't had anything to feed my kids. They're so skinny, even little Timafi; you remember she was chubby. They're just sticks now."

Sweatshop workers, carpenters, and others whose income was based on day wages were out of luck, too. So were those who made a living from the informal economy, like the guys who sold ten-minute phone cards outside gas stations for a cent or two profit per transaction, because both they and their potential customers had been off the streets for days.

By the weekend, the madness began to exhaust itself, though not the anxiety about who would win the presidency or by what process.

⌘

Meanwhile, the international community put on boxing gloves and strode right to the center of the ring. The Electoral Observation Mission of the Organization of American States (OAS) had described itself as "proactively" involved in the preparations and execution.[6] It and the United States had paid most of the bill.[7] Though the final results of the first round of voting were to be announced on December 20, the OAS requested that the Haitian government delay its announcement pending its investigation. This investigation would later throw out the results of the first round without a recount, an unprecedented approach.[8] On January 24, State Department spokesperson P. J. Crowley would say, "We want to see the government of Haiti embrace the recommendations of the OAS verification mission report." That same day, the State Department revoked the visas of some dozen or two dozen (reports differ) Haitian government officials; the gesture was believed to be a pressure tactic, though the public pretext was those officials' alleged connections to violence and corruption.[9] The following week, the U.S. government sent Secretary of State Clinton to the island to make clear whom it wanted to see make the runoff.

As for what the OAS and the United States were seeking to gain from their manipulation, we will need to wait to see how their policies unfold. What is clear is that the United States did not want a protégé of Préval to win. WikiLeaks documents revealed that Washington was increasingly fed up with Préval for his refusal to submit absolutely to U.S. positions, particularly regarding the Chávez government in Venezuela.[10] A memo from the U.S. Embassy to the State Department said, "[Préval's] reflexive nationalism, and his disinterest in managing bilateral relations in a broad diplomatic sense, will lead to periodic frictions as we move forward our bilateral agenda. Case in point, we believe that in terms of foreign policy, Preval is most interested in gaining increased assistance from any available resource. He is likely to be tempted to frame his relationship with Venezuela and Chávez-allies in the hemisphere in a way that he hopes will create a competitive atmosphere as far as who can provide the most to Haiti."[11]

By contrast, Martelly made clear in his campaign statements that he would pursue a neoliberal course and align closely with the United States. The United States may also have believed that it could control Martelly, and that it could in turn count on him to control a restive population. By all appearances, the United States does not like Martelly, but never mind. As Mark Weisbrot, codirector of the Center for Economic and Policy Research who was closely tracking events, wrote me, "It's a chess game to them. Haiti is just a pawn, but the pawns matter in their calculus."[12]

Antonal Mortimé, executive secretary of the Platform of Haitian Human Rights Organizations, said, "We're ready for democracy. We're so ready that people in the countryside walked for miles and miles to vote. It's the [foreign] institutions here to accompany us that aren't able or willing to help us get there."[13]

Byzantine maneuvers by the OAS and the governments of Haiti and the United States would go on to replace Célestin, Préval's chosen candidate, with Martelly in the second round in February 2011. Martelly would win with an official count of 16.7 percent of registered voters.[14] By then the process would be so sullied that even the electoral council would refuse to ratify the election—a requirement for certification—but the Haitian government would approve it anyway.

※

Some camp dwellers found a silver lining during the wild week of anxiety and violence. At least they didn't have to worry about being evicted immediately, because the wave of camp closures was on temporary reprieve. "They're all engaged in other business; they've forgotten we're here," said Vania Dessables, the coordinator of a camp on Route de Frères. "But just wait till elections are over."

The election appeared to have had another beneficiary. The shutdown meant that, for once in the super-dense capital with almost no recreational spaces, boys had endless open streets on which to play soccer. Block after block was full of fleet-footed youth moving between the broken cinderblocks which served as goalposts.

On a foot tour of the still-smoldering town with Djab and Marco, I called out to one group of young soccer players, "This electoral craziness gave you your soccer field. You lucked out!"

"No way!" one called back. "We'd rather have free elections!"

25

We Will Never Fall
Asleep Forgetting

(Tales from Twelve Months Out)

January 2011

When Wilson came to the Toussaint Louverture Airport to collect me in his *taptap*, his news update was even more politically retrograde than usual. He told me jubilantly about the January 16 return of Duvalier after twenty-five years in France. The order-über-alles Wilson explained, "The thing about Duvalier, you had peace as long as you weren't in politics. If you didn't speak out, they wouldn't arrest you. You had no problem."

Baby Doc had likely returned, at least in part, to try to liberate $6 million in stolen assets from his frozen bank account in Switzerland. He appeared to have been trying to beat a Swiss law, dubbed the "Duvalier law," which was to go into effect on February 1, making it easier for that government to seize the funds. To fight for his loot, Duvalier would have had to go to Haiti and leave again without being prosecuted. Instead, the government charged him with corruption and embezzlement (though it is unclear if the case will ever go to trial). Duvalier's return was surely political, too, though the end goal was not yet clear. From the moment of his return, he defied house arrest in his sumptuous new digs to tool around town in a luxury automobile.

The peace of which Wilson spoke was the peace of the jail cell or the cemetery, as he himself immediately made clear. "Now you see that man standing there? He was one who got into politics and paid the price." He pointed to someone by the airport gates, who, as chance would have it, was my former colleague Robert (Bobby) Duval. Bobby had spent seventeen months in 1976 and 1977 in Fort Dimanche, a prison that few ever left except as corpses. He never knew of what crime he was accused, but it could have been anything. People were regularly imprisoned, tortured, or killed for literally any reason: not stopping in front of the palace for the 8 a.m. playing of the national anthem; protesting that a cow got into their garden, if that cow's owner had a friend in government; or dancing with a woman in whom a Tonton Macoute had an interest. (At least one of my neighbors in Millet Mountain was targeted for each of these reasons.) When an intensive campaign by Jimmy Carter won liberty for Bobby and several others, this normally burly man weighed less than one hundred pounds. He went on to found the League of Former Haitian Political Prisoners (Ligue des Anciens Prisonniers Politiques Haïtiens).

When I returned to the *taptap* after greeting Bobby, I tried to tell Wilson how wrong he was, but he protested with a logic I couldn't contest. "But compared to now, life was good. Everything wasn't so expensive. Food was cheaper. The state owned its own factories. The country hadn't deteriorated like it has. It's the people today who've left this country in rubble."

At forty-seven, Wilson had lived through thirteen years of the tyranny. However, the vagaries of memory and an odd interpretation of cause and effect converged to give him and many of his compatriots a favorable view of the traumatic history. One factor in this perspective was that government negligence in addressing earthquake victims' needs was so grave that any other leadership looked better, even a man who had committed crimes against humanity. Another was a faulty analysis of causality. Levels of poverty and social exclusion were not lower under Duvalier because his policies had been kinder, but because the tsunami of economic globalization that has everywhere ravaged the destitute majority struck as he was leaving office. An additional factor in the forgiving attitude was that 70 percent of Haiti's population was under thirty at the time of Duvalier's return, and simply had no knowledge of what the dictatorship had been like.

Grassroots and nonprofit organizations would go on to hold public colloquia featuring survivor testimony, film and photo exhibitions, and discussions, to educate those who hadn't lived under Duvalier and to reignite popular opposition among those who had. One program announcement would read, "We will never fall asleep forgetting."[1] (Those of us from the United States might also do well never to fall asleep forgetting that the U.S. government gave the Duvaliers almost unbroken financial and political support throughout their reign.) Bobby and others who survived abuse, and families of some who had been killed—nearly twenty plaintiffs in all—brought charges for torture, rape, and murder. Many prominent international groups joined Haitian human rights groups in supporting the cases. Later, the government would throw those charges out, claiming that the statute of limitations had expired.[2]

Wilson, Bobby, and I converged at the airport just after the nation had marked the first anniversary of the earthquake. Bad news stalked the land. Cholera was killing at least one person every thirty minutes.[3] With only 38 percent of the aid collected by relief and development organizations having been spent, the Disaster Accountability Project noted that "the leadership of the major disaster relief and aid organizations operating in Haiti allowed cholera to become a threat because they did not do their jobs."[4] Back in the United States, the Department of Homeland Security announced it would resume deportations of people with "serious criminal convictions." Given health and sanitation conditions in Haiti, especially in its deportee holding cells, human rights and refugee organizations sounded cries of alarm. Nevertheless, the United States proceeded. Among the many deported was Wildrick Guerrier, on January 20. In an overcrowded police holding cell, he quickly developed the telltale signs of cholera: severe diarrhea and vomiting. Despite well-known World Health Organization epidemic protocol and attempted interventions by a family member, the man was left untreated and died a few days later.[5] The United States said it would continue deportations.

Though Haitian and UN forces were sporadically using violence against demonstrators, citizens could still revel in the general absence of political repression. Soon, though, all bets might be off. During his campaign, Martelly had spoken of his desire to reinstate the army that Aristide had dismantled in 1995. Haiti already had a police force to maintain public order, and the country was not expected to go to war, so Martelly's wish could only mean one thing: reclaiming a tool in a toolbox of repression that past presidents had used to keep a firm grip on their power. Forces were already preparing for violence. In clandestine training camps, former soldiers and new inductees were learning a combination of military protocol, martial arts, and basic training.[6] Just who was funding them was a million-dollar question. Another was how much the new political configuration of Martelly, Duvalier, and a paramilitary might collaborate in persecuting opponents.

But this is where Haiti's long tradition of dissidence came in handy. When I lamented to Konpè Filo the probable outcome of the presidential elections, he smiled wryly and said, "Don't you worry." Filo—whom I'd first met in a safe house in Brooklyn in the early '80s, after he had been jailed, tortured, and exiled—knew something about the matter.

I was with Filo and another friend, who had also been arrested and tortured under a despot past, at a cozy, smoky Pétionville club. A compas band played sultry ballads in minor keys from days of yore, provoking delirium in the rum-filled couples who were tightly intertwined on the dance floor. Surreally enough, we were entering Carnival season. One distinctive feature of Carnivals during periods of political repression had been that veiled protest songs had passed as celebratory street music. All day and much of the night, bands and street revelers had sung the coded lyrics over and over, exciting the popular imagination. This night in Pétionville, the musicians worked into their show a Carnival chant from the Duvalier era. It was a call-and-response number where "Yes!"—in English—was the safe stand-in for "Let's bring him down!"

Beyond my two friends, I spotted others in the club who had been part of explosive rebellions. They had seen over and over how hope and determination could make a way from no way. They had lived long enough to know that no shiny future was around the corner, but neither was defeat, unless people chose to acquiesce. Being Haitians, they knew that that wasn't likely to happen.

When the band came back around to the refrain, they pumped their arms in the air and shouted: "Yes!"

Epilogue

Bringing It Back Home

The people this book depicts deserve a clean, happy ending. None is forthcoming. Yet. Here is where we leave some of our cast of characters.

To the naked eye, nothing has changed in Tibebe's life in the year since *twelve*. Her poverty is unrelentingly what Haitians call *kraze zo*, bone crushing. She still lives on the slab where her house used to sit. Her foot has never recovered from two injuries shortly after the earthquake, and her heart has been giving her trouble, too.

But something profound has shifted in Tibebe's life. Since the *event*, she has "been inspired," as she says, with a flood of poetry. In order to write that poetry down, and to be what she calls "inside society," Tibebe has long dreamed of literacy. So vocal and passionate has she been about her dream since we met fifteen years ago that I've latched onto it, too. Five different times over the years, we've pooled our resources to try to get her into classes. Each time something intervened, in successive episodes that together create a rough sketch of the hazards of being a Haitian woman without money or power. Once, the money granted by a U.S. foundation to start a literacy class for a group of rape survivors, which included Tibebe, mysteriously vanished. Once, a health emergency meant that Tibebe had to redirect the fees that had been given to pay a private tutor.

Once, a grassroots organization was poised to start a course, but just then the earthquake transpired. Once, she couldn't get to class because public transportation didn't go close to the locale, and it would have required a hefty walk that her injured foot couldn't sustain. Once, the high crime levels in a neighborhood where a program was starting kept her away. However, thanks to a new tutor and Tibebe's dedication, during our most recent visit she proudly produced a notebook. Sounding out each letter, she wrote in Creole: Beveli Bel. Then she penned, "Alas, there is much disappointment in life for someone that can't read." I whooped and gave her a high-five. Her smile was as bright as a fireworks display.

Like Tibebe, Suze is still busy responding to 911-type calls from women. And like Tibebe, Suze's work for rights and security for women and children has been broadly publicized in the United States. Some of that has been through big-name TV and magazines that the two women say published their words and images without their permission. They say they feel used and will no longer give interviews to foreigners they don't know.

Suze is, however, pleased with other international attention she has received, such as a human rights award from a women's center in the United States. When I delivered the news and a plaque on behalf of the center, she laughed shyly and said, "Who would have ever thought that Suze, a *timalerèz*, poor little woman, would one day be famous all over the United States?"

Famous or not, Suze still lives with three of her four surviving children and her granddaughter Timafi in the little shack she constructed out of sticks and a couple of tarps at the edge of the sewer in Martissant. By day, she worries about how she will feed everyone at least once. By night, when it's dry, she and the kids do their best to sleep crammed together on two small mattresses, despite the heat and bugs and fear of attackers. When it rains, they remain wide awake, sitting in the spot on one mattress where it leaks least.

The pain of never having found her eldest son after the earthquake seems to devastate Suze less now, but maybe she has just learned to mask it better. Her blood pressure has been dangerously high of late, and several lapses in medications when she didn't have the cash confined her to bed. She gets a little money from the two women's centers where she works and a little more from friends, but still her fate feels very bleak. She regularly gets a faraway look in her eyes and makes that clucking sound in her throat and says, "Honestly, I don't know what to do."

Djab's landlord repaired the apartment, so his wife and their son Karl, now a perpetual-motion three-year-old, returned to Port-au-Prince, and they all live together again. They still get by on Djab's short-term contracts with local nonprofits. Djab never mentions the holes left from January 12, when he lost his oldest son, his close friend Jean Anil Louis-Juste, and who knows how many others. Perhaps the holes have been filled somewhat by a new daughter, a vibrantly alive little tot named Peralta, after Charlemagne Péralte, leader of the rebel force against the 1915–34 U.S. occupation.

Sometimes, when Haiti's grim state weighs heavily, I stop in to visit Djab and his family. Peralta clambers onto my lap and we sit on the stoop in the little courtyard, which is still filled with rubble. Djab and Karl both have a lot to say, Djab on politics and little Karl on random observations that are not always intelligible, and everyone laughs a lot. Laughter flows freely in Port-au-Prince again, I've noticed.

Djab still raises hell with the Toussaint Louverture Front, campaigning for workers' unionizing efforts, protesting the latest violence by UN forces, and raising a ruckus about how the government has been sidelined by the international community. Members of the front talk endlessly about how the global capitalist economy is suffocating Haiti and everything else in its grasp. It doesn't matter whether anyone on high thought to invite them to take part in re-creating their homeland. They're fully engaged in the process, regardless.

⌘

This book remains unfinished because the end of the story is not yet written. This is true for the individuals discussed above, and it is true for Haiti. The natural disaster of *twelve* and the crises it has propelled mark a fulcrum in an as yet uncertain future.

Historian Rebecca Solnit tells us that the written Chinese word for "crisis" combines the ideograms for "disaster" and "opportunity."[1] This interpretation would not be big news to Suze, Tibebe, Djab, or many of their fellow countrymen and women. Labor organizer Yannick Etienne once told me, "This earthquake was one of the worst things that

Zan-7 (Ancestors) theater troupe at a right-to-housing rally in a displaced persons camp. Photograph by Ben Depp.

could have happened, but we have to turn it into something positive. We have to make sure that people are agents of change, and right now this is a good opportunity, positive in a political sense. There are so many things that can be done to shake up the traditional way things have always worked here."

Given the bleak landscape, the rest of us might be tempted to think that the Haitian people are losing their shot at the opportunities in the disaster. But any number of factors could reverse the recent downward trajectory of the majority's well-being and power. It may be that the final-drop phenomenon is at work. Many small gestures of noncompliance and resistance, some almost invisible and weightless on their own, are slowly rising. Who knows how or when the spread of the reservoir, from the accumulation of all those drops, may break the dam and change the landscape altogether?

But regardless of what changes social movements are able to force within their country, Haitians will remain trapped as long as the rules of global political and economic power remain unchanged. For that reason, how the disaster/opportunity dyad plays out is up to us, too. We all have an important role in it, for Haiti and our own country. Yannick said, "As Haiti alone, we can't get to the radical solutions that we need. It has to be a worldwide movement, in America, Europe, and Africa. This is why solidarity is so important. One hand has to give to the other."

Those of us from the United States carry an added burden because of the disproportionate power our country has over everyone else. People throughout the world have told me that the most useful action U.S. Americans can take is to work for change at home, because altering popular belief systems and government policies in this country will reverberate around the planet.

If for no other reason, we have to work together because we are all strapped to one globe. Martin Luther King, Jr., said that none of us is free until all of us are free. None of us is environmentally or economically or physically secure, either, until all of us are. We are all living the blowback of pollution, climate change, undemocratic global governance, corporate control, and war. None of us can save ourselves in isolation given the globalized, systemic nature of the problems. Personal or local acts alone won't cut it.

Ricot Jean-Pierre of the Haitian Platform to Advocate Alternative Development presented another way to think about this when I interviewed him a few weeks after the *event*.

How can we as peoples develop ways to support each other when we have common problems? How can we get together to show that the battle is against a common enemy, which is the source of poverty and marginalization? We want to create another world that's based on solidarity and equality between women and men, rich and poor, North and South—not just one above and another below being exploited. We need to develop other forms of cooperation between and among people and countries, with solidarity integrated into them. We need to learn how we each can complement and learn from the other.

Close collaboration between peoples from Haiti and other countries makes at least two additional contributions. First is what we get to learn from Haitians' long and powerful organizing experience that we can use to fortify our own. Haitians are superb teachers in how to refuse to believe the lies, refuse to be silenced, refuse to be intimidated, refuse to accept the unacceptable, refuse to acquiesce. They are masterful examples of the potential of imagining what we are told is unimaginable, and of changing what we are told can't be changed. They are vivid reminders that we don't have to have money or connections or influence to make a difference. We just need hope, conviction, and the knowledge that none of us is alone.

Second is that we become part of an alternative model of human relationship, in which we recognize that we are all sisters and brothers except for an accident of birth and all compatriots except for an accident of history. We get the chance to experience what Malians refer to as *maaya*, meaning both "being human" and "relationship to others." A common Malian saying is, "Life is a cord. We make the cord between ourselves, and you have to hold on to it. Don't drop the cord." What can we do so that we don't forget this lesson? How can we take the concepts of interdependence and unity further so that people dedicate themselves to good global citizenry beyond the catastrophe, from New Orleans to Haiti and beyond?

Together, we have the chance to disprove Margaret Thatcher's famous dictum that "there is no alternative" and create another world. Transformation is afoot in Haiti, just as it has been across the United States with Occupy, the Middle East with the Arab Spring, Europe with anti-austerity protests, and in a surge of movements all over, where people know that we are not condemned to live in the world as it is. We are many and everywhere and energized, those who know that the time to be on the right side of history is now.[2]

※

I was struggling with final edits of this manuscript when in came an e-mail from Ricot to encourage me along. He concluded his note with, "We are a people who has liberty written in our blood, and we'll continue showing the world the path to take to be liberated from slavery. Because this isn't the battle of Haitian people only, but of all peoples. We will stand firm so that everyone on the planet can find the light to illuminate the route of liberty."

And then he signed off: "*Kenbe fèm*." Hold strong.

Notes

Introduction

1. "Haiti: The Politics of Rebuilding," YouTube video, 23:26, from *Fault Lines*, Al Jazeera, posted by "AlJazeeraEnglish," February 11, 2010, http://www.youtube.com/watch?v=AuUt12usDVs.

2. Deborah Sontag, "Countless Lost Limbs Alter Life in Haiti's Ruins," *New York Times* online, February 22, 2010, http://www.nytimes.com/2010/02/23/world/americas/23amputee.html?pagewanted=all.

3. Abhijit Bhattacharjee and Roberta Lossio, "Terms of Reference," in *Evaluation of Ocha Emergency Response to the Haiti Earthquake* (UN Office for the Coordination of Humanitarian Affairs, July 28, 2010), 1, http://ochanet.unocha.org/p/Documents/Evaluation%20of%20OCHA%20Response%20to%20the%20Haiti%20Earthquake.pdf.

4. Ida Minerva Tarbell, *A Short Life of Napoleon Bonaparte, Issue 1* (New York: S. S. McClure, 1895), 85.

5. Carl A. Brasseaux, quoted in Jordan Flaherty, *Floodlines: Community and Resistance from Katrina to the Jena Six* (Chicago: Haymarket Books, 2010), 260.

6. Jeremy Brecher, Tim Costello, and Brendan Smith, *Globalization from Below* (Cambridge, MA: South End Press, 2000), 23.

7. Sukumar Muralidharan, "Some 'Heresies' of Development: An Interview with Professor Roberto Mangabeira Unger," *Frontline: India's National Magazine*, September 1-14, 2001.

2. What We Have, We Share

1. Rory Carroll and Inigo Gilmore, "Miracle Survivor Found as Haiti Rescue Teams Ordered to Stand Down," *Guardian* online, January 23, 2010, http://www.guardian.co.uk/world/2010/jan/23/haiti-earthquake-miracle-survivor-rescue.

2. UN Office of the Coordination of Humanitarian Affairs, Advocacy and Visual Media Unit, *Haiti Earthquake Population Movements out of Port-au-Prince Map* (New York, February 21, 2010).

3. Pearl of the Antilles

1. Remy Sietchiping, UN-HABITAT, *The Poor, Urban Planning and Adaptation to Climate Change: Tales of Haitian Cities* (lecture slide show, Fifth World Bank Urban Research Symposium, Marseille, France, 2009), 7, http://siteresources.worldbank.org/INTURBANDEVELOPMENT/ Resources/336387-1256566800920/sietchiping.pdf.

2. Emile Nau, Ducis Viard, and Eugène Nau, *Histoire des caciques d'Haïti* [History of the Caciques of Haiti] (Port-au-Prince: Éditions Panorama, 1894), quoted in Carolyn Fick, *The Making of Haiti: The Saint Domingue Revolution from Below* (Knoxville: University of Tennessee Press, 1990), 288.

3. The French introduced the highly labor-intensive sugarcane to the French West Indies. This led the colonists to increase the number of Africans they brought into the region each year to roughly thirty-seven thousand. Fick, *Making of Haiti*, 22.

4. Paul Farmer, *The Uses of Haiti* (Monroe, ME: Common Courage Press, 2005); Peter Hallward, *Damming the Flood: Haiti, Aristide, and the Politics of Containment* (London: Verso, 2007); and Alex Dupuy, *Jean-Bertrand Aristide, the International Community and Haiti* (New York: Rowman & Littlefield, 2007).

5. Matthew J. Smith, *Red and Black in Haiti: Radicalism, Conflict, and Political Change, 1934–1957* (Chapel Hill: University of North Carolina Press, 2009), 8–10; and Mary A. Renda, *Taking Haiti: Military Occupation and the Culture of U.S. Imperialism, 1915–1940* (Chapel Hill: University of North Carolina Press, 2001), 34.

6. UN Development Programme, *Human Development Report 2011: Human Development Statistical Annex* (New York, 2011), 129, http://hdr.undp.org/en/media/HDR_2011_EN_ Tables.pdf.

7. Ibid., 129.

8. Central Intelligence Agency, *The World Factbook*, "Haiti," https://www.cia.gov/library/ publications/the-world-factbook/geos/ha.html (accessed November 1, 2011).

9. International Fund for Agricultural Development, *Enabling the Rural Poor to Overcome Poverty in Haiti* (Rome, 2008), 2, http://www.ifad.org/operations/projects/regions/pl/factsheet/ haiti_e.pdf.

10. Library of Congress, Federal Research Division, *Country Profile: Haiti* (May 2006), 11, http://lcweb2.loc.gov/frd/cs/profiles/Haiti.pdf.

11. UNICEF, *UNICEF Humanitarian Action: Partnering for Children in Emergencies* (2010), 117, www.unicef.org/infobycountry/files/HAR_Mid-Year_Review_2010.pdf; and UN, *Human Development Report 2011*, 160.

12. Concern Worldwide, International Food Policy Research Institute, and Welthungerlife, *2011 Global Hunger Index* (Washington, DC, 2011), 16, http://www.ifpri.org/sites/default/files/ publications/ghi11.pdf; and UN, *Human Development Report 2011*, 129.

4. Maroon Man

1. Albert Thrasher, *"On to New Orleans!" Louisiana's Heroic Slave Revolt* (New Orleans: Cypress Press, 1995). Cited in Jordan Flaherty, *Floodlines: Community and Resistance from Katrina to the Jena Six* (Chicago: Haymarket Books, 2010).

2. James C. Scott, *Weapons of the Weak: Everyday Forms of Peasant Resistance* (New Haven, CT: Yale University Press, 1985).

3. For extended discussions of U.S. government relations with the Duvaliers see John R. Ballard, *Upholding Democracy: The United States Military Campaign in Haiti, 1994–1997* (Westport, CT: Praeger, 1998), 35–36; James Ferguson, *Papa Doc, Baby Doc: Haiti and the Duvaliers*

(Oxford: Basil Blackwell, 1988); and Michel-Rolph Trouillot, *Haiti, State against Nation: The Origins and Legacy of Duvalierism* (New York: Monthly Review Press, 1990).

4. Frei Betto, interview by Tarso Luis Ramos, "Frei Betto's Brazil," *Europe solidaire sans frontières* online, September 2006, http://www.europe-solidaire.org/spip.php?page=article_impr&id_article=3695.

5. Arundhati Roy, "Confronting Empire," presentation, World Social Forum, Porto Alegre, Brazil, January 27, 2003.

6. See, for example, Paul Farmer, *The Uses of Haiti* (Monroe, ME: Common Courage Press, 2006); Tim Weiner, "Haitian Ex-Paramilitary Leader Confirms CIA Relationship," *New York Times* online, December 3, 1995; Allan Nairn, "Haiti under the Gun: How U.S.-Backed Paramilitaries Rule through Fear," *Nation*, January 8-15, 1996, 11; John Kifner, "Haitians Ask If U.S. Had Ties to Attaché," *New York Times*, October 6, 1994; Allan Nairn, "Our Man in Fraph—Behind Haiti's Paramilitaries," *Nation*, October 24, 1994; and Marcia Myers, "Claiming CIA Ties, Haitian Sues over Detention in U.S.: Paramilitary Leader Had Opposed Return of President Aristide," *Baltimore Sun* online, December 12, 1995.

7. Dan Coughlin and Kim Ives, "WikiLeaks Haiti: Let Them Live on $3 a Day," *Nation* online, June 1, 2011, http://www.thenation.com/article/161057/wikileaks-haiti-let-them-live-3-day.

8. Mimi Lytje, "Debt Cancellation for Haiti: An Important Victory but an Unfinished Agenda," Jubilee USA Network, August 2009, http://www.jubileeusa.org/fileadmin/user_upload/Resources/Haiti/Haiti_Policy_Update_August_2009.pdf.

9. "IMF Executive Board Cancels Haiti's Debt and Approves New Three-Year Program to Support Reconstruction and Economic Growth," press release by International Monetary Fund, no. 10/299, July 21, 2010, http://www.imf.org/external/np/sec/pr/2010/pr10299.htm.

10. Yves Dejean, "Creole and Education in Haiti," in *The Haitian Creole Language: History, Structure, Use, and Education*, ed. Arthur K. Spears and Carole Berotte Joseph (Lexington Books, 2010).

11. Lise Marie Dejean, "Minister of the Status and Rights of Women," in Beverly Bell, *Walking on Fire* (Ithaca, NY: Cornell University Press, 2001), 162.

5. We Will Carry You On

1. Witnessed by Carolle Charles, as reported in an e-mail to author, June 11, 2012.

2. Patrick Bellegarde-Smith, *Haiti: The Breached Citadel* (Boulder, CO: Westview Press, 1990), 83.

3. Myriam J. A. Chancy, *Framing Silences: Revolutionary Novels by Haitian Women* (New Brunswick, NJ: Rutgers University Press, 1997), 40.

4. Madeleine Bouchereau, *Haïti et ses femmes* [Haiti and Its Women] (Port-au-Prince: Presse Libre, 1957), referenced in Chancy, *Framing Silences*, 39. An e-mail from Chancy also cited evidence from "Voix des femmes" [The Women's Voice] circa 1929-33 and anecdotal information from interviews of elder Haitian women. E-mail to author, May 28, 2012.

5. Carolle Charles, "Gender and Politics in Contemporary Haiti: The Duvalierist State, Transnationalism, and the Emergence of a New Feminism, 1980-1990," *Feminist Studies* 21, no. 1 (Spring 1995): 147.

6. Ibid., 135-58.

7. Analysis adapted from Charles, "Gender and Politics," 148-52.

8. See, for example, Marie M. B. Racine and Kathy Ogle, *Like the Dew That Waters the Grass: Words from Haitian Women* (Washington, DC: EPICA, 1999); Beverly Bell, *Walking on Fire: Haitian Women's Stories of Survival and Resistance* (Ithaca, NY: Cornell University Press, 2001), and *Poto Mitan*, Tèt Ansanm Productions, directed by Renée Bergan and Mark Schuller, 2009.

6. You Can't Eat Okra with One Finger

1. Camille Chalmers, Marie Carmelle Fils-Aimé, and Sony Estéus, "Haiti: After the Catastrophe, What Are the Perspectives? Statement by the Coordinating Committee of Progressive

Organisations" (open statement, Port-au-Prince, January 27, 2010), http://mrzine.monthlyreview.
org/2010/haiti040210.html.

2. The exact figure was 90,997. UN Office for the Coordination of Humanitarian Affairs,
Advocacy and Visual Media Unit, *Haiti Earthquake Population Movements out of Port-au-Prince
Map* (New York, February 21, 2010).

7. Fragile as a Crystal

1. United States Geological Service, "Magnitude 7.0—Haiti Region 2010 January 12: Summary," last modified January 28, 2012, http://earthquake.usgs.gov/earthquakes/eqinthenews/
2010/us2010rja6/#summary.

8. Children of the Land

1. The Central Intelligence Agency claims 66 percent, while Haitian peasant farmer organizations typically use a figure of 80 percent. Central Intelligence Agency, *The World Factbook*,
"Central American and the Caribbean: Haiti," last updated October 21, 2011, https://www.cia.
gov/library/publications/the-world-factbook/geos/ha.html.

2. Nathanial Gronewold, "No Shortage of Blame as Haiti Struggles to Feed Itself," *New York
Times* online, November 19, 2011, http://www.nytimes.com/gwire/2009/11/19/19greenwire-
no-shortage-of-blame-as-haiti-struggles-to-fee-21377.html?pagewanted=all.

3. Government of the Republic of Haiti, *Haiti: Executive Summary of the PDNA after the
Earthquake, Sector Evaluation of Damage, Losses and Needs* (Port-au-Prince, 2010), 5, http://
siteresources.worldbank.org/INTLAC/Resources/PDNAExecutiveSummary.pdf.

4. Pal Sletten and Willy Egset, *Poverty in Haiti* (FAFO, 2004), 11, www.fafo.no/pub/
rapp/755/755.pdf.

5. World Health Organization, *World Health Statistics 2010* (Geneva, 2010), 146–47, www.
who.int/whosis/whostat/EN_WHS10_Full.pdf.

6. Organization of American States, *Modernization of Cadastre and Land Rights Infrastructure in Haiti: A Rapid and Inclusive Approach* (March 2010), 4, http://www.ifud.org/wp-content/
uploads/2010/05/Modernization-of-Cadastre-and-Land-Rights-Infrastructure-in-Haiti-Project-
Proposal-v9-2010.pdf.

7. UN Conference on Trade and Development, *Rebuilding Haiti: A New Approach to International Cooperation*, UN Conference on Trade and Development Policy Update, no. 13 (March
2010), 1, http://www.unctad.org/en/docs/presspb20103_en.pdf.

8. International Monetary Fund, *Haiti: Selected Issues, IMF Staff Country Report No. 01/04*
(January 2001), 43–44, http://www.imf.org/external/pubs/ft/scr/2001/cr0104.pdf.

9. Allan Ebert, "Porkbarreling Pigs in Haiti: North American 'Swine Aid' an Economic Disaster for Haitian Peasants," *Multinational Monitor* online, vol. 6, no. 18 (December 1985).

10. World Food Programme, "Haiti," http://www.wfp.org/countries/Haiti/Overview (accessed June 13, 2012).

11. Concern Worldwide, International Food Policy Research Institute, and Welthungerlife,
2011 Global Hunger Index (Washington, DC, 2011), 17, http://www.ifpri.org/sites/default/
files/publications/ghi11.pdf; and UN Office for the Coordination of Humanitarian Affairs Haiti,
"Cross-Cutting Issues," *Humanitarian Bulletin* (September 21–October 18, 2011), 3, http://
reliefweb.int/sites/reliefweb.int/files/resources/OCHA%20Haiti_Humanitarian%20Bulletin_
11_ENG.pdf.

12. Plate-forme Haïtienne de Plaidoyer pour un Développement Alternatif [Haitian Platform
to Advocate Alternative Development] et al., "Forum Social Mondial pour la Souveraineté Alimentaire: Appel des Mouvements Sociaux Haïtiens" [World Social Forum for Food Sovereignty:
Call to Haitian Social Movements], Port-au-Prince, January 2011.

9. Grains and Guns

1. See, for example, Patrick Elie, "Aristide's War on Drugs," *Washington Post*, August 15, 1992; and Dennis Bernstein and Howard Levine, "The CIA's Haitian Connection," *San Francisco Bay Guardian*, November 3, 1993.

2. Barack Obama, "Why Haiti Matters," *Newsweek*, January 25, 2010, 24.

3. Ansel Herz, "WikiLeaks Cables Reveal: U.S. Worried about International Criticism of Post-Quake Troop Deployment," *Haiti Liberté* online, June 15–21, 2011, http://www.haiti-liberte. com/archives/volume4–48/U.S.%20Worried%20about%20International.asp; U.S. Embassy of Haiti, "TFHA01: Embassy Port au Prince Earthquake Sitrep as of 1800 Day 4" (cable to White House, Port-au-Prince, January 16, 2010), Reference ID: 10PORTAUPRINCE50, http://wikileaks.org/cable/2010/01/10PORTAUPRINCE50.html; and U.S. Embassy of Haiti, "TFHA01: Embassy Port-au-Prince Earthquake Sitrep as of 1600, Day 8" (cable to White House, Port-au-Prince, January 19, 2010), Reference ID: 10PORTAUPRINCE66, http://wikileaks.org/ cable/2010/01/10PORTAUPRINCE66.html.

4. U.S. Embassy of Haiti, "Demarche Request: Haiti: U.S. Humanitarian Assistance to Haiti" (cable to White House, Port-au-Prince, January 22, 2010), Reference ID: 10STATE6918, http://wikileaks.org/cable/2010/01/10STATE6918.html.

5. Ianthe Jeanne Dugan and Corey Dade, "Medical Care for Haitians Falls Short, Group Warns," *Wall Street Journal* online, January 22, 2010, http://online.wsj.com/article/SB1000142 4052748704320104575015141368581502.html; and John Kruzel, "U.S. Forces in Haiti to Grow to 20,000," American Forces Press Service, January 21, 2010, http://www.defense.gov/news/ newsarticle.aspx?id=57661.

6. "Doctors Without Borders Plane with Lifesaving Medical Supplies Diverted Again from Landing in Haiti," press release by Doctors Without Borders, January 19, 2010, http://www.doc torswithoutborders.org/press/release.cfm?id=4176.

7. Ansel Herz, "WikiLeaks Haiti: The Earthquake Cables," *Nation* online, June 15, 2011, http://www.thenation.com/article/161459/wikileaks-haiti-earthquake-cables.

8. Medical Education Cooperation with Cuba (MEDICC), *Field Notes from Haiti: After the Earthquake* (2010), http://medic.org/ns/documents/MEDICC_Field_Notes_from_Haiti.pdf, 3.

9. Herz, "WikiLeaks Haiti"; and U.S. Embassy of Haiti, "Embassy Port au Prince Earthquake Sitrep as of 1800, Day 8" (cable to White House, Port-au-Prince, January 21, 2010), Reference ID: 10PORTAUPRINCE70, http://wikileaks.org/cable/2010/01/10PORTAUPRINCE70.html.

10. U.S. Embassy of Haiti, "Embassy Port au Prince Earthquake Sitrep as of 1800, Day 9" (cable to White House, Port-au-Prince, January 22, 2010), Reference ID: #10PORTAUPRINCE74, http://wikileaks.org/cable/2010/01/10PORTAUPRINCE74.html. See also Herz, "WikiLeaks Cables Reveal."

11. James M. Roberts and Ray Walser, *American Leadership Necessary to Assist Haiti after Devastating Earthquake*, web memo, Heritage Foundation, no. 2754, January 13, 2010, http:// s3.amazonaws.com/thf_media/2010/pdf/wm_2754.pdf.

12. U.S. Embassy of Haiti, "Why We Need Continuing MINUSTAH Presence in Haiti" (cable to White House, Port-au-Prince, October 1, 2008), Reference ID: 08PORTAUPRINCE1381, http://wikileaks.org/cable/2008/10/08PORTAUPRINCE1381.html.

13. Herz, "WikiLeaks Haiti."

14. Aislinn Laing and Tom Leonard, "US Accused of 'Occupying' Haiti as Troops Flood In," *Telegraph* online, August 5, 2011, http://www.telegraph.co.uk/news/worldnews/centralameri caandthecaribbean/haiti/7020908/US-accused-of-occupying-Haiti-as-troops-flood-in.html.

15. Kenneth H. Merten, "On-the-Record Briefing: Kenneth H. Merten, Ambassador to Haiti," U.S. Department of State, February 12, 2010, http://reliefweb.int/node/345174.

16. UN High Commissioner for Refugees, *Driven by Desperation: Transactional Sex as a Survival Strategy in Port-au-Prince Camps* (May 2011), 16, http://www.unhcrwashington.org/ atf/cf/%7Bc07eda5e-ac71–4340–8570–194d98bdc139%7D/SGBV-HAITI-STUDY-MAY2011. PDF.

17. UN, "Emergency Shelter and Sanitation Are Main Priorities Two Months after Quake," *UN News Centre* online, March 12, 2010, http://www.un.org/News/dh/infocus/haiti/haiti_quake_update.shtml.

18. Institute for Justice and Democracy in Haiti, Bureau des Avocats Internationaux [International Lawyers' Office], Lamp for Haiti, Earle Mack School of Law at Drexel University, *Neglect in the Encampments: Haiti's Second Wave Humanitarian Disaster* (Washington, DC, March 23, 2010), http://ijdh.org/archives/10671.

19. UN Office of the Special Envoy for Haiti, *Has Aid Changed? Channeling Assistance to Haiti before and after the Earthquake* (June 2011), 20, http://reliefweb.int/sites/reliefweb.int/files/resources/has_aid_changed_en.pdf; Oxfam International, *Predictable Funding for Humanitarian Emergencies: A Challenge to Donors* (October 24, 2005), www.oxfam.org/en/policy/bn051024-CERF-predictablefunding; and Thalif Deen, "UN, Relief Groups Fear Aid Falling Behind Pledges," *IPS News*, January 3, 2005, http://ipsnews.net/print.asp?idnews=26894.

20. Calculated based on USAID and UN data from January 2010. Yesica Fisch and Martha Mendoza, "Haiti Government Gets 1 Penny of US Quake Dollar," Associated Press, January 27, 2010, http://www.boston.com/business/articles/2010/01/27/haiti_govt_gets_only_1_cent_of_every_us_aid_dollar/.

21. Jonathan Katz, "Billions for Haiti, a Criticism for Every Dollar," Associated Press, March 6, 2010.

22. AFP writers, "Ecuador President Blasts Aid 'Imperialism' on Haiti Trip," *Laredo Sun* online, January 30, 2010, http://www.laredosun.us/notas.asp?id=3475.

23. George Russell, "With Haiti in Ruins, Some U.N. Relief Workers Live Large on 'Love Boat,'" *Fox News* online, April 8, 2010, http://www.foxnews.com/world/2010/04/08/haiti-ruins-relief-workers-live-large-love-boat/.

24. UN Office for the Coordination of Humanitarian Affairs, *Haiti Earthquake Situation Report #13* (January 25, 2010), 3–4, http://reliefweb.int/sites/reliefweb.int/files/resources/115D7B69E7070F56492576B7001ABCA2-Full_Report.pdf.

25. Oxfam International, *Tèt Ansanm Pou Yon Nouvèl Ayiti: Reflections on the Reconstruction of Haiti* (Port-au-Prince, March 5, 2010).

26. International Donors Conference Towards a New Future for Haiti, "Over US $5 Billion Pledged for Haiti's Recovery," March 31, 2010, http://www.haiticonference.org/story.html.

27. Katz, "Billions for Haiti."

28. Tim Padgett, "The Failed State That Keeps Failing: Quake-Ravaged Haiti Still without a Government," *Time World* online, September 10, 2011, http://globalspin.blogs.time.com/2011/09/10/the-failed-state-that-keeps-failing-quake-ravaged-haiti-still-without-a-government/; See also, for example, Gerald Helman and Steven Ratner, "Saving Failed States," *Foreign Policy* 89 (2002): 3; Robert Rotberg, ed., *When States Fail: Causes and Consequences* (Princeton, NJ: Princeton University Press, 2004); Tim Weiner, "Life Is Hard and Short in Haiti's Bleak Villages," *New York Times* online, March 14, 2004, http://www.nytimes.com/2004/03/14/world/life-is-hard-and-short-in-haiti-s-bleak-villages.html?pagewanted=all&src=pm; and Felix Salmon, "Don't Give Money to Haiti," Reuters online, January 15, 2010, http://blogs.reuters.com/felix-salmon/2010/01/15/dont-give-money-to-haiti/.

29. Fund for Peace, "The Failed States Index 2011," http://www.fundforpeace.org/global/?q=fsi-grid2011 (accessed June 16, 2011).

30. David Brooks, "The Underlying Tragedy," *New York Times* online, January 14, 2010, http://www.nytimes.com/2010/01/15/opinion/15brooks.html?_r=1.

31. International Donors Conference, "US $5 Billion Pledged."

32. Jordan Flaherty, *Floodlines: Community and Resistance from Katrina to the Jena Six* (Chicago: Haymarket Books, 2010), 81.

33. Brandon Steward, "Video of the Week: New Orleans School Choice Experiment," *Foundry* online, Heritage Foundation, August 19, 2010, http://blog.heritage.org/2010/08/19/video-of-the-week-the-new-orleans-school-choice-experiment/.

34. Milton Friedman, "The Promise of Vouchers," *Wall Street Journal* online, December 5, 2005, http://online.wsj.com/article/SB113374845791113764.html?mod=2-1239-1.

35. Katz, "Billions for Haiti."

36. The World Bank, "International Community, World Bank Commit to Haiti's Long-Term Recovery," March 31, 2010, http://go.worldbank.org/CF42HJ40F0.

37. Martin Kaste, "After Quake in Haiti, Who's the Boss?" NPR online, March 31, 2010, http://www.npr.org/templates/story/story.php?storyId=125328026.

38. Government of the Republic of Haiti, "Action Plan for the National Recovery and Development of Haiti" (March 2010), 5, 9, 27, www.haiticonference.org/Haiti_Action_Plan_ENG.pdf.

39. Interim Haiti Recovery Commission, "About the Board," http://en.cirh.ht/about-us/about-the-board.html (accessed June 6, 2012).

40. Réné Préval, *Order* (Republic of Haiti, 2010), en.cirh.ht/files/pdf/ihrc_decree_20100421.pdf.

41. Haiti Support Group, "Beyond Relief, Beyond Belief," *Haiti Support Group Briefing*, no. 69 (January 2012), 1.

42. Interim Haiti Recovery Commission, http://en.cirh.ht/ (accessed June 6, 2012).

43. Government of the Republic of Haiti, "Action Plan," 53, www.haiticonference.org/Haiti_Action_Plan_ENG.pdf.

44. Includes grants, contracts, and in-kind donations such as commodities and services from the U.S. government. KPMG, LLP, *Save the Children Federation, Inc. Financial Statements* (December 31, 2010), 3, http://www.savethechildren.org/atf/cf/%7B9def2ebe-10ae-432c-9bd0-df91d2eba74a%7D/FINANCIAL%20STATEMENT%2012.31.2010.PDF; and Catholic Relief Services, *2010 Annual Report* (2010), 40, http://crs.org/2010-annual-report/.

45. USAID, "Where Does USAID's Money Go?" March 31, 2010, http://www.usaid.gov/policy/budget/money/WhereDoesUSAIDsMoneyGoFY2010Mar31.xlsx; and KPMG, LLP, *Consolidated Financial Statements, World Vision, Inc. and Affiliates September 30, 2009 and 2010* (2010), http://www.worldvision.org/resources.nsf/Main/annual-review-2010-resources/$FILE/AR_2010AuditedFinancialStatement.pdf.

46. Katz, "Billions for Haiti."

47. World Bank, Caribbean Country Management Unit, *Haiti: Social Resilience and State Fragility, A Country Social Analysis* (April 27, 2006), v, http://siteresources.worldbank.org/EXTSOCIALDEV/Resources/3177394-1168615404141/SocialResilienceandStateFragilityinHaiti-ACountrySocialAnalysis.pdf.

48. "Readout of President Clinton's Meeting with the NGO Community working in Haiti," press release by Clinton Foundation, March 8, 2010, http://haiti.clintonfoundation.org/news_detail.php?id=93&source=1.

49. "Liste actualisée des ONG actives en Haïti" [Updated List of Active NGOs in Haiti], Ministère de la Planification et de la Coopération Externe [Ministry of Planning and External Cooperation], October 22, 2011, http://www.mpce.gouv.ht/.

10. The Ones Who Must Decide

1. Antonal Mortimé, interview with Jonas Scherrens, *Broederlijk Delen*, January 25, 2010.

2. "The Position of Various Public Organizations and Institutions after the Catastrophe of January 12," e-mailed to Beverly Bell, Port-au-Prince, February 13, 2010.

3. GARR et al., "Position des mouvements sociaux haïtiens sur le processus de 'reconstruction' d'Haïti" [Haitian Social Movements' Position on the Process of the "Reconstruction" of Haiti], Plate-forme Haïtienne de Plaidoyer pour un Développement Alternatif [Haitian Platform to Advocate Alternative Development], March 18, 2010, http://www.papda.org/article.php3?id_article=625.

4. Jean Valéry Vital-Herne, "To Whom It May Concern," Port-au-Prince, March 19, 2010, quoted in *Haitian Led Reconstruction & Development: A Compilation of Recommendation*

Documents from Several Haitian Civil Society and Diaspora Conferences, Organizations and Coalitions, prepared by a Washington, DC–based ad hoc Haiti advocacy coalition (March 29, 2010), 14, http://ajws.org/assets/uploaded_documents/haitian_led_reconstruction_and_development.pdf.

5. Groupe d'Appui aux Réfugiés et Repatriés [Support Group for Refugees and the Repatriated] et al., "Pozisyon Divès Òganizasyon sou Konjonkti a" [Position of Multiple Organizations on the Current Context], Port-au-Prince, July 24, 2011.

6. Termes de référence pour l'évaluation des besoins post désastre (PDNA1) après le tremblement du terre de 12 Janvier 2010 en Haïti [Terms of Reference for the Post-disaster Evaluation of Needs (PDNA1) following the January 12, 2010, Earthquake in Haiti], February 15, 2010.

7. Government of the Republic of Haiti, *Action Plan for National Recovery and Development of Haiti: Key Initiatives for the Future* (Port-au-Prince, March 2010), 3, http://www.haiticonference.org/Haiti_Action_Plan_ENG.pdf.

8. Rudolph Henri Boulos et al., *Strategic Plan for National Salvation: An Intergenerational Pact of Shared Progress and Prosperity, English Summary* (Port-au-Prince, February 7, 2010), www.haitipolicy.org/Rencontre/Menu/Plan.html.

9. "The Position of Haitian Social Movements on the PDNA Process and the Process of Reconstruction in Our Country," Port-au-Prince, March 13, 2010.

10. Plate-forme Femmes Citoyennes Haïti Solidaire [Solidarity Platform of Haitian Women Citizens], *Pour que l'égalité entre les femmes et les hommes soit enfin intégrée à la vision et aux plans d'action pour une nouvelle Haïti* [In Order for Equality between Women and Men to Be Finally Integrated into the Vision and Action Plans for a New Haiti] March 17, 2010, http://www.oregand.ca/files/femmescitoyenneshaitisolidaire-doc-de-travail—17.03.2010.pdf.

11. Coordination Nationale de Plaidoyer pour les Droits des Femmes, CONAP [National Coordination for Advocacy on Women's Rights], "Haïti—un processus sans véritable légitimité" [Haiti—a Process without Real Legitimacy], March 22, 2010, http://www.oregand.ca/veille/2010/03/pdna-processus-sans-legitimite.html.

11. Our Bodies Are Shaking Now

1. Nick Stratton, an ally of the group COURAGE, wrote, "Virtually no statistics on male rape and/or male prostitution/transactional sex in Haiti exist, whereas many organizations, institutions, and the ministry for the feminine condition are all working on rape of women and girls. The only victims of pedophilia in Haiti who report are girls, because male/boy victims are afraid of being seen as a *masisi* [hate speech for "gay"], since victims of sexual violence are penetrated the majority of the time. For male adults who are raped, they do not report because their masculinity will be questioned. If you add poverty in the camps into the equation, the result is as serious as for girls and women, except with an added layer of stigmatization ('intersectionality' in black feminist theory)." Nick relayed a call from the group COURAGE for research and "action amongst scholars, activists, and Americans in solidarity with Haitians." Nick Stratton, e-mail, June 16, 2012.

2. Joseph Guyler Delva and Marine Hass, "UN Chief Urges Donors to Keep Haiti Funds Flowing," Reuters online, March 14, 2010, http://www.reuters.com/article/2010/03/15/us-quake-haiti-un-idUSTRE62D28120100315.

3. Claudia Felten-Biermann, "Gender and Natural Disaster: Sexualized Violence and the Tsunami," in Society for an International Development, *Development* (2006), 82–86; UN High Commissioner on Refugees, *Sexual Violence against Refugees: Guidelines on Prevention and Response* (Geneva, 1995); and the New York City Alliance against Sexual Assault, "Factsheets: Katrina, Natural Disasters and Sexual Violence," http://www.svfreenyc.org/research_factsheet_111.html (accessed October 28, 2010).

4. Mac McClelland "I'm Gonna Need You to Fight Me on This: How Violent Sex Helped Ease My PTSD," *Good* online, June 27, 2001, http://www.good.is/posts/how-violent-sex-helped-ease-my-ptsd.

5. Dave Gibson, "Rape Is the Order of the Day in Haiti . . . as It Always Has Been," *Examiner* online, February 7, 2010, http://www.examiner.com/article/rape-is-the-order-of-the-day-haiti-as-it-always-has-been?render=print.

6. See, for example, Jordan Flaherty, "Lies in the News: The Flood and Its Aftermath," in *Floodlines: Community and Resistance from Katrina to the Jena Six* (Chicago: Haymarket Books, 2010), 31–51; and Rebecca Solnit, "Reconstructing the Story of the Storm: Hurricane Katrina at Five," *Nation* online, August 26, 2010, http://www.thenation.com/article/154168/reconstructing-story-storm-hurricane-katrina-five.

7. John Burnett, "More Stories Emerge of Rapes in Post-Katrina Chaos," NPR online, December 21, 2005, http://www.npr.org/templates/story/story.php?storyId=5063796; Alec Gifford, "40 Rapes Reported in Hurricane Katrina, Rita Aftermath," WSDU online, December 23, 2005, http://www.wdsu.com/news/5627087/detail.html; "Press Release: Beaten, Sexually Assaulted, and Living in a Hurricane Evacuation Shelter or a Makeshift Tent City," press release by Louisiana Coalition against Domestic Violence, September 13, 2005, http://www.ncdsv.org/images/BeatenSexuallyAssaultedLivingHurricane.pdf; and Lucinda Marshall, "Were Women Raped in New Orleans?" *Counter Currents* online, September 15, 2005, http://www.counter currents.org/us-marshall150905.htm.

8. See Brian Thevenot and Gordon Russel, "Rape. Murder. Gun Fights," *Times Picayune*, September 26, 2005, A1, http://www.nola.com/katrina/pages/092605/0926PAGEA01.pdf; Brian Thevenot, "Myth-Making in New Orleans," *American Journal Review* online, http://ajr.org/article.asp?id=3998; and David Carr, "More Horrible Than Truth: News Reports," *New York Times* online, September 19, 2005, http://www.nytimes.com/2005/09/19/business/media/19carr.html?pagewanted=all.

9. Susan Brownmiller, *Against Our Will: Men, Women, and Rape* (New York: Ballantine Books, 1975), 31.

10. See, for example, Tim Weiner, "Haitian Ex-Paramilitary Leader Confirms CIA Relationship," *New York Times*, December 3, 1995; Allan Nairn, "Haiti under the Gun: How U.S.-Backed Paramilitaries Rule through Fear," *Nation*, January 8–15, 1996, 11; John Kifner, "Haitians Ask If U.S. Had Ties to Attaché," *New York Times*, October 6, 1994; Allan Nairn, "Our Man in Fraph— Behind Haiti's Paramilitaries," *Nation*, October 24, 1994; and Marcia Myers, "Claiming CIA Ties, Haitian Sues over Detention in U.S.: Paramilitary Leader Had Opposed Return of President Aristide," *Baltimore Sun*, December 12, 1995.

11. Centre Haïtien de Recherches et d'Actions pour la Promotion Féminine [Haitian Center for Research and Action for the Promotion of Women], *Violences exercées sur les femmes et les filles en Haïti* [Violence against Girls and Women in Haiti] (Port-au-Prince: Les Imprimeries Henri Dechamps, November 1996), 59. For more information see Beverly Bell, "Women Targeted in Growing Military Violence in Haiti," International Liaison Office for President Aristide, May 1994; and Beverly Bell, "Haitian Women Speak Out against Violence," in *National NOW Times*, National Organization for Women, June 1994.

12. Commission Nationale de Verité et de Justice [National Commission of Truth and Justice], *Si m pa rele* [If I Don't Cry Out], 91, http://ufdcweb1.uflib.ufl.edu/UF00085926/00001/109j.

13. U.S. Embassy of Haiti, "Confidential Cablegram" (cable, Port-au-Prince), April 12, 1994, 2 and 3.

12. The Creole Connection

1. Paul Collier, "Haiti's Rise from the Rubble," September/October 2011, *Foreign Affairs* online, http://www.foreignaffairs.com/articles/68043/paul-collier/haitis-rise-from-the-rubble.

2. Andrew Price, "Somali Pirates: Down to Help Haiti Too," *Good*, January 28, 2010, http://www.good.is/post/somali-pirates-down-to-help-haiti-too/.

3. The World Bank, "Migration and Remittances Data," http://siteresources.worldbank.org/INTPROSPECTS/Resources/334934-1110315015165/RemittancesData_Inflows_Apr12(Public).xlsx (accessed June 17, 2012).

4. Lawrence Barchue, "Senegal Offers Land to Haitians," *BBC News* online, January 17, 2010, http://news.bbc.co.uk/2/hi/8463921.stm.

5. NBC News and News Services, "Baptist Group Denies Trafficking in Haitian Children," MSNBC online, February 1, 2010, http://www.msnbc.msn.com/id/35162046/ns/world_news-haiti/t/baptist-group-denies-trafficking-haitian-kids/#.T8KZgbAeOH0.

6. Ken Korman, "Notes from New Orleans," *Gambit* online, February 8, 2011, http://www.bestofneworleans.com/gambit/notes-from-new-orleans/Content?oid=1558896.

7. Evan Hansen, "High Tech, Low Tech, Condescension, Understanding," *Haiti Rewired*, February 2, 2010, http://haitirewired.wired.com/profiles/blogs/high-tech-low-tech.

8. Laura Roper, Jennifer Utz, and John Harvey, *The Tsunami Learning Project: Lessons for Grantmakers in Natural Disaster Response* (Grantmakers without Borders, 2006), http://www.gwob.net/issues/pdf/tlp_full-report.pdf.

14. Social Fault Lines

1. My regular visitations to the palace were due to having served as an international liaison for President Aristide during his first term.

2. Woods Hole Oceanographic Institute, "Image: WHOI Expert: Haiti Quake Occurred in Complex, Active Seismic Region," last modified February 1, 2012, http://www.whoi.edu/page.do?pid=7545&tid=441&cid=101118&ct=61&article=66766; and United States Geological Service, "Magnitude 7.0—Haiti Region 2010 January 12: Summary," last modified January 28, 2012, http://earthquake.usgs.gov/earthquakes/eqinthenews/2010/us2010rja6/#summary (accessed January 31, 2012).

3. University of San Francisco School of Law, Institute for Justice and Democracy in Haiti, Bureau des Avocats Internationaux [International Lawyers' Office], Lamp for Haiti, "We've Been Forgotten: Conditions in Haiti's Displacement Camps Eight Months after the Earthquake," September 2010, 1.

4. Ibid.

15. Monsanto Seeds, Miami Rice

1. The Calypso tomato seeds are treated with Thiram, according to an e-mail from Monsanto representative Elizabeth Vancil to Emmanuel Prophete, director of seeds at the Haitian Ministry of Agriculture, and others, released by the Haitian Ministry of Agriculture, date unavailable. U.S. Environmental Protection Agency, *Reregistration Eligibility Decision for Thiram* (Washington, DC, 2004), vi, www.epa.gov/oppsrrd1/REDs/0122red_thiram.pdf; and Andrea Mojica, EPA chemical review manager for Thiram, phone conversation with Other Worlds' staffperson Deepa Panchang, January 9, 2012.

2. Vancil to Prophete, released by Haitian Ministry of Agriculture.

3. "Peasant Leader, Chavannes Jean-Baptiste to Visit U.S. following on a Massive March against Monsanto," press release by Food First, June 9, 2010, www.foodfirst.org/en/node/2969.

4. "Monsanto Company Donates Conventional Corn and Vegetable Seeds to Haitian Farmers to Help Address Food Security Needs," press release by Monsanto, May 13, 2010, http://monsanto.mediaroom.com/index.php?s=43&item=839. See also Haiti Grassroots Watch, "Monsanto in Haiti, Part 1," March 30, 2011, http://haitigrassrootswatch.squarespace.com/6Mon1eng.

5. Edward Walters and Dina Brick, *A Rapid Seed Assessment in the Southern Department of Haiti* (Catholic Relief Services, March 10, 2010), 22, http://oneresponse.info/Disasters/Haiti/Agriculture/publicdocuments/CRS.%20Rapid%20Seed%20Assessment.%20Mars-10.pdf.

6. Via Campesina, "Peasants Worldwide Rise Up against Monsanto, GMOs," October 16, 2009, http://viacampesina.org/en/index.php?option=com_content&view=article&id=797:peasants-worldwide-rise-up-against-monsanto-gmos&catid=49:stop-transnational-corporations&Itemid=76.

7. Donald L. Bartlett and James B. Steele, "Monsanto's Harvest of Fear," *Vanity Fair* online, May 2008, http://www.vanityfair.com/politics/features/2008/05/monsanto200805.

8. The four companies control 49.9 percent of the global commercial seed market. Kristina Hubbard, *Out of Hand: Farmers Face the Consequences of a Consolidated Seed Industry* (National Family Farm Coalition, December 2009), 13, farmertofarmercampaign.com/Out%20of%20Hand.FullReport.pdf.

9. The figure is based on estimates from Monsanto's own documents and media reports. Center for Food Safety, *Monsanto vs. US Farmers* (2005), 23 and 24, http://www.centerforfoodsafety.org/pubs/CFSMOnsantovsFarmerReport1.13.05.pdf.

10. "Haitian Farmers Increase Agriculture Productivity through Support of U.S. Government," press release by USAID, October 19, 2010, www.usaid.gov/press/releases/2010/pr101019.html; and "Monsanto Company," press release by Monsanto.

11. Maud Beelman, "U.S. Contractors Reap the Windfalls of Post-War Reconstruction," *CorpWatch* online, October 30, 2003, http://www.corpwatch.org/article.php?id=8910.

12. Washington Technology, "2009 Top 100," http://washingtontechnology.com/toplists/top-100-lists/2009.aspx (accessed October 28, 2011).

13. Fariba Nawa, "Expensive (and Dubious) Advice," *CorpWatch* online, May 2, 2006, http://www.corpwatch.org/article.php?id=14078.

14. Beelman, "U.S. Contractors Reap."

15. "USA Rice Efforts Result in Rice Food-Aid for Haiti," press release by USA Rice Federation, January 20, 2010, http://www.usarice.com/index.php?option=com_content&view=article&id=957:usa-rice-efforts-result-in-rice-food-aid-for-haiti-&catid=84:usarice-newsroom&Itemid=327.

16. Figures are from 2006 through 2010. U.S. Department of Agriculture, *Rice Outlook* (August 13, 2010), 36, http://usda.mannlib.cornell.edu/usda/ers/RCS//2010s/2010/RCS-08-13-2010.pdf in Oxfam, *Planting Now: Challenges and Opportunities for Haiti's Reconstruction* (October 2010), 8, http://www.oxfam.org/sites/www.oxfam.org/files/bp140-planting-now-agriculture-haiti-051010-en_0.pdf.

17. Environmental Working Group, "2011 Farm Subsidy Database," http://farm.ewg.org/region?fips=00000&regname=UnitedStatesFarmSubsidySummary.

18. Mark Weisbrot, Jake Johnston, and Rebecca Ray, *Using Food Aid to Support, Not Harm, Haitian Agriculture* (Center for Economic and Policy Research, April 2010), 2, http://www.cepr.net/documents/publications/haiti-2010-04.pdf.

19. The USDA estimates ninety thousand metric tons, "mostly from the U.S. and Vietnam" would be donated in 2010. The World Food Program Food Aid Information System reports that over 110,000 MT of food aid rice was donated to Haiti, with 57,000 MT provided by the United States. Carlos G. Suarez & Nicolas Rubio, *Haiti: Rice Production and Trade Update* (USDA Foreign Agricultural Service, Global Agricultural Information Network), gain.fas.usda.gov/Recent%20GAIN%20Publications/Rice%20Production%20and%20Trade%20Update_Santo%20Domingo_Haiti_11-9-2010.pdf. Carlos G. Suarez and Nicolas Rubio, *Haiti: Rice Production and Trade Update* (USDA Foreign Agricultural Service, Global Agricultural Information Network), gain.fas.usda.gov/Recent%20GAIN%20Publications/Rice%20Production%20and%20Trade%20Update_Santo%20Domingo_Haiti_11-9-2010.pdf; and Center for Economic and Policy Research, "Local Purchases of Rice as Food Aid Overstated," November 4, 2011, www.cepr.net/index.php/blogs/relief-and-reconstruction-watch/local-purchases-of-rice-as-food-aid-overstated.

20. USAID, *U.S. International Food Assistance Report 2002* (Washington, DC, February 2004), 31.

21. Ibid.

22. Jonathan M. Katz, "With Cheap Food Imports, Haiti Can't Feed Itself," Associated Press, March 20, 2010, http://www.huffingtonpost.com/2010/03/20/with-cheap-food-imports-h_n_507228.html.

16. Home

1. UN Office for the Coordination of Humanitarian Affairs, *Haiti Earthquake Situation Report #33* (April 12, 2010), 1, http://www.cinu.org.mx/haiti/docs/OCHASituationReport No33Haiti%20Earthquake12April2010.pdf.

2. Ibid., 7.

3. Mark Schuller, *Unstable Foundations: Impact of NGOs on Human Rights for Port-au-Prince's Internally Displaced People* (October 4, 2010), http://ijdh.org/wordpress/wp-content/uploads/2010/10/Report-unstable-foundations-final-2.pdf.

4. University of San Francisco School of Law, Institute for Justice and Democracy in Haiti, Bureau des Avocats Internationaux [International Lawyers' Office], Lamp for Haiti, *"We've Been Forgotten": Conditions in Haiti's Displacement Camps Eight Months after the Earthquake* (September 2010), 10, http://ijdh.org/archives/14633.

5. Inter-American Commission on Human Rights, *Follow-up Report on the Situation of Human Rights in Haiti*, April 15, 2011, 598, reliefweb.int/sites/reliefweb.int/files/resources/Full_Report_689.pdf.

6. Government of the Republic of Haiti, *Action Plan for National Recovery and Development of Haiti: Key Initiatives for the Future* (Port-au-Prince, March 2010), 32, http://www.haiticonference. org/Haiti_Action_Plan_ENG.pdf.

7. The Shelter Cluster estimated "5,657 transitional shelters constructed" by July 2010, while other sources gave a much lower number. UN Office for the Coordination of Humanitarian Affairs, *Haiti: Humanitarian Bulletin #7* (July 17, 2010), 1, reliefweb.int/node/361457/pdf.

8. Lois Romano, "State Department's Cheryl Mills on Rebuilding Haiti," *Washington Post* online, May 20, 2010, http://www.washingtonpost.com/wp-dyn/content/article/2010/05/09/AR2010050903009.html.

9. Bureau des Avocats Internationaux [International Lawyers' Office], "Haiti Earthquake Survivors Peacefully Demonstrate to Call Attention to the Forced Expulsions and Horrific Conditions in Camps," August 12, 2010, http://ijdh.org/archives/14046; and Bureau des Avocats Internationaux, "Internally Displaced Haitians Faced with Forced Expulsions and Looming Hurricanes Will Beat Pots and Pans to Protest Horrific Conditions in Camps," August 26, 2010, http://ijdh.org/archives/14472.

17. For Want of Twenty Cents

1. UN Department of Economic and Social Affairs, "World Population Prospects, the 2010 Revision," May 4, 2011, http://esa.un.org/unpd/wpp/Sorting-Tables/tab-sorting_mortality. htm.

2. Lucy Bassett, "Nutrition Security in Haiti: Pre- and Post Earthquake Conditions and the Way Forward," *En Breve*, World Bank, no. 157 (June 2010), https://openknowledge. worldbank.org/bitstream/handle/10986/10180/566860BRI0Box31571English1Printable. pdf?sequence=1; "WFP Issues Report of Child Nutrition in Haiti," *Examiner* online, January 5, 2011, http://www.examiner.com/global-hunger-in-national/wfp-report-on-child-nutrition-haiti.

3. UN Department of Public Information, "Press Conference by United Nations Special Rapporteur on Right to Food," October 26, 2007, http://www.un.org/News/briefings/docs/2007/071026_Ziegler.doc.htm.

4. In a 2002 study, the research institute Fafo estimated 173,000 children in domestic servitude, from ages five to seventeen. In 2009, the U.S. Department of State estimated 90,000 to 300,000. UNICEF estimated 225,000 in 2010 before the earthquake. Tone Sommerfelt, ed., *Child Domestic Labour in Haiti: Characteristics, Contexts and Organisation of Children's Residence, Relocation and Work, Revised Draft* (Fafo, 2002), 6, http://www.fafo.no/ais/other/haiti/childlabour/EEDH_Report_draft_english.pdf; U.S. Department of State, *Trafficking in Persons Report* (2009), 306, http://www.state.gov/documents/organization/123365.pdf; and UNICEF Humanitarian Action and Recovery, *Haiti 2010–2011: Mid-Year Review of 2010 Humanitarian*

Action Report (2010), 6, http://www.unicef.org/infobycountry/files/UNICEF_Haiti_Humani
tarian_and_Recovery_-_Mid-Year-Review_of_the_2010_HAR.pdf.

18. The Super Bowl of Disasters

1. Ansel Herz and Kim Ives, "WikiLeaks Haiti: The Post-Quake 'Gold Rush' for Reconstruction Contracts," *Nation* online, June 15, 2011, www.thenation.com/article/161469/wikileaks-
haiti-post-quake-gold-rush-reconstruction-contracts.

2. Alex Dupuy, "One Year after the Earthquake, Foreign Help Is Actually Hurting Haiti,"
Washington Post, January 7, 2011.

3. Mike Clary, "Broward Rivals Battle for Work in Post-Quake Haiti," *Sun-Sentinel*, July
14, 2010.

4. Emma Perez-Trevino, "Beating Death Lawsuit Ends in Settlement," *Brownsville (TX)
Herald* online, January 7, 2010; and Martha Brannigan and Jacqueline Charles, "U.S. Firms Want
Part in Haiti Cleanup," *Miami Herald*, February 9, 2010.

5. See Jeremy Scahill, *Blackwater: The Rise of the World's Most Powerful Mercenary Army*
(New York: Nation Books, 2007); Jeremy Scahill, "US Mercenaries Set Sights on Haiti," *Nation*
online, February 1, 2010, http://www.thenation.com/article/us-mercenaries-set-sights-haiti; and
Anthony Fenton, "Private Contractors 'Like Vultures Coming to Grab the Loot,'" *IPS News*, February 19, 2010, http://ipsnews.net/news.asp?idnews=50396.

6. "Al Jazeera Reports on the Haiti 'Summit' for Private Contractors," YouTube video, 3:32,
Al Jazeera, posted by "WebofDem," May 6, 2010, http://youtu.be/kkNCdy0GXyc.

7. Federal Procurement Data System, "Haiti Earthquake Report," updated September 15,
2011, https://www.fpds.gov/downloads/top_requests/Haiti_Earthquake_Report.xls.

8. Ibid.

9. Isabel Macdonald, "Disaster Capitalism in Haiti Leaves Displaced with Few Good Choices," *Colorlines*, June 20, 2011, http://colorlines.com/archives/2011/06/disaster_capitalism_in_
haiti_leaves_displaced_with_few_good_choices.html; Jane Regan, "Haiti: Housing Exposition
Exposes Waste, Cynicism," *Huffington Post*, October 3, 2012, http://www.huffingtonpost.com/
jane-regan/haiti-housing-exposition-_b_1911898.html.

10. "Housing/Haiti/2011," YouTube video, Al Jazeera, posted by "CinthyaTV," June 27,
2011, http://youtu.be/kg5S-FiX8e4.

11. Macdonald, "Disaster Capitalism in Haiti."

12. Team member of MIT / Harvard University design team for Exemplar Community Pilot
Project, phone interview by Deepa Panchang, October 28, 2011.

13. "FHFA Sues 17 Firms to Recover Losses to Fannie Mae and Freddie Mac," press release by
Federal Housing Finance Agency, September 2, 2011, www.fhfa.gov/webfiles/22599/PLSLitiga
tion_final_090211.pdf.

14. Macdonald and Doucet, "The Shelters That Clinton Built."

15. Isabel Macdonald and Isabeau Doucet, "The Shelters That Clinton Built," *Nation* online,
July 11, 2011, http://www.thenation.com/article/161908/shelters-clinton-built; and "Clinton
Foundation Accused of Sending Haiti Shoddy Trailers Found Toxic after Katrina," *Democracy
Now* video, 59:05, July 12, 2011, http://www.democracynow.org/2011/7/12/clinton_foundation_
accused_of_sending_haiti.

16. Jane Madden, "Corporations Must Consider Haiti's Long Term Needs," *Philanthropy
News Digest* online, March 10, 2010, http://foundationcenter.org/pnd/commentary/co_item.
jhtml?id=287300002.

17. "New USAID-Funded Haiti Apparel Center to Provide Training to Thousands of Haitians in the Garment Industry," press release by USAID, August 11, 2010, http://www.usaid.gov/
press/releases/2010/pr100811_1.html.

18. USAID, *Haiti Earthquake: Fact Sheet #48* (April 2, 2010), http://www.usaid.gov/our_
work/humanitarian_assistance/disaster_assistance/countries/haiti/template/fs_sr/fy2010/
haiti_eq_fs48_04-02-2010.pdf.

19. Center for Economic and Policy Research, "USAID/OTI's Politicized, Problematic, Cash-for-Work Programs," December 21, 2010, http://www.cepr.net/index.php/blogs/cepr-blog/usaidotis-politicized-problematic-cash-for-work-programs; Antèn Ouvriye [Workers' Antenna], *Submission to the United Nations Universal Periodic Review: Labor Rights* (Transnational Legal Clinic, University of Pennsylvania Law School, 2011), http://ijdh.org/archives/17948; and Office of Inspector General, *Audit of USAID's Cash-for-Work Activities in Haiti* (San Salvador, September 24, 2010), www.usaid.gov/oig/public/fy10rpts/1–521–10–009-p.pdf.

20. Haiti Grassroots Watch, "Is Cash-for-Work Working?" http://www.ayitikaleje.org/Dossier2Story2 (accessed October 31, 2011); and Haiti Grassroots Watch, "Cash for Work—at What Cost," http://www.ayitikaleje.org/haiti-grassroots-watch-engli/2011/7/18/cash-for-work-at-what-cost.html (accessed October 31, 2011).

- 21. Office of Inspector General, *Audit*, 2.

22. Mary Bridges et al., *Innovations in Corporate Global Citizenship: Responding to the Haiti Earthquake* (World Economic Forum, July 2010), 16 and17, www3.weforum.org/docs/WEF_HaitiResponse_Report_2010.pdf.

23. Interim Haiti Recovery Commission, "Minutes of the Board Meeting of the Interim Haiti Recovery Commission (IHRC)," Karibe Hotel, Pétionville, June 17, 2010, en.cirh.ht/files/pdf/ihrc_board_minutes_june_17_2010.pdf; and Interim Haiti Recovery Commission, "IHRC Board Meeting Minutes," http://en.cirh.ht/board-meeting-minutes.html (accessed October 31, 2011).

24. Ian Davis, "Government as Business," *McKinsey Quarterly*, October 2007, http://www.mckinsey.com/locations/UK_Ireland/~/media/Reports/UKI/Ian_Davis_government_as_a_business_the_times.ashx.

25. Risma Umar et al., *Tsunami Aftermath: Violations of Women's Human Rights in Nanggroe Aceh Darussalam, Indonesia* (Asia Pacific Forum on Women, Law, and Development, 2006), www.apwld.org/pdf/tsumai_vwhr.pdf.

26. David Dietz and Darrell Preston, "The Insurance Hoax," Bloomberg online, September 2007, http://www.bloomberg.com/apps/news?pid=nw&pname=mm_0907_story1.html; and Jay Feinman, *Delay, Deny, Defend: Why Insurance Companies Don't Pay Claims and What You Can Do about It* (New York: Penguin Group, 2010).

27. "Interim Haiti Reconstruction Commission (IHRC)," 2010, http://fr.groups.yahoo.com/group/VINOUSH/message/13186.

20. Beyond Medical Care

1. Lucy Bassett, *Nutrition Security in Haiti: Pre- and Post-Earthquake Conditions in Haiti and the Way Forward* (World Bank, June 2013), 3, http://siteresources.worldbank.org/INTLA/resources/2578031269390034020/EnBreve_157_English_web.pdf.

2. World Health Organization, "Haiti," http://www.fachc.org/pdf/mig_haitians.pdf, http://www.who.int/countries/hti/en/ (accessed June 15, 2012); and Central Intelligence Agency, *The World Factbook 1999*, "Haiti," http://www.umsl.edu/services/govdocs/wofact99/156.htm (accessed June 15, 2012).

3. Library of Congress—Federal Research Division, *Haiti Country Profile* (May 2006), 11, http://lcweb2.loc.gov/frd/cs/profiles/Haiti.pdf.

4. Pan-American Health Organization, *Health Situation in the Americas: Basic Indicators 2010* (2010), 10, http://new.paho.org/hq/index.php?option=com_content&task=blogcategory&id=1775&Itemid=1866; World Health Organization, *World Health Statistics 2010*, 146; and UN Development Program, *Human Development Report 2006: Beyond Scarcity: Power, Poverty and the Global Water Crisis* (2006), 303, http://hdr.undp.org/en/reports/global/hdr2006/.

5. World Health Organization, *World Health Statistics 2010*, 41.

6. World Health Organization, Commission on Social Determinants of Health, *Closing the Gap in a Generation: Health Equity through Action on the Social Determinants of Health* (Geneva, August 20, 2008), 26, http://whqlibdoc.who.int/publications/2008/9789241563703_eng.pdf.

7. *Break the Chains of Haiti's Debt* (Jubilee USA, May 20, 2006), 5, http://www.jubileeusa. org/fileadmin/user_upload/Resources/Policy_Archive/haitireport06.pdf; International Monetary Fund, *Haiti: Selected Issues* (Washington, DC, 2005), 88; and World Bank, *Haiti: External Financing Report: October 1, 2000–September 30, 2001* (Washington, DC, 2002), vii.

8. U.S. Treasury Department internal e-mail, quoted in NYU School of Law Center for Human Rights and Global Justice, Partners in Health, RFK Memorial Center for Human Rights, and Zanmi Lasante, *Wòch nan Soley: Denial of the Right to Water in Haiti* (2008), 11, http://www. chrgj.org/projects/docs/wochnansoley.pdf.

9. Dr. Evan Lyon, "Partners in Health Physician on Haiti: 'Cholera Will Not Go Away until Underlying Situations That Make People Vulnerable Change,'" interview with Amy Goodman, Democracy Now, rush transcript, October 26, 2010, http://www.democracynow. org/2010/10/26/partners_in_health_physician_cholera_will.

10. R. S. Hendriksen, K. B. Price, J. M. Schupp, J. D. Gillece, R. S. Kaas, D. M. Engelthaler, et al., "Population Genetics of *Vibrio Cholerae* from Nepal in 2010: Evidence on the Origins of the Haitian Outbreak," *mBio* 2, no. 4 (2011): e00157–11. R. Piarroux, R. Barrais, B. Faucher, R. Haus, M. Piarroux, J. Gaudart, et al. "Understanding the Cholera Epidemic, Haiti," *Emerging Infectious Diseases* 17, no. 7 (2011):1161–67.

11. Just Foreign Policy, "Haiti Cholera Counter," May 30, 2012, http://www.justforeignpolicy. org/haiti-cholera-counter.

12. Partners in Health, "Partners in Health History," http://www.pih.org/pages/partners-in-health-history/ (accessed October 21, 2011); and S. Koenig et al., "Successes and Challenges of HIV Treatment Programs in Haiti: Aftermath of the Earthquake." *HIV Ther* 4 (March 2010): 145–60, http://www.ncbi.nlm.nih.gov/pmc/articles/PMC3011860/pdf/nihms 258513.pdf.

13. Paul Farmer, *Haiti after the Earthquake* (New York: Public Affairs, 2011), 4.

21. Hold Strong

1. Jonathan Katz, "Haiti: A Year after the Quake, Waiting to Rebuild," Associated Press, January 11, 2011, http://www.msnbc.msn.com/id/41023645/ns/world_news-haiti/t/haiti-year-after-quake-waiting-rebuild/.

22. Mrs. Clinton Will Never See Me Working There

1. Paul Farmer, *Aids and Accusation: Haiti and the Geography of Blame* (Berkeley and Los Angeles: University of California Press, 1992).

2. Jonathan M. Katz, "Can the Garment Industry Save Haiti?" Associated Press, February 21, 2010, http://www2.ljworld.com/news/2010/feb/22/can-garment-industry-save-haiti/.

3. Solidarity Center, *A Post-Earthquake Living Wage Estimate for Apparel Workers in the SONAPI Export Processing Zone* (Port-au-Prince, March 3, 2011), www.solidaritycenter.org/ Files/haiti_livingwagesnapshot030311.pdf; and Dan Coughlin and Kim Ives, "WikiLeaks Haiti: Let Them Live on $3 a Day," *Nation* online, June 1, 2011, http://www.thenation.com/ article/161057/wikileaks-haiti-let-them-live-3-day.

4. Nathan Associates Inc., *Bringing HOPE to Haiti's Apparel Industry: Improving Competitiveness through Factory-level Value-Chain Analysis* (2009), 37.

5. Women make up 62 percent of the garment industry. UNIFEM says that nearly 45 percent of Haitian households are headed by women, while the UN Shelter Cluster uses an estimate of 60 percent. World Bank figures put the average number of children at 3.42. International Finance Corporation, *Better Work Haiti: Garment Industry 1st Compliance Synthesis Report* (July 9, 2010), 3, http://www.nathaninc.com/sites/default/files/HOPE-for-haitis-apparel-industry.pdf; UNIFEM, "UNIFEM Fact Sheet: At a Glance—Women in Haiti," July 2010, *UN Women* online, http://www.unifem.org/materials/fact_sheets.php?StoryID=1146; Inter-Agency Standing Committee, *Generic Presentation on the IASC Gender Marker for HQ and Regional Offices* (March 18,

2011), 15; and "Data: Fertility Rate, Total (Births Per Woman)," chart, World Bank, 2011, http://data.worldbank.org/indicator/SP.DYN.TFRT.IN.

6. Central Intelligence Agency, *The World Factbook*, "Haiti," https://www.cia.gov/library/publications/the-world-factbook/geos/ha.html (accessed March 9, 2012).

7. Coughlin and Ives, "WikiLeaks Haiti."

8. John Bray, *International Companies and Post-Conflict Reconstruction: Cross-Sectoral Comparisons* (Washington, DC: World Bank, Conflict Prevention and Reconstruction, February 2005), 26, http://www.international-alert.org/sites/default/files/publications/Int_companies&post-conflict.pdf, quoted in Mark Schuller, "Deconstructing the Disaster after the Disaster: Conceptualizing Disaster Capitalism," in *Capitalizing on Catastrophe: Neoliberal Strategies in Disaster Reconstruction*, ed. Nandini Gunewardena and Mark Schuller (Lanham, MD: AltaMira Press, 2008), 23.

9. Government of the Republic of Haiti, *Action Plan for National Recovery and Development of Haiti* (March 2010), www.haiticonference.org/Haiti_Action_Plan_ENG.pdf.

10. Paul Collier, "The Fundamentals Favour Economic Development," in *Haiti: From Natural Catastrophe to Economic Security; A Report for the Secretary-General of the United Nations* (January 2009), www.focal.ca/pdf/haiticollier.pdf.

11. Paul Collier and Jean-Louis Warnholz, "Building Haiti's Economy, One Mango at a Time," *New York Times* online, January 28, 2010, www.nytimes.com/2010/01/29/opinion/29collier.html.

12. USAID, "Caracol Industrial Park," November 2011, haiti.aid.gov/work/docs/haiti_book_3rd_draft_112411.pdf (accessed October 4, 2012).

13. The twenty-three-thousand figure is from J. F. Hornbeck, *Report for Congress: The Haitian Economy and the HOPE Act* (Congressional Research Service, June 24, 2010), 14, fpc.state.gov/documents/organization/145132.pdf. Determination of working age population: In Haiti's latest census, conducted in 2003, the working age population (generally defined as ages fifteen to sixty-four) was 58.4 percent of the total population. Applying this same percentage to the World Bank's estimate of Haiti's current population, the working age population is now about 5.7 million people. Institut Haïtien de Statistique et d'Informatique [Haitian Institute for Statistics and Information Technology], "Le 4ième Recensement Général de la Population et de l'Habitat" [Fourth General Census of the Population and Habitat], 2003, http://ihsi.ht/rgph_resultat_ensemble_population.htm.

14. Just-Style, "Haiti Poised to Become a Regional Export Champion?" January 5, 2011, http://www.just-style.com/analysis/haiti-poised-to-become-a-regional-export-champion_id109933.aspx.

15. "Update 1-T-shirt Maker Gildan Shifts Ops after Haiti Quake," Reuters, January 13, 2010, http://www.reuters.com/article/2010/01/13/gildan-idUSN1315247020100113.

16. Heidi Coryell Williams, "By a Thread," Alta Gracia website, February 25, 2012, http://altagraciaapparel.com/news/entry/by-a-thread; and Steven Greenhouse, "Factory Defies Sweatshop Label, but Can It Thrive?" *New York Times* online, July 17, 2010, http://www.nytimes.com/2010/07/18/business/global/18shirt.html?_r=1&scp=1&sq=Factory%20Defies%20Sweatshop%20Label&st=cse.

17. Check out the websites of United Students against Sweatshops, Witness for Peace, U.S. Labor Education and Action Project, Worker Rights Consortium, and Institute for Global Labour and Human Rights.

24. Elections

1. Jake Johnston and Mark Weisbrot, *Haiti's Fatally Flawed Election* (Washington, DC: Center for Economic and Policy Research, February 2011), 1, http://www.cepr.net/documents/publications/haiti-2011-01.pdf.

2. "Why Martelly Hates Aristide So Much?" YouTube video, 0:40, posted by "welcome-2Haiti," February 6, 2011.

3. Johnston and Weisbrot, *Haiti's Fatally Flawed Election*.

4. National Human Rights Defense Network, *RNDDH Report on the Presidential and the Parliamentary Elections Nov. 28th, 2010* (December 3, 2010), www.rnddh.org/IMG/pdf/Rapport_Elections_2010-3.pdf; and Lawyers' Earthquake Response Network, Bureau des Avocats Internationaux [International Lawyers' Office], and Institute for Justice and Democracy in Haiti, *Summary Submission to the UN Universal Periodic Review of Haiti* (Twelfth Session of the UPR Working Group of the Human Rights Council, October 3–13, 2011), 5, http://ijdh.org/archives/17920.

5. Sustainable Organic Integrated Living, "Burning Tires in the Time of Cholera," *Winter Newsletter 2010*, http://hosted.verticalresponse.com/793713/ea3a9f4179/1470889033/d46ba33652/ (accessed November 2, 2011).

6. "The Joint Mission OAS/CARICOM in Haiti Provides an Update after More Than Three Months of Activity," press release by the Organization of American States, November 19, 2010, http://www.oas.org/en/media_center/press_release.asp?sCodigo=E-447/10.

7. Through USAID, the United States contributed $14 million to the election's $29 million price. Johnston and Weisbrot, *Haiti's Fatally Flawed Election*.

8. "OAS Overturned Haitian Presidential Election in a 'Political Intervention,' New CEPR Paper Suggests," press release by Center for Economic and Policy Research, October 17, 2011, http://www.cepr.net/index.php/press-releases/press-releases/oas-overturned-haitian-presidential-election-in-a-qpolitical-interventionq-new-cepr-paper-suggests.

9. Jill Dougherty, "U.S. Pulls Visas of Some Haitian Officials," CNN U.S. online, January 24, 2010, http://www.cnn.com/2011/US/01/21/haiti.visas.revoked/index.html.

10. Dan Coughlin and Kim Ives, "WikiLeaks Haiti: The PetroCaribe Files," *Nation* online, June 1, 2011, http://www.thenation.com/article/161056/wikileaks-haiti-petrocaribe-files?page=0,2.

11. Mark Weisbrot, "The US Embassy Cables: WikiLeaks' Lesson on Haiti," December 17, 2010, *Guardian* online, http://www.guardian.co.uk/commentisfree/cifamerica/2010/dec/17/haiti-wikileaks.

12. Mark Weisbrot, e-mail to author, June 16, 2012.

13. Alexis Erkert, "Working for Human Rights in Haiti: A Struggle with Wide Scope and Deep Roots," *Peace Office Newsletter*, Mennonite Central Committee Peace Office Publication, vol. 41, no. 2 (April–June 2011): 4.

14. Dan Beeton, "Haiti's Elections: Parties Banned, Media Yawn," *NACLA Report on the Americas*, March/April 2011, 52.

25. We Will Never Fall Asleep Forgetting

1. Sendika Travayè Anseyan Invèsitè Ayiti [Haitian University Teacher Workers' Union] et al., "3-Day Program of Activities on the Duvalier Period," announcement e-mail to Beverly Bell, February 9, 2010.

2. Trenton Daniel, "Rights Groups Blast Haiti Judge on Duvalier Case," Associated Press, January 30, 2012, http://ijdh.org/archives/24594.

3. Haiti Grassroots Watch, "Behind the Cholera Epidemic," December 21, 2010, http://haitigrassrootswatch.squarespace.com/haiti-grassroots-watch-engli/2010/12/21/behind-the-cholera-epidemic.html.

4. Caroline Preston and Nicole Wallace, "American Donors Gave $1.4-Billion in 2010 to Aid Haiti," *Chronicle of Philanthropy* online, January 6, 2011, http://philanthropy.com/article/Haiti-Aid-Falls-Short-of-Other/125809/; and Disaster Accountability Project, "We Donated to Haiti Relief and We're Angry," *Change.org*, http://www.change.org/petitions/we-donated-to-haiti-relief-and-were-angry (accessed October 23, 2011).

5. "Death by Deportation," press release by the Florida Immigrant Advocacy Center, Miami, January 31, 2011.

6. Isabeau Doucet, "Haiti, a Nation in Fragments, Faces the Future," *Indypendent* online, April 6, 2011, http://www.indypendent.org/2011/04/05/haiti-a-nation-in-fragments-faces-the-future/.

Epilogue

1. Rebecca Solnit, *A Paradise Built in Hell: The Extraordinary Communities That Arise in Disaster* (New York: Penguin Books, 2009), 142.

2. "The time to be on the right side of history is now" is a line from Mary Oishi's poem "Grandpa's Will," unpublished, 1965. Borrowed with gratitude.

Index

Abraham, Suze
  advocacy work, 96, 143, 144, 145
  pseudonym, 10
  rape of her granddaughter, 95–96, 101
  stories of, 60, 171–75, 193–94, 202–3
Action Plan for National Recovery and Development, 81–83, 89–90, 134, 180
activists. *See* community groups; social movements
Agricultural Missions, 126
agriculture, 63–71
  Creole pigs, 67–68, 143
  ecological, 69, 70
  food aid and, 27, 70, 108, 110, 128–30
  food sovereignty, 65, 68–70, 111, 124–27, 187, 188
  import tariffs and, 27, 30, 67, 128
  land ownership, 29, 30, 45, 63–64, 67, 71
  land reform, 29, 35, 36, 45, 63–71, 138, 185–87
  neglect, government, 65–66
  rice, 37, 127–30
  seeds, 64, 66, 67, 69, 70, 124–30
  sugarcane, 28, 208n3
  water, 66, 69, 70, 71, 129
  See also food aid; peasants; *specific names of organizations*

Agronomist, The (film), 42
Amen to Brave Women Martyrs (Fanm Martir Ayibobo Brave), 8, 20
Anita (film), 42
Antènne Ouvriye (Workers' Antenna), 179
APROSIFA (Association for the Promotion of Integrated Family Health), 54, 165–67
Arawak Indians, 8, 28
Aristide, Jean-Bertrand
  army, dismantling of, 199
  author and, 92, 216n14.1
  coups d'etat against, 36–37, 72
  Lavelas Family (Fanmi Lavelas) party, 190–91
  Martelly, Michel and, 100, 192
  Ministry for the Status and Rights of Women, 48
  popular pressure and, 91–92
  public health under, 160–62
Artibonite Valley, 49, 128, 129, 130
assembly industry, 30, 37, 75–76, 176–83, 194
  See also economics; labor unions
Association for the Promotion of Integrated Family Health (APROSIFA), 54, 165–67

Athelus, Elitane, 8
Auguste, Rose Anne, 54, 165

"Baby Doc." *See* Duvalier, Jean-Claude ("Baby Doc")
Ban Ki-moon, 80, 97
banks. *See* loan funds; *specific names of institutions*
Bartlett, Stephen, 126
Bassin Zim Education and Development Fund, 125
Batay Ouvriye (Workers' Struggle), 33, 91, 179, 181
Beaubrun, Djab, 20, 57–59, 61, 113, 157–58, 196, 203
Bel Air, 55, 170
Belair, Sanite, 44
Bellerive, Jean-Max, 81, 83, 171
Berkshire Hathaway, 149
Betto, Frei, 34
Beyond Borders, 144
biofuel crops, 70
Bonheur, Marie Bertine, 77
Boumba, Nixon, 119–23, 178
Brazil, 34–35, 76, 138
Brooks, David, 80
Brown, Michael, 77
Buffett, Warren, 149
Bureau des Avocats Internationaux (International Lawyers' Office), 100, 135–36, 137
Bush, Barbara, 135
Bush, George W., 77

Cacos, 29
Cajuste, Alina "Tibebe," 11, 60, 96, 123, 143, 191, 201–2
camps. *See* displaced persons camps
CARE, 83
Caribbean Basin Initiative, 180
Carrefour, 155
Carrefour-Feuilles, 53–54, 165–66
Carter, Jimmy, 198
cash-for-work, 78, 150–51
Catholic Church, 2, 12–13, 30, 36, 125
    See also religions
Catholic Relief Services, 83, 125
Célestin, Jude, 192, 195
Center for Economic and Policy Research, 192–93, 195
Center for Research and Action for Development (CRAD), 43
Center for the Promotion of Women Workers (CPFO), 178

Central Plateau, 25, 53, 68, 124–26
Chalmers, Camille, 107, 108, 181, 182
Charles, Rony, 129, 130
Chávez, Hugo, 76, 195
Chemonics International, 127
CHF International, 150–51
children
    health care, 24, 140–41, 166–67
    kidnapping of, 104
    mortality rates, 66, 141
    orphans, 24, 143
    poverty, 121, 141, 143
    protection of, 24, 25, 44, 140–45
    rape of, 93–97, 98, 99
    rights for, 35, 140–45
    Timafi, 95–96, 101, 172, 174, 194, 202
    See also education; schools; women's movements; *specific names of organizations*
child slaves (*restavèk*), 42, 60, 93, 123, 142–45, 171–72
    See also children; violence
cholera, 161–62, 186–87, 193, 199
churches, 2, 12–13, 38, 51, 59, 172, 189
    See also religions
church movement, progressive, 36, 50–51, 88–89
    See also religions; social movements
CIMO (anti-riot squads), 134
class
    development and, 80
    legal codification of, 67
    overview, 5, 6, 8, 9
    perpetuation of inequality, 3–4, 36–37, 68, 118–23
    rape and, 97
    religions and, 30, 36
    women's movements and, 44–45, 47, 187–88
    See also inequality; poverty
Clayton Homes trailers, 149–50
clinics. *See* health care; hospitals
Clinton, Bill
    "build back better," 7–8
    corporate ties, 91–92, 147, 149, 151–52
    demonstrations against, 90
    Interim Haiti Recovery Commission (IHRC), 82
    NGOs estimate, 84
    rice imports, 129, 182
Clinton, Hillary Rodham, 74, 80, 135, 149, 183, 194
Clinton Foundation, 148, 149, 152
Clinton Global Initiative, 149

Coalition against Third World Debt, 38
Coalition of Haitian Women Citizens in Soli-
    darity (La Plateforme Femmes Citoyennes
    Haïti Solidaire), 90
Collier, Paul, 180
colonialism, 8, 29–30, 38, 66, 73–85, 90
    See also economics; France; Spain
Columbus, Christopher, 28, 36
Commission of Women Victim to Victim (KO-
    FAVIV), 93–94, 96–97, 100, 143–44
communications networks, 3, 14, 87, 119,
    147, 148
community groups
    collaboration by, 86–88, 135
    international, 51, 107–9
    NGOs and, 84
    relief efforts, 4–5, 19–26, 49–56, 108–11
    See also social movements; solidarity; specific
        names of organizations
CONAP (National Coordination for Advocacy
    on Women's Rights), 46
Concertation Nationale contre la Violence Faite
    aux Femmes (National Coalition against
    Violence against Women), 46
consciousness-raising, 37, 87, 172
contractors. See corporations and contractors
Cooper, Anderson, 24
Cooperative Farming Production Network of
    the Lower Artibonite (RACPABA), 129
cooperatives, 71, 91, 129–30, 138
Coordination Nationale de Plaidoyer pour les
    Droites des Femmes (CONAP), 46
Coordination Régionale des Organisations du
    Sud-Est (CROSE), 71
Coriolan, Anne-Marie, 43
corporations and contractors, 5, 6, 30, 78–79,
    127–28, 146–53
    See also assembly industry; development;
        disaster capitalism; food aid; foreign aid
Correa, Rafael, 79
corruption
    cash-for-work and, 151
    disaster capitalism and, 127, 146–53
    Duvalier and, 33–34
    elections, 190–93, 194, 195
    food distribution systems, 77–78
    funding requests, 104
coups d'état, 29, 36–37, 72, 73, 82, 100
COURAGE (KOURAJ), 95
CPFO (Center for the Promotion of Women
    Workers), 178
CRAD (Centre de Recherche et d'Action pour
    le Développement), 43

Creole language, 30, 31, 38, 87, 97
Creole pigs, 67–68, 143
crime, 5, 22, 202
    See also rape; violence
Crowley, P. J., 194
Cry of the Excluded (Grito de los Excluidos), 71
Cuba, 75, 76, 103, 122

death squads, 100
    See also Tonton Macoutes
death tolls, earthquake, 2, 27–28
debt, foreign, 29, 38, 82, 160–61
dechoukaj campaign, 36
Défi Michée (Micah Challenge), 88
Dejean, Lise-Marie, 39–40
Deloné, Nadine, 177, 182
Delva, Eramithe, 96, 97, 101
democracy
    agriculture and, 65, 68–71
    corruption and, 153
    elections, 35, 36, 188, 190–96
    future of, 203–6
    government, Haitian and, 82–85
    history of struggle for, 33–40
    reconstruction and, 4, 7–8, 108
    women's movements and, 44–47, 188–89
    See also social movements
Democratic Popular Movement (MODEP),
    119, 178
demonstrations. See protests
Department of Homeland Security, 199
Deronzil, Jonas, 128–29, 130
Desir, Marco, 57, 58, 155, 157–58, 172
Dessalines, Jean-Jacques, 6, 29
Deutsche Bank, 148–49
development
    Action Plan for National Recovery and
        Development, 81–83, 89–90, 134, 180
    alternative, 26, 35, 87–90, 107, 129–30,
        136–39, 186–89
    assembly industry as, 176, 180–83
    failed state discourse, 80
    models for, 7
    See also agriculture; foreign aid; reconstruc-
        tion; social movements; specific names of
        organizations; specific projects
Digicel, 148
Disaster Accountability Project, 199
disaster capitalism
    cash-for-work contracts, 150–51
    Chemonics International and, 127
    food aid and, 128–29
    foreign aid and, 73, 78–85

disaster capitalism *(continued)*
  Interim Haiti Recovery Commission (IHRC)
    and, 148
  minimum wage and, 178
  Monsanto seed donation, 125
  overview, 5–6, 30
  privatization and, 81–82, 91–92, 151–52
  U.S. government contracts, 146–53
diseases
  cholera, 161–62, 186–87, 193, 199
  HIV/AIDS, 162, 165
  public health and, 160, 162
  sexually transmitted, 121
  tuberculosis, 163
  See also health care; public health
displaced persons, 131–39
  homelessness, 60–61, 143
  participation by, 35, 88, 89, 108
  rural impact, 25, 50, 53, 88
displaced persons camps, 131–39
  conditions in, 132–33, 156–57, 162,
    193–94
  creation of, 2, 24–25
  evictions from, 133–36, 196
  health care in, 164–65
  locations, 118, 131, 132
  organization of, 25, 132
  portrayal of residents, 135
  potential permanence of, 133
  See also housing; rape
Doctors Without Borders, 75, 122
  See also health care
domestic violence, 41–42, 46, 188–89
  See also rape; women's movements
Dominican Republic, 3, 28, 59, 182
Dominique, Jean, 8, 34
Dumas, Wilson, 14, 62, 169, 197–98
Duval, Robert (Bobby), 198, 199
Duvalier, François ("Papa Doc"), 9, 33, 45
Duvalier, Jean-Claude ("Baby Doc")
  Creole pigs, 67–68
  fall of, 9, 64
  resistance under, 19, 33–34, 41, 70–71
  return of, 197–99, 200
  women's rights under, 45

economics, 27–32
  agriculture and, 69–70
  gift economy, 21, 26
  globalization, 30, 38–39, 198
  neoliberalism, 69, 81–82, 91–92, 151–52,
    195
  structural adjustments, 30
  trade, 27, 30, 67, 124–30

  See also colonialism; development; disaster
    capitalism; free trade zones; *specific names
    of industries*
Ecumenical Foundation for Peace and Justice
  (Fondation Oecuménique Pour la Paix et
  la Justice), 144
education
  child slaves (*restavèk*), 143, 171
  in displaced persons camps, 25
  government neglect of, 30, 66
  national budget for, 161
  New Orleans, 80–81
  right to, 174–75
  social movements and, 35, 37, 45, 88, 90, 138
  See also literacy; schools
elections, 35, 36, 188, 190–96
Elie, Patrick, 72–73, 85
embargoes, 29, 161
eminent domain, 137
employment. *See specific industries; specific
  kinds of employment*
EnfoFanm (WomenInfo), 43
environmental issues
  free trade zones, 177
  housing and, 138
  neglect of, 66
  peasants and, 68, 69, 70
  social movements and, 35, 88
  World Environment Day, 124
Estimé, Jean-Robert, 127
Etienne, Yannick, 33, 91, 181, 203–4, 205
Etienne, Yolette, 19–20, 21–22, 26, 168
export assembly industry. *See* assembly
  industry

failed state, 80
Fanmi Lavalas (Lavalas Family), 190–91
Fanm Martir Ayibobo Brave, 8, 20
Fanm Viktim Leve Kanpe (FAVILEK), 100
Farmer, Paul, 161, 163
farmers. *See* peasants
Fatiman, Boukman, 8
Fatiman, Cécile, 8, 44
Federal Emergency Management Agency
  (FEMA), 77, 78, 149
Felix, Tania, 55, 77
Feminine League for Social Action (Ligue
  Féminine d'Action Sociale), 44–45
feminism. *See* women's movements
Filippi, Loris de, 75
Filo, Konpè, 21, 39, 200
Fils-Aimé, Marc-Arthur, 37
First National Congress of Democratic Move-
  ments, 184

first responders, 4, 13, 16, 19–26, 50–53
  See also refugees
Fondasyon Limyè Lavi (Light of Life
  Foundation), 143, 144
Fondasyon Men nan Men (FONDAMA),
  125–26
Fondasyon Zanmi Timoun (Friends of Children Foundation), 144
Fondation Oecuménique Pour la Paix et la
  Justice (Ecumenical Foundation for Peace
  and Justice), 144
food aid
  agriculture and, 27, 70, 108, 110, 128–30
  benefits to U.S. corporations, 128
  community groups and, 50, 54
  food distributions, 23–24, 54, 55, 77–78,
    121
  See also agriculture; foreign aid; humanitar-
    ian aid; solidarity
food imports, 27, 30, 67, 128, 129, 182
food production. *See* agriculture
food sovereignty, 65, 68–70, 111, 124–27,
  187, 188
foreign aid, 72–85
  Cuban government, 75, 76, 103, 122
  embargo and, 161
  environmental projects, 66
  insufficiency of, 4, 20, 78
  military and, 74–75
  misdirection of, 77, 109–11
  monetary, 110–11, 161–62, 199
  money pledged, 77, 78–79, 80, 82
  recommendations for, 85, 108–11, 129, 130
  water and sanitation, 161, 162
  See also food aid; nongovernmental organiza-
    tions (NGOs); reconstruction; social
    movements
foreign debt, 29, 38, 82, 160–61
  See also France; United States
Fort Dimanche, 198
Fòs Refleksyon ak Aksyon sou Koze Kay
  (FRAKKA), 135
France
  colonial rule, 5, 8, 104
  Duvalier exile to, 34, 197
  post-colonial relations, 28–29, 30
  Sarkozy, Nicolas, 90
  sugarcane industry, 208n3
  U.S. occupation and, 76
free trade zones, 30, 177, 180
  See also development; economics
French language, 30, 38, 82, 84
Friends of Children Foundation (Fondasyon
  Zanmi Timoun), 144

Fund for Peace, 80
Fwaye Maurice Sixto (Maurice Sixto Home),
  144

garment industry. *See* assembly industry
GARR (Support Group for Refugees and the
  Repatriated), 136, 138
gender. *See* rape; transactional sex; women's
  movements
Gerbier, Iderle Brénus, 187–88
gift economy, 21, 26
  See also mutual aid; solidarity
globalization, economic, 30, 38–39, 198
  See also economics
Globalization from Below, 7
Gonaïves, 34
government, Haitian
  bypassing of, 78
  emergency response, 20
  foreign privatization of, 151–52
  neglect, 6, 28, 65–66
  services, 66, 68, 160, 186
  weakness of, 79–80, 81–85, 170
  See also health care; housing; schools; water
Grand Goâve, 2
Grantmakers Without Borders, 111
grassroots movements. *See* social movements;
  women's movements
Gressier, 2, 62, 138
Grito de los Excluidos (Cry of the Excluded),
  71
Groupe d'Appui aux Réfugiés et Repatriés
  (GARR), 136, 138
guerilla insurrections, 29–30
  See also revolution
Guerrier, Wildrick, 199

Haiti Advocacy Working Group, 108
Haitian National Network for Food Sovereignty
  and Security (RENHASSA), 124–25,
  187–88
Haitian Platform to Advocate Alternative
  Development (PAPDA), 26, 107, 181,
  182, 205
Haitian Women's Solidarity (SOFA), 40, 41,
  43, 46, 100
Haitian Youth Music Relief, 105
Haiti Economic Lift Program (HELP), 180
Haiti Grassroots Watch, 150
Haiti Response Coalition, 108
Haiti Summit, 147
Haiti Support Group, 82
Heads Together Haitian Peasants (Tèt Kole),
  49–50, 64, 65, 70–71, 185–87

health care, 159–67
   accompaniment program, 163
   APROSIFA, 165–67
   children's health, 140–43
   class and, 160–67
   Cuban team, 75, 103, 122
   first responders, 13, 21, 23
   improvement of, 162–65
   national budget for, 160–61
   NGOs and, 84
   rape victims and, 97, 100
   relief workers, 75, 103
   See also clinics; hospitals; public health;
      specific names of organizations
health care access
   children, 140–41
   class and, 122
   doctors and nurses, 31
   overview of issues, 159–60, 164–65
   peasants and, 49, 66, 187
HELP (Haiti Economic Lift Program), 180
Henrilus, Jean-Jacques, 49, 71
Henry Reeve Team of Medical Specialists in
   Disasters and Epidemics, 103
Heritage Foundation, 76, 80
Highlight Best Practices for Housing, 148–49
   See also housing
Hinche, 124, 188
HIV/AIDS, 162, 165
homelessness. *See* displaced persons; displaced
   persons camps
Hometown Associations, 103
hope, 8–9, 11, 91, 168, 175, 200, 203–6
hospitals
   access to, 122, 141, 164–65, 187
   accompaniment program, 163
   destruction of, 13, 159
   Léogâne hospital, 141
   military presence and, 75
   National Hospital, 160
   Partners in Health (Zanmi Lasante), 53, 164
   University Hospital, 75, 122, 165
Hotel Montana, 119
housing
   disaster capitalism and, 148–50
   government policies, 134–36, 137
   loss of, 60–61, 172
   models for, 138, 148–49
   rape and, 96–97, 98, 99, 101
   rights, 131–39, 148–50
   rural, 50
   shantytowns, 28, 155
   visions for, 136–39
   See also displaced persons camps

humanitarian aid, 4–5, 7, 22–23, 49–56,
      72–73, 103–5
   See also displaced persons camps; food aid;
      housing
human rights
   basic principles, 7
   Duvalier, Jean-Claude ("Baby Doc"),
      197–200
   NGOs and, 85
   Platform of Haitian Human Rights Organiza-
      tions (POHDH), 87
   social movements and, 34–37, 50, 91
   systemic change, 111
   See also women's movements; *specific names
      of issues; specific names of organizations*
hunger, 110, 121, 139, 142, 174
   See also agriculture; food aid; poverty
Hurricane Katrina, 5, 104, 135, 152
   See also New Orleans

IMF (International Monetary Fund), 27, 38,
      67, 69
import tariffs, 27, 30, 67, 128
   See also economics; foreign debt; free trade
      zones; trade
inclusion, 7, 8, 65, 71, 83, 90
inequality
   death tolls and, 27
   health, 159–60
   language and, 38
   NGOs and, 84
   overview, 3–6, 7, 8, 11
   perpetuation of, 3–4, 27–31, 36–37, 68, 90,
      118–23
   See also class; poverty; protests; social move-
      ments; *specific social groups*
Institute Culturel Karl Lévêque (ICKL), 37
Institute for Justice and Democracy in Haiti,
      100
Institute of Technology and Animation
      (ITECA), 138–39
Inter-American Commission on Human Rights
   of the Organization of American States,
      135
Inter-American Development Bank, 38, 81,
      148, 152, 161–62, 180
Interim Haiti Recovery Commission (IHRC),
      82–83, 148–49, 151–52
International Labour Organisation, 182
International Lawyers' Office (Bureau des Avo-
      cats Internationaux), 100, 135, 137
International Monetary Fund (IMF), 27, 38,
      67, 69
International Peace Operations Association, 147

International Women's Day, 188
investment. *See* assembly industry; corporations and contractors
Izméry, Antoine, 8

Jacmel, 2, 42, 43
Jean, Wyclef, 190
Jean-Baptiste, Bazelais, 125
Jean-Baptiste, Chavannes, 65, 66–67, 68, 69
Jean-Baptiste, Rosnel, 65
Jean-François, Lenz, 55–56, 170–71
Jean-Pierre, Ricot, 26, 205, 206
Jean-Rabel, 49, 63–64, 69
Jeanty, Yolette, 48
Jérémie, 95, 101
Joanis, Mirlène, 178–79
Jubilee South, 38

Karl Lévêque Cultural Institute (ICKL), 37
King, Martin Luther, Jr., 205
Klein, Naomi, 5, 73
KOFAVIV (Commission of Women Victim to Victim), 93–94, 96–97, 100, 143–44
KONAFAP (National Coalition of Peasant Women), 187, 188
konbit (collective work group), 52
Korn/Ferry International, 152
KOURAJ (COURAGE), 95
Kramer, Sasha, 23–24

labor unions, 36, 39, 178, 179–80, 182, 183
    See also assembly industry
Lamartinière, Marie-Jeanne, 44
Lambi Fund, 14, 85, 89, 110
Landless Workers' Movement, 138
land reform
    demands for, 35, 36, 69
    land ownership, 29, 30, 63–64, 67, 71, 137
    models for, 138
    urban, 137
    women's movements and, 45, 185–87
    See also agriculture; housing
Lavalas Family (Fanmi Lavalas) party, 190–91
Léogâne, 2, 59, 62, 149–50
Lespinasse, Colette, 136, 138
Lexima-Constant, Guerda, 143, 144, 145
liberation theology, 36, 37
    See also religions
Light of Life Foundation (Fondasyon Limyè Lavi), 143, 144
Ligue Féminine d'Action Sociale (Feminine League for Social Action), 44–45
literacy, 31, 35, 36, 60, 166, 174, 201–2
    See also education; schools

loan funds, 52, 166
looting, 23
Louisama, Gerta, 185–87
Louis-Juste, Jean Anil, 57–58, 203
Louverture, Toussaint, 6
Lyon, Evan, 162

Mackandal, François, 8
malnutrition. *See* hunger
Manigat, Mirlande, 192–93
Marcelin, Magalie, 41–43, 46, 48
Marie-Jeanne, 44
maroons, 8, 32–33, 44, 64
    See also revolution; slavery
Marron Inconnu, Le (Unknown Maroon), 32–33
Martelly, Michel, 192–93, 195, 199–200
Martineau Jean-Claude, 31
massacres, 49, 64
Maurice Sixto Home (Fwaye Maurice Sixto), 144
McKinsey and Company, 151–52
media portrayals, 4, 98–99, 108, 171, 202
medical services. *See* health care
mental health, 2, 17–19, 60, 98, 170–71, 174, 175
Mercy Corps, 83
Merlet, Myriam, 43
Merten, Kenneth, 77–78, 146
Mexico, 39, 67
Micah Challenge (Défi Michée), 88
Michaud, Yvette, 188–89
military, 199–200
Millet Mountain (Mòn Pitimi), 2–3, 4, 140–42
Mills, Cheryl, 135
minimum wage, 37, 176–78, 179
Ministry for the Status and Rights of Women, 40, 43, 48
Ministry of Agriculture, Natural Resources, and Rural Development, 83–84, 124, 125, 164
Ministry of Education, 164
Ministry of Planning and External Cooperation, 84–85
Ministry of Public Health, 159, 161, 164
Mirebelais, 162, 164
MODEP (Democratic Popular Movement), 119, 178
Montès, Jean, 105
Mortimé, Antonal, 87, 88, 195
Mouscardy, Guercy, 168
MPNKP (National Peasant Movement of the Papaye Congress), 65, 71, 125

MPP (Peasant Movement of Papaye), 53, 65, 68, 71, 125
Mulet, Edward, 81
Munger, Amber, 20
mutual aid, 4–5, 19–26, 49–57, 71, 102–11
    See also gift economy; solidarity

Naiman, Robert, 110
Nathan Associates, Inc, 177
National Cathedral, 12–13
National Coalition against Violence against Women (Concertation Nationale contre la Violence Faite aux Femmes), 46
National Coalition of Peasant Women (KONA-FAP), 187, 188
National Coordination for Advocacy on Women's Rights (CONAP), 46, 90
National Human Rights Defense Network (RNDDH), 190–93
National Peasant Movement of the Papaye Congress (MPNKP), 65, 71, 77, 125
National Truth and Justice Commission, 42, 100
Nèg Mawon (Maroon Man), 32–33
Nelio, Getro, 22, 121, 133–34, 139, 169
New Orleans
    community organizations, 51, 89
    comparisons with Haiti, 5–7, 102, 112, 133, 135
    Cuban aid, 103
    disaster capitalism in, 147
    FEMA trailers, 149
    McKinsey and Company, 152
    people-to-people solidarity, 102–11
    relationship with Haiti, 5–6, 103
    resilience, 168
    schools, 80–81
    solidarity in, 23, 51
    violence in, 99
    See also Hurricane Katrina
noiriste movement, 33
nongovernmental organizations (NGOs), 79, 82–85, 91, 109, 133
    See also reconstruction; specific names of organizations

OAS (Organization of American States), 194–95
Obama, Barack, 73
offshore assembly industry. See assembly industry
Other Worlds, 10, 136
Ouanaminthe, 177
Oxfam, 19, 168

Palace of Justice, 2, 62
Panchang, Deepa, 108
Papaye, 25, 45, 188
PAPDA (Haitian Platform to Advocate Alternative Development), 26, 107, 181, 182, 205
participation, citizen. See democracy; displaced persons; women's movements
Partners in Health (Zanmi Lasante), 53, 59, 85, 122, 161, 162–65
peacekeeping operations. See United Nations
Peasant Movement of Papaye (MPP), 53, 65, 68, 71, 125
peasants
    Cacos, 29
    Creole pigs, 67–68, 143
    development and, 68
    displaced persons and, 25, 50, 53, 88
    health care access, 49, 66, 187
    status of, 63–67, 70–71
    use of term, 11
    women, 184–89
    See also agriculture; social movements; women's movements; specific names of organizations
people-to-people solidarity, 18–23, 50–53, 87, 102–11
Péralte, Charlemagne, 6
Pérard, Josette, 14, 62, 89
Pétionville, 120–21, 200
Petit Goâve, 2
Piatre, 49–50, 53, 64, 69
Pierre, Doudou, 124–25
Pierre, Msgr. André, 12–13
pigs, Creole, 67–68, 143
Plateforme Femmes Citoyennes Haïti Solidaire, La, 90
Platform of Haitian Human Rights Organizations (POHDH), 87, 195
police
    evictions, 133–34
    first responders, 14, 20
    history of, 29
    rape responses, 95, 96, 101
    violence by, 134, 178, 185, 193, 199
popular movements. See social movements
Post-Disaster Needs Assessment, 66, 81
poverty, 9, 28–31, 66, 121
    See also assembly industry; child slaves (restavèk); class; development; inequality
power, political
    author's personal, 11
    reconstruction and, 5, 79–85, 109–11
    social movements, 7, 87–92
    struggle for, 28–31, 33–40

See also protests; United States; violence;
 specific types of organizations
Préval, René
  elections, 192
  foreign aid, 74, 79
  jokes about, 59, 118
  minimum wage increase, 178
  public health and, 160
  U.S. opposition to, 195
  privatization, 81–82, 91–92, 151–52
  profiting from the earthquake. *See* corpora-
    tions and contractors; disaster capitalism;
    privatization
prostitution. *See* transactional sex
Protestant denominations, 88, 155
  See also religions
protests
  electoral theft, 193–94
  history of, 33–40
  housing, 131–32, 139
  minimum wage, 178, 179
  against Monsanto seed, 124
  police response to, 178, 185, 193, 199
  privatization, 92
  restavèk (child slaves), 144
  See also social movements; women's move-
    ments
public health, 85, 159, 160–67, 186–87, 193, 199
  See also cholera; diseases; health care

Quisqueya University, 2

race 5, 6, 28–30, 33, 80
racism 6, 28–30, 33, 80–81, 98–99, 104
RACPABA (Cooperative Farming Production
  Network of the Lower Artibonite), 129
radio, 34, 36, 144, 193
rape, 93–101
  of child slaves (*restavèk*), 142–43
  disaster profiteers and, 22
  housing and, 174
  legal battles, 42, 46
  of males, 214n1
  prevalence of, 172
  prevention of, 25
reconstruction, 72–85
  citizen involvement in, 7–8, 87, 88–89,
    90–91, 170–71, 203
  control by foreign powers, 79–85, 147
  Interim Haiti Recovery Commission
    (IHRC), 82–83
  Strategic Plan for National Salvation, 90
  U.S. role in, 71–81
  women's movements and, 90–91

See also corporations and contractors;
  disaster capitalism; foreign aid; social
  movements
refugees. *See* displaced persons; displaced
  persons camps; housing
Regional Coordination of the Southwest
  (CROSE), 71
religions
  Catholic Church, 6, 12–13, 30, 36, 119, 154
  class inequities, 30, 36, 38, 186
  liberation theology, 36, 37
  Protestant denominations, 2, 88, 156
  Vodou, 6, 8, 30, 154, 155
  See also churches
rescues, 4, 13, 16, 17, 19, 20–22, 23
  See also first responders
Réseau National de Défense des Droits Humains (RNDDH), 190–93
Réseau National Haïtien de Sécurité et
  Souveraineté Alimentaire (RENHASSA),
  124–25, 187–88
resilience, 19–25, 113, 115–17, 120, 158,
  168–75, 200
resistance. *See* protests
restavèk (child slaves), 42, 60, 93, 123,
  142–45, 171–72
revolution, 8, 28–30, 32–33, 44, 66, 104
  See also hope; land reform; massacres;
    protests
Rezo Asosyasyon Koòperatif pou Komès ak
  Pwodwi Agrikòl Ba Latibonit (RACPA-
  BA), 129
rice, 37, 54, 67, 77, 121, 127–30, 157
  See also agriculture; food aid
RNDDH (National Human Rights Defense
  Network), 190–93
Robertson, Pat, 104
Roy, Arundhati, 35
rural communities. *See* agriculture; land reform;
  peasants

SAJ / Veye Yo (Solidarity among Youth /
  Watch Out), 55–56, 57
Sandinistas, 36
sanitation, 160–62, 186–87, 193, 199
  See also cholera; health care; public health;
    water
Sanon, Reyneld, 136, 137
Sarkozy, Nicolas, 90
Save the Children, 83
schools
  child slaves (*restavèk*), 141, 142, 171
  Clayton Homes trailers and, 149–50
  destruction of, 2, 18

schools *(continued)*
  enrollment in, 31
  fees, 173, 174–75
  New Orleans, 80–81
  NGOs and, 84
  reopening of, 77, 122
  rural, 66
  See also education; literacy
Schuller, Mark, 133
search-and-rescue operations, 4, 19, 20–21
  See also first responders; rescues
seeds. *See* agriculture
shantytowns, 28, 155
  See also housing
Shock Doctrine, The, 5, 73
slavery, 5–6, 8, 28, 29, 32–33, 44, 206
  See also child slaves (*restavèk*); maroons; revolution
social movements, 3–5, 7–8, 32–40, 86–92, 135–38, 183, 204–6
  See also community groups; democracy; protests; *specific causes; specific names of organizations*
Solidarite Fanm Ayisyen (SOFA), 40, 43
solidarity
  community groups, 51
  donations by individuals, 103–5
  humanitarian aid, 22–24
  mutual aid, 4–5, 19–26, 49–57, 71
  in New Orleans, 23, 51
  obstacles to, 39
  people-to-people, 102–11
  rescues, 4, 13, 16, 17, 19, 20–22, 23
  See also community groups; foreign aid; humanitarian aid
Solidarity among Youth / Watch Out (SAJ / Veye Yo), 55, 77
Solnit, Rebecca, 203
sovereignty
  food sovereignty, 65, 68–70, 111, 124–27, 187, 188
  revolution and, 28–29
  social movements and, 35
Spain, 5, 8, 28, 29
state violence. *See* violence; *specific names of perpetrators*
Strategic Plan for National Salvation, 90
structural violence, 27–31, 142–43, 160
subsidies, 37, 67, 82, 125, 127–28
sugarcane industry, 28, 208n3
Support Group for Refugees and the Repatriated (GARR), 136, 138
sweatshop industry. *See* assembly industry

tariffs, import, 27, 30, 67, 128
  See also trade
tent camps. *See* displaced persons camps
Tète Kole Ti Peyizan Ayisyen (Heads Together), 49
textile industry. *See* assembly industry
Thelusmond, Ronel, 83–84
Timafi, 95–96, 171, 174, 194, 202
Tonton Macoutes, 34, 36, 198
trade, 27, 30, 67, 124–30
  See also free trade zones
transactional sex, 78, 96, 121, 151, 178, 214n1
Triple Canopy, 147
tuberculosis, 163

unemployment, 177, 180
Unger, Roberto, 8
unions, labor, 36, 178, 179, 182, 183
United Nations
  Conventions, 45, 144
  coordination and, 84, 135
  economic planning, 69
  evictions and, 134
  expenditures, 79
  Food and Agriculture Organization, 66
  food distributions, 54, 77–78
  Guiding Principles on Internal Displacement, 135
  Human Development Index, 31
  military occupation, 29, 74, 76, 162
  protection of women, 97
  search-and-rescue operations, 20
  Universal Declaration of Human Rights, 135
  See also foreign aid
United States
  coups d'états and, 29, 36–37, 73, 100
  Creole pigs, 67–68, 143
  deportations to Haiti, 199
  elections and, 195
  food distributions, 54, 77
  import tariffs, 27, 30, 67, 128
  material aid, 76–77
  military presence, 74–78, 97, 162
  occupations, 8, 29, 44, 76
  people-to-people solidarity, 102–11, 204–6
  reconstruction, 72–81
  social movements and, 88–92
  support of the Duvaliers, 34, 36, 100, 197–99
  See also assembly industry; corporations and contractors; foreign aid; nongovernmental organizations (NGOs)
Universal Declaration of Human Rights, 135

University Hospital, 75, 165
U.S. Agency for International Development
(USAID), 68, 78, 125, 128–29, 150–51,
178

Vancil, Elizabeth, 125
Venezuela, 76, 195
Via Campesina, 71, 126
Viaud, Kertus, 13, 23
Viaud, Loune, 59, 163–65
Villard-Appolon, Malya, 94, 96–97, 100
Vincent, Jean-Marie, 8
violence
    domestic, 41–42, 46, 188–89
    elections and, 193–94
    evictions, 133–34
    against gay men, 95
    Haitian army, 29, 36–37, 42, 100, 199,
        200–201
    legal settlements, 146
    media coverage of, 98–100
    New Orleans, 99
    police, 134, 178, 185, 193, 199
    prevention of, 25, 166
    structural, 29–31, 142–43, 160
    See also child slaves (restavèk); rape;
        women's movements
Vodou, 6, 8, 30, 154, 155

Walking on Fire, 123
water
    access to, 133, 160
    agricultural, 66, 69, 71

assembly industry and, 179
cholera and, 161–62, 186–87, 193, 199
Watershed Initiative for National Natural
    Environmental Resources (WINNER),
    127
"weapons of the weak," 109
weapons of the weak, 33
Weisbrot, Mark, 195
WomenInfo (EnfoFanm), 43
Women's Commission of Heads together
    Haitian Peasant (Tèt Kole Ti Peyizan
    Ayisyen), 185–86
Women's House (Kay Fanm), 41–43, 46, 48,
    100
women's movements, 34, 41–48, 90–91, 97,
    100, 178–79, 184–89
    See also labor unions; protests; rape; trans-
        actional sex; violence; specific names of
        organizations
Women Victims Get Up Stand Up (FAVILEK),
    100
Workers' Antenna (Antènne Ouvriye), 179
World Bank, 38, 39, 69, 81–83, 89–90, 134,
    180
    See also assembly industry; foreign debt; free
        trade zones; trade
World Health Organization (WHO), 160
World Social Forums, 35, 39
World Trade Organizaton (WTO), 39, 71
World Vision, 83

Zapatistas, 39
Ziegler, Jean, 142

CPSIA information can be obtained
at www.ICGtesting.com
Printed in the USA
LVHW112259020922
727305LV00005B/230

9 780801 477690